Habitat Gray wolves live throughout a large part of North America.

Behavior Wolves live in family groups called packs. The pack hunts together.

COVERING Wolves have two coats of fur that keep them warm in winter. They can stay warm in temperatures as cold as –40° C.

GROOMING Wolves sometimes bathe in rivers or streams to wash mud from their fur.

Science

Gray Wolf

Harcourt
SCHOOL PUBLISHERS

Orlando   Austin   New York   San Diego   Toronto   London

Visit *The Learning Site!*
www.harcourtschool.com

Gray Wolf

Consulting Authors

Michael J. Bell
Assistant Professor of Early Childhood Education
College of Education
West Chester University of Pennsylvania

Michael A. DiSpezio
Curriculum Architect
JASON Academy
Cape Cod, Massachusetts

Marjorie Frank
Former Adjunct, Science Education
Hunter College
New York, New York

Gerald H. Krockover
Professor of Earth and Atmospheric Science Education
Purdue University
West Lafayette, Indiana

Joyce C. McLeod
Adjunct Professor
Rollins College
Winter Park, Florida

Barbara ten Brink
Science Specialist
Austin Independent School District
Austin, Texas

Carol J. Valenta
Senior Vice President
St. Louis Science Center
St. Louis, Missouri

Barry A. Van Deman
President and CEO
Museum of Life and Science
Durham, North Carolina

Ohio Reviewers and Consultants

Linda Bierkortte
Teacher
Parkmoor Urban Academy
Columbus, Ohio

Napoleon Adebola Bryant, Jr.
Professor Emeritus of Education
Xavier University
Cincinnati, Ohio

Laurie Enia Godfrey
Director of Curriculum Development
Lorain City Schools
Lorain, Ohio

Christine Hamilton
Curriculum Specialist
Toledo Public Schools
Toledo, Ohio

Jerome Mescher
Science/Math Coordinator
Hilliard City Schools
Hilliard, Ohio

Cheryl Pilatowski
Science Support Teacher/Coordinator
Toledo Public Schools
Toledo, Ohio

Lisa Seiberling
Elementary Science Coordinator
Columbus Public Schools
Columbus, Ohio

Kathy Sparrow
Science Learning Specialist, K-12
Akron Public Schools
Akron, Ohio

Matthew Alan Teare
Science Resource Teacher
Miles Park Elementary School
Cleveland Municipal School District
Cleveland, Ohio

Shirley Welshans
Teacher
Parkmoor Urban Academy
Columbus, Ohio

Getting Ready for Science **X**

Lesson 1—What Are Inquiry Skills? 2
Lesson 2—What Are Tools for Inquiry? 10
Lesson 3—What Is the Scientific Method? 18
Chapter Review and Test Preparation **24**

EARTH AND SPACE SCIENCES
UNIT A:

  26

Chapter 1

The Water Cycle **28**

Lesson 1—What is the Water Cycle? 30
Lesson 2—How Is the Water Cycle
  Related to Weather? 38
Lesson 3—How Do Land Features Affect
  the Water Cycle? 46
Lesson 4—How Can Weather Be Predicted? 42
Science Projects for Home or School 65
Chapter Review and Test Preparation **66**

Science Spin
Weekly Reader

Technology
Into the Eye of the
Storm, 62

People
Saving the Earth, 64

Chapter 2

Changes to Earth's Surface **68**

Lesson 1—What Are Some of Earth's Landforms? 70
Lesson 2—What Causes Changes to Earth's
  Landforms? 78
Lesson 3—What Is the Geological Timescale? 88
Science Projects for Home or School 99
Chapter Review and Test Preparation **100**
Ohio Expeditions **102**

Science Spin
Weekly Reader

Technology
Wipeout! Splash, 96

People
Watching a Volcano,
98

LIFE SCIENCES
UNIT B:

110

Chapter 3

Plant Growth and Reproduction 112

Lesson 1—What Are Some Plant Types? 114
Lesson 2—How Do Plants Grow? 122
Lesson 3—How Do Plants Reproduce? 130
Lesson 4—How Do Plants of the Past
      Compare with Those of Today? 140
Science Projects for Home or School 151
Chapter Review and Test Preparation 152

Science Spin
Weekly Reader

Technology
Farms of the Future, 148

People
Birds Help Trees, 150

Chapter 4

Understanding Ecosystems 154

Lesson 1—What Are the Parts of an Ecosystem? 156
Lesson 2—What Factors Influence Ecosystems? 164
Lesson 3—What are the Roles of Living Things? 174
Lesson 4—How Do Living Things Get Energy? 182
Science Projects for Home or School 195
Chapter Review and Test Preparation 196
Ohio Expeditions 198

Science Spin
Weekly Reader

Technology
Aquarius: An
Underwater Lab
with a View, 192

People
Meet a Young
Conservationist,
194

PHYSICAL SCIENCES

UNIT C: 206

Chapter 5

Matter and Its Properties 208

Lesson 1—How Can Physical Properties Be
Used to Identify Matter? 210
Lesson 2—How Does Matter Change States? 218
Lesson 3—What are Mixtures and Solutions? 226
Science Projects for Home or School 237
Chapter Review and Test Preparation 238

Science Spin
Weekly Reader

Technology
Fighting Fires with
Diapers, 234

People
Marie Curie:
Scientific Pioneer,
236

Chapter 6

Changes in Matter 240

Lesson 1—What Is Matter Made Of? 242
Lesson 2—What Are Physical Changes in Matter? 252
Lesson 3—How Does Matter React Chemically? 260
Science Projects for Home or School 271
Chapter Review and Test Preparation 272
Ohio Expeditions 274

Science Spin
Weekly Reader

Technology
What a Taste Test,
268

People
High Flying Scientist,
270

References

Health Handbook R1
Reading in Science Handbook R16
Math in Science Handbook R28
Science Safety R36
Glossary R37
Index R43

OHIO EXPEDITIONS

Your Guide to Science in Ohio

UNIT A: Earth and Space Sciences

Unit Opener Rockbridge Nature Preserve   26

OHIO EXPEDITIONS
On Location—Glacial Grooves   102
On Location—Serpent Mound   104
On Location—Shoreline Erosion   106

Projects and Investigations   108

UNIT B: Life Sciences

Unit Opener Reynoldsburg
Tomato Festival   110

OHIO EXPEDITIONS
On Location—Franklin Park Conservatory   198
On Location—Holden Arboretum   200
On Location—The Lakeside Daisy   202

Projects and Investigations   204

UNIT C: Physical Sciences

Unit Opener Neil Armstrong
Air and Space Museum   206

OHIO EXPEDITIONS
On Location—Building Fort Ancient   274
On Location—The Canal at Roscoe Village   276
On Location—The Y Bridge of Zanesville   278

Projects and Investigations   280

What do YOU wonder?

Does "doing science" require special skills? What science skills is this young snorkeler using?

What Are Tools for Inquiry?

Fast Fact

Out-of-This-World Tools The wheels of the Mars Rovers were tools for exploration. They exposed layers of soil. Scientists used the soil data to draw conclusions about Mars. In the Investigate, you will draw conclusions about ways to measure.

Measuring with Straws

Materials
- plastic straws
- classroom objects
- marker
- 2 cups
- water

Procedure

1. Use straws to measure length and width (distance). For example, you might measure this textbook or another flat object. Record your measurements.

2. Now use straws to measure the distance around a round object (its circumference). Hint: Flatten the straws before you start. Record your measurements.

3. Next, work with a partner to find a way to use straws to measure the amount of water in a cup (its volume). Record your measurements.

Draw Conclusions

1. Compare your measurements with those of other students. What can you conclude?

2. **Inquiry Skill** Scientists measure carefully so they can record changes accurately. Why do all scientists need to use the same unit of measurement when working on the same problems?

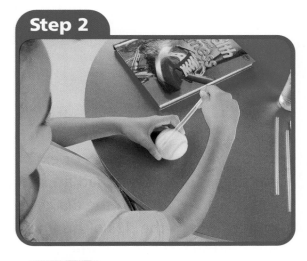

Step 2

Step 3

Investigate Further

How could you mark a straw to divide it into smaller units? How would this change the way you collect data? What might be a reason to do this?

Reading in Science

SI-1 Select appropriate tools; **ST-1** Explain how technology improves lives; **ST-2** Explain how technology meets needs

VOCABULARY

standard measure p. 4
microscope p. 6
pan balance p. 8
spring scale p. 8

SCIENCE CONCEPTS

► how scientists use tools to measure, observe, and manipulate

► how to use tools properly and safely

READING FOCUS SKILL

MAIN IDEA AND DETAILS

Look for tools that scientists use.

Main Idea

detail   detail   detail

Tools for Measuring Distance

Long ago, people sometimes used body parts to measure distance. For example, King Henry I of England had an iron bar made. It was as long as the distance from his nose to the tips of his fingers. Copies of the bar were made. The king told everyone to use the bars to measure things. This bar became the standard length for one yard. A **standard measure** is an accepted measurement.

When it was introduced, the meter, another unit of length, was not based on a body part. It was defined as 1/10,000,000 of the distance from the North Pole to the equator. Imagine measuring that distance!

These units of measurement may seem strange. Yet they helped people agree on the lengths of objects and the distances between places.

MAIN IDEA AND DETAILS Why do we have standard units of measure?

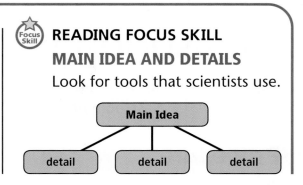

▼ A flexible measuring tape can measure circumference.

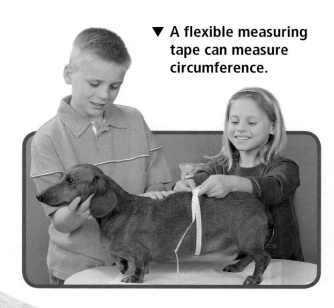

Geologists and surveyors use this tool to measure large distances.

◄ A ruler measures length. Place the first line of the ruler at one end of the object. The point on the ruler where the object ends is its length.

Tools for Measuring Volume

Cooks use cups and spoons to measure ingredients for a recipe. Scientists measure volume with tools, too. To find the volume of a liquid, you put it into a container such as a measuring cup, a beaker, or a graduate. The numbers on the side of the container show the volume of the liquid. Never use tools from your science lab for measuring food or medicine!

To measure the volume of a solid, multiply its length by its width by its height. For example, one box has a length of 4 centimeters and a width of 2 centimeters. Its height is 2 centimeters. The volume is 4 cm x 2 cm x 2 cm = 16 cubic centimeters.

 MAIN IDEA AND DETAILS How do you measure the volume of a solid? Of a liquid?

Personal Measuring Tools

Think of other ways you could measure distance or volume, using items you have at home or in the classroom. Test your new measuring tools, and exchange ideas with other students.

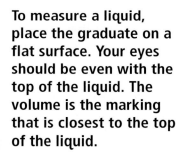

To measure a liquid, place the graduate on a flat surface. Your eyes should be even with the top of the liquid. The volume is the marking that is closest to the top of the liquid.

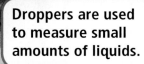

Droppers are used to measure small amounts of liquids.

Tools for Observing and Handling

Sometimes scientists need to observe an object closely. Certain tools can help them observe details they might not be able to see using just their eyes.

A hand lens makes things look larger than they are. It magnifies them. Hold the lens a few centimeters in front of your eye. Then move the object closer to the lens until you can see it clearly. Never let the lens touch your eye. Never use it to look at the sun!

Forceps let you pick up a sharp or prickly object without getting hurt. They can also protect a delicate object from too much handling. However, you must squeeze the forceps gently.

A magnifying box is sometimes called a bug box. Students often use it to observe live insects. An insect can move around in the box while you watch.

A **microscope** makes an object look several times bigger than it is. The microscope on the next page has lenses that can magnify a little or a lot. Two knobs help you adjust the image until you can see it clearly.

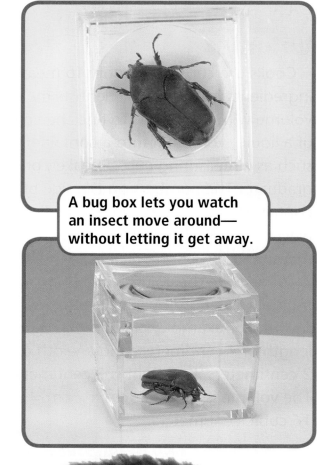

A bug box lets you watch an insect move around— without letting it get away.

Focus Skill **MAIN IDEA AND DETAILS** How do the tools on these pages help scientists?

A hand lens allows you to see many details. When you use forceps to hold an object, you can observe it without your fingers getting in the way.

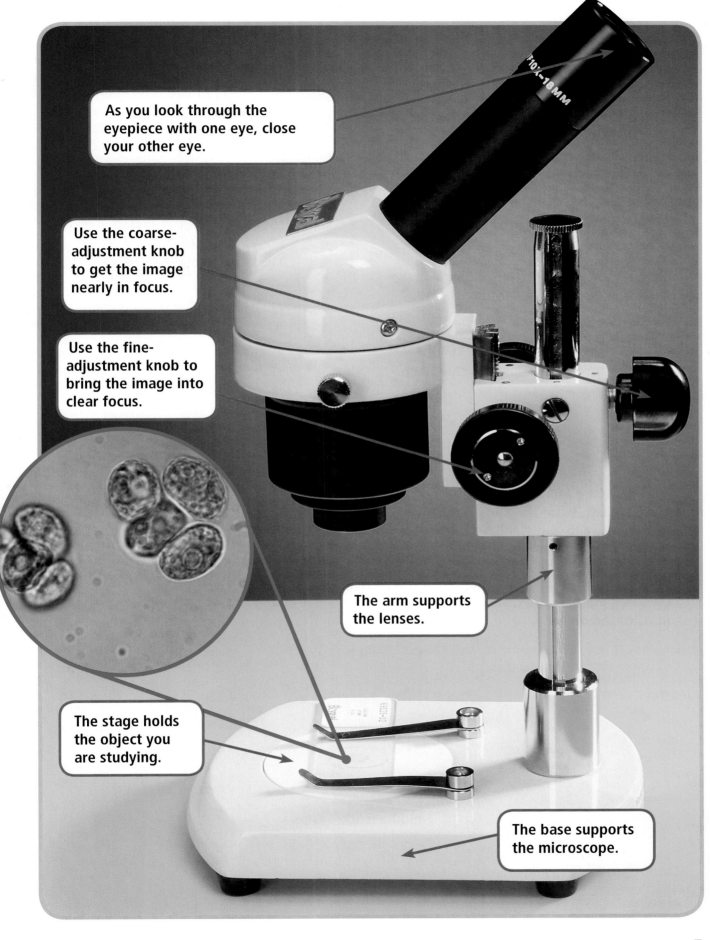

As you look through the eyepiece with one eye, close your other eye.

Use the coarse-adjustment knob to get the image nearly in focus.

Use the fine-adjustment knob to bring the image into clear focus.

The arm supports the lenses.

The stage holds the object you are studying.

The base supports the microscope.

Other Tools

Many other tools can help you measure. A thermometer can measure the temperature of the air or of a liquid. Be sure to touch the thermometer as little as possible. Otherwise, it will just measure the warmth of your fingers. Be careful! Glass thermometers break easily.

A **pan balance** measures mass. Mass is the amount of matter in an object. It is measured in grams (g). A **spring scale** measures forces, such as weight. The pull is measured in newtons (N).

 MAIN IDEA AND DETAILS What do a pan balance and a spring scale each measure?

The number closest to the top of the liquid is the temperature.

This girl is using a spring scale to measure the rabbit's weight. ▶

▼ Before you use a pan balance, make sure the pointer is at the middle mark. Place the object in one pan, and add standard masses to the other pan. When the pointer is at the middle mark again, add the numbers on the standard masses. The total is the mass of the object.

pans

middle mark

standard masses

1. MAIN IDEA AND DETAILS Copy and complete this graphic organizer.

MAIN IDEA: Scientists use many different tools to measure, observe, and handle.

Two tools for measuring	Two tools for observing	One tool for handling

A _____ **B** _____ **C** _____ **D** _____ **E** _____

2. SUMMARIZE Write two sentences that tell what this lesson is mostly about.

3. DRAW CONCLUSIONS How would scientific experiments change if scientists had no tools to use?

4. VOCABULARY Write a fill-in-the-blank sentence for each vocabulary word. Trade sentences with a partner.

Test Prep

5. Critical Thinking How can you decide which tool to use in a certain experiment?

6. Which tool would help you measure how different colors absorb the energy in sunlight?

A. beaker   **C.** pan balance
B. meterstick   **D.** thermometer

Links

Writing

Persuasive Writing
You are a scientist, but you can afford only two of the tools described in this lesson. Choose two tools, and write a persuasive **paragraph** about why they are the most important.

Math

Solve a Problem
You are using a measuring wheel to determine the width of a street. A rotation of the wheel is one meter (3.3 ft). The wheel rotates $9\frac{1}{2}$ times. About how wide is the street?

Art

Looking Closer
Draw an object as you would see it with your eyes. Then draw the same object as you think it would look under a hand lens. Now draw it under the highest-power microscope lens.

 For more links and activities, go to www.hspscience.com

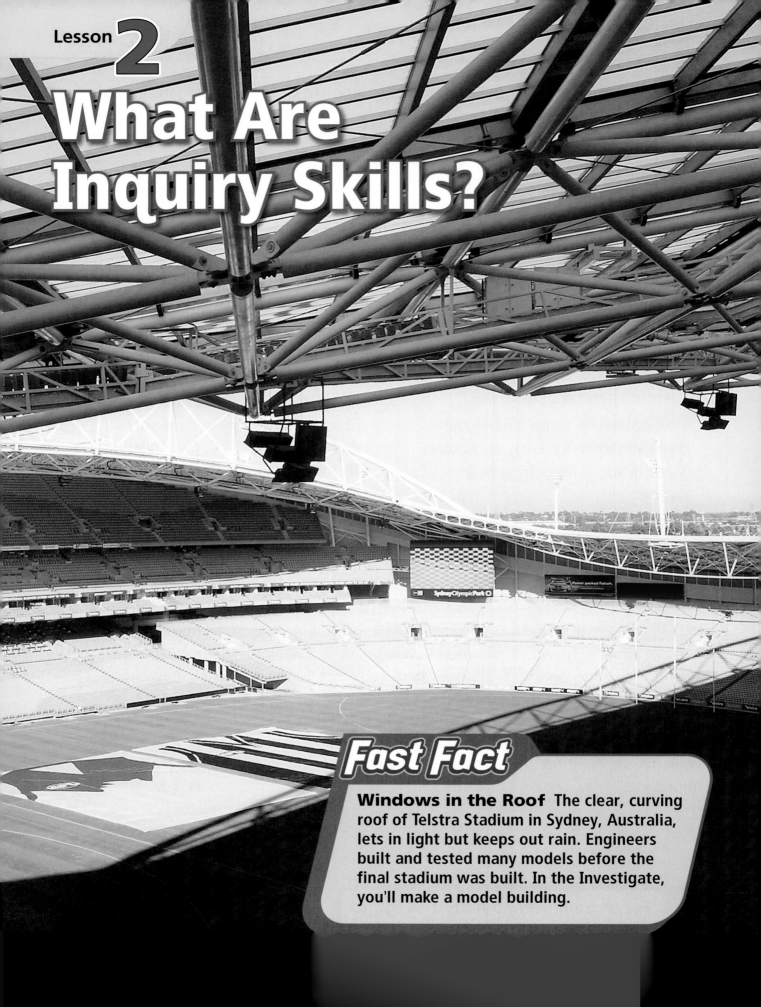

What Are Inquiry Skills?

Fast Fact

Windows in the Roof The clear, curving roof of Telstra Stadium in Sydney, Australia, lets in light but keeps out rain. Engineers built and tested many models before the final stadium was built. In the Investigate, you'll make a model building.

Build a Straw Model

Materials • 16 plastic straws • 30 paper clips • 30 cm masking tape

Procedure

1 You will work with a group to construct a model of a building. First, discuss questions such as these: What should the building look like? What are some ways to use the paper clips and the tape with the straws? What will keep the building from falling down?

2 Have one group member record all the ideas. Be sure to communicate well and respect each other's suggestions.

3 Predict which techniques will work best and try them out. Observe what works, draw conclusions, and record them.

4 Plan how to construct a model building, and then carry out the plan.

Draw Conclusions

1. Why was it important to share ideas before you began construction?

2. **Inquiry Skill** Scientists and engineers often use models to better understand how parts work together. Models help find problems before building. What did you learn about constructing a building by making the model?

Step 3

Step 4

Investigate Further

Choose one additional material or tool to use in constructing your model. Explain how it will improve your model.

Reading in Science

VOCABULARY
observation p. 12
inference p. 12
hypothesis p. 15
experiment p. 15

SCIENCE CONCEPTS
▶ how scientists think
▶ how asking questions helps scientists learn and understand

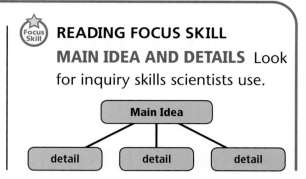

READING FOCUS SKILL

MAIN IDEA AND DETAILS Look for inquiry skills scientists use.

Inquiry Skills

Scientists practice certain ways of thinking, or *inquiry skills.* You use these skills, too. Keep reading to learn more about inquiry skills.

Observe Did you notice the clouds when you woke up today? If so, you made an observation. An **observation** is information from your senses. You can observe how tall or smooth an object is.

Infer Did you ever try to explain why something is a certain color or why it smells like old socks? You were not observing. You were inferring. An **inference** is an untested conclusion based on your observations.

Scientists might observe that one star looks brighter than others. They could infer that the brighter star is bigger, hotter, or closer to Earth than the others.

Predict You often use your knowledge to guess what will happen next. You are predicting. You figure out patterns of events. Then you say what you think will happen next. For example, scientists might observe a series of small earthquakes. Then they use that information to predict a nearby volcano eruption.

MAIN IDEA AND DETAILS Why do scientists observe, infer, and predict?

◀ You use inquiry skills to infer when a flower's buds will open. You might even predict what color they will be.

12

▲ How are these plants different and the same? What
words and numbers can be used to describe them?

Compare Scientists—and you—
often compare things. You describe ways
the things are different and the same.
For example, you learn about two rocks
by comparing the minerals in them.

Classify/Order Is your music
collection sorted in some way, such as
by performer or type of music? Then
you've classified it. You sorted it, based
on an observation. Scientists also classify,
or sort, things. For example, they might
group rocks by color or texture.

You might also put objects or events in
order. You could put planets in order by
their size or their distance from the sun.
You might put sounds in order by their
pitch or their loudness. Putting things in
order helps you see patterns.

Use Numbers Where would
scientists be without numbers? They
use exact numbers to show the mass of
a seed. They use estimates to show the
mass of a planet. Scientists—and you—
use numbers to experiment and learn.

 MAIN IDEA AND DETAILS Name a
way you use each skill on this page in
your daily life.

Use Time and Space Relationships How do the orbits of planets relate to one another? What are the steps in the water cycle? How does a pulley work? To answer these questions, you need to understand time and space relationships. Scientists—and you—need to understand how objects and events affect each other. You also need to know the order in which events happen.

Measure You often need to measure the results of your experiments. How tall did each plant grow? How far did the block slide on sandpaper and on waxed paper? Measuring allows you to compare your results to those of others anywhere. Scientists use the International System (SI) of measurements. It is also called the *metric system.*

Formulate or Use Models Have you ever used a little ball and a big ball to show Earth orbiting the sun? Have you ever drawn the parts of a cell? You were making models. Models help you understand how something works. For example, a globe is a model of Earth.

Scientists often formulate, or make, models. Models help them understand things that are too big, small, fast, slow, or dangerous to observe in person.

 MAIN IDEA AND DETAILS How would you use these three skills to make a diorama of an ecosystem?

▼ These students are measuring how fast loaded and unloaded toys move. Which variables are they controlling? Which variable changes?

◀ What is a possible hypothesis for an investigation using these materials?

Plan and Conduct a Simple Investigation Your CD player will not work. You think of several possible causes, such as dead batteries. Then you plan and conduct a simple investigation. You find and fix the problem. Scientists also use this approach.

Hypothesize Suppose you have a more complex problem. Your class is making sandwiches to sell at a school fair. You must decide how to keep the sandwiches fresh.

A **hypothesis** is a statement of what you think will happen and why. You hypothesize that small, resealable bags work best because they keep air out. Next, you test your hypothesis.

You set up an **experiment** to test your hypothesis. You put different sandwiches in different wrappings. A day later, the meat and cheese sandwich in the resealable bag is freshest. However, maybe it was the cheese, and not the bag, that kept the sandwich fresh. You can't be sure!

Identify and Control Variables To make a fair test, you must identify the variables—the things that can change—in an experiment. Then you need to control—keep the same—all the variables except the one you change and the one you observe. So, only the kind of sandwich wrapping should change.

 MAIN IDEA AND DETAILS Why is it important to control variables?

Insta-Lab

Full Measure
Select an object in the classroom. Measure it as many ways as you can. Record the measurements. Give them to your teacher. You will be given another list. Try to find the object that the new list describes.

Draw Conclusions For the sandwich experiment, suppose the results support your hypothesis. You can draw a conclusion based on the data you collected. Small, resealable bags do keep sandwiches fresher than other wrappings. You are ready for the school fair!

Gather/Record/Interpret/ Display Data In this experiment, you gathered data by checking the freshness of each sandwich. You recorded the results for each wrapping so you would not mix them up. Then you interpreted the data by drawing a conclusion.

If this investigation were for a science class, you would display the results. You might organize the results into a graph, table, or map.

Communicate You would probably tell your friends which sandwich wrapping works best. If this experiment were for a science fair, you would use other tools to share information—writing, pictures, and graphs. You might even display some sandwiches. They would help communicate how well each kind of wrapping worked.

 MAIN IDEA AND DETAILS Why is communication an important skill?

▼ These students are using words, objects, and pictures to communicate. They are sharing how they conducted their experiment with toys and what conclusions they drew.

1. MAIN IDEA AND DETAILS Write details to complete this organizer.

> **MAIN IDEA: Scientists use many different inquiry skills.**

A _____ **B** _____ **C** _____

2. SUMMARIZE Write a sentence that tells the most important information in this lesson.

3. DRAW CONCLUSIONS You cannot understand a friend's science project. What inquiry skill or skills does your friend need to strengthen?

4. VOCABULARY Create a word puzzle with the vocabulary words.

Test Prep

5. Critical Thinking Which skills could help you find out what kind of muscle tissue is on a slide?

6. Which inquiry skill helps you notice a change?
   A. communicate   **C.** observe
   B. hypothesize   **D.** predict

Links

Writing

Narrative Writing
Write a **story** about how you or an imaginary person your age could use several inquiry skills to solve a problem. At the end of the story, name the skills used.

Math

SI Units
Find out more about the International System (SI) of units. What SI units are most like these common units: inches, yards, miles, quarts?

Health

Get Moving
What do you believe is the main reason some people do not like to exercise? Now think of a way to find out whether your reason (hypothesis) is accurate. Write the steps you would take.

 For more links and activities, go to **www.hspscience.com**

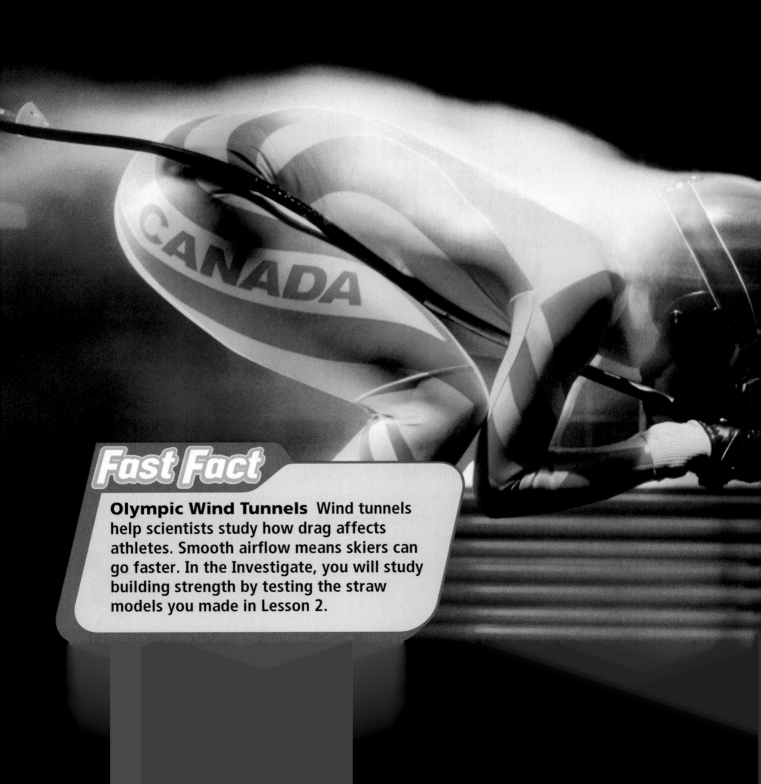

What Is the Scientific Method?

Fast Fact

Olympic Wind Tunnels Wind tunnels help scientists study how drag affects athletes. Smooth airflow means skiers can go faster. In the Investigate, you will study building strength by testing the straw models you made in Lesson 2.

Testing a Straw Model

Materials
- straw models from Lesson 2
- paper cups
- large paper clips
- pennies

Procedure

1. Bend a paper clip to make a hanger for a paper cup, as shown.

2. With your group, predict how many pennies your straw model can support. Then hang the cup on your model, and add one penny at a time. Was your prediction accurate?

3. Now work together to think of ways to strengthen your model. You might also look for other places on your model to hang the cup. Record your ideas.

4. Form a hypothesis about what will make the model stronger. Then experiment to see if the results support the hypothesis.

5. Discuss what made your straw model stronger, and draw conclusions.

6. Communicate your findings to the class.

Draw Conclusions

1. Were you able to increase the strength of your model? How?

2. **Inquiry Skill** Scientists experiment to test their hypotheses. What did you learn from your experiments in this activity?

Step 1

Step 2

Investigate Further

Will your model support more pennies if their weight is spread across the structure? Plan and conduct an experiment to find out.

VOCABULARY
scientific method p. 20

SCIENCE CONCEPTS
▶ how to explain the steps in the scientific method
▶ how the scientific method helps scientists gain knowledge

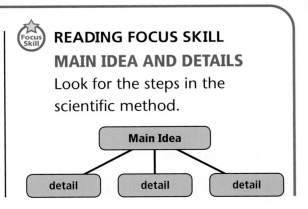

READING FOCUS SKILL

MAIN IDEA AND DETAILS
Look for the steps in the scientific method.

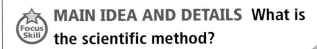

Using the Scientific Method

The **scientific method** is a way scientists find out how things work and affect each other. The five steps of this method help test ideas. You learned the terms used in this method in Lesson 2. Now you will see how scientists—and you—can put these terms to work.

❶ Observe and Ask Questions

After observing the straw models your class built, you might ask:

• Is a cube stronger than a triangle?

• Are straws more likely to bend if they are placed at an angle?
• Is a shorter straw stronger?
• Why do buildings use triangles?

MAIN IDEA AND DETAILS What is the scientific method?

▼ You can find triangle shapes in bridges and other structures. Why is that?

② Form a Hypothesis

Maybe you wonder whether a pyramid or a cube is stronger. Now form a hypothesis. A hypothesis is a statement that tells what will happen and why. A hypothesis must be testable. Here is a possible hypothesis: *Pyramids hold more weight than cubes because triangles are stronger than squares.*

③ Plan an Experiment

How can you test your hypothesis? You think of a plan and then write it as steps. For example, you might hang a cup on each model and then add one penny at a time to each cup.

Next, you need to think about all the variables. Make sure that you are changing only one each time you do the experiment.

In this experiment, both models are made of straws. Both are made the same way. The cups are the same. Only one variable will be tested—the shape of the structures. The complete plan should list all the materials. After that, it should list what to do in order.

④ Conduct an Experiment

Now it's time to conduct, or carry out, your experiment. You follow the steps in the correct order. At each step, you record everything you observe, especially any results you didn't expect.

 MAIN IDEA AND DETAILS How do you plan an experiment?

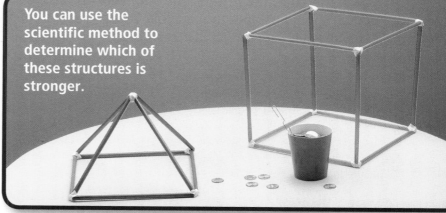

You can use the scientific method to determine which of these structures is stronger.

Insta-Lab

Observe and Ask Questions

Write down three questions about anything you can see while seated at your desk. Discuss the questions with two classmates. Choose one question none of you could answer. Plan a way to find the answer.

21

⑤ Draw Conclusions and Communicate Results

The final step is drawing conclusions. You look at the hypothesis again. Then you look at the observations you recorded. Do the results support your hypothesis? Was the pyramid able to support more pennies than the cube?

In this experiment, you could give the results in numbers. Other times, you might describe the results in other ways. For example, you might explain that a liquid turned blue or a plant wilted.

Scientists share the results of their investigations. That allows others to double-check the results. Then scientists can build new ideas on knowledge they are sure is reliable.

You can share your findings in a written or oral report. Charts, graphs, and diagrams help explain your results and conclusions. A written procedure allows others to repeat what you did.

MAIN IDEA AND DETAILS Why should a report on an investigation be clear and detailed?

▼ Your report should describe your hypothesis, the steps you carried out, the results, and your conclusions. Another person should be able to read your report, repeat your investigation, and get similar results.

1. MAIN IDEA AND DETAILS Draw and complete this graphic organizer.

> **MAIN IDEA: The scientific method consists of five steps.**

> **Step 1: A**_____ and ask questions.

> **Step 2: Form a B**_____.

> **Step 3: Plan an experiment.**

> **Step 4: Conduct an C**_____.

> **Step 5: D**_____ and communicate results.

2. SUMMARIZE Write a summary of this lesson, beginning with this sentence: *The scientific method helps us gain new knowledge.*

3. DRAW CONCLUSIONS Will the scientific method be different 100 years from now? Why or why not?

4. VOCABULARY Write a fill-in-the-blank sentence for the vocabulary term.

Test Prep

5. Critical Thinking Name a problem in a young person's life that could be solved by using the scientific method.

6. When you use the scientific method, what are you testing?

A. conclusions   **C.** hypothesis
B. experiment   **D.** observations

Links

Writing

Expository Writing

Choose an investigation you conducted or observed. Write a **report** on it. Describe how each step of the scientific method was completed—or how it should have been.

Math

Solve a Problem

A penny weighs 2.8 grams (0.1 oz). Suppose a pyramid supports 10 pennies and a cube supports 6. How much more weight will the pyramid support than the cube?

Social Studies

Super Scientists

Choose a scientist who interests you and research his or her life, challenges, and accomplishments. Then make a poster to share interesting facts about this scientist with others.

For more links and activities, go to www.hspscience.com

Review and Test Preparation

Vocabulary Review

Use the terms below to complete the sentences. The page numbers tell you where to look in the chapter if you need help.

microscope p. 6
spring scale p. 8
inference p. 12
hypothesis p. 15
experiment p. 15
scientific method p. 20

1. Forces are measured by a _____.

2. A _____ is a testable explanation of an observation.

3. When you make an observation and then draw a conclusion, you make an _____.

4. To observe very small details, you might use a _____.

5. Scientists find out how things work and affect each other by using the _____.

6. A scientific test in which variables are carefully controlled is an _____.

Check Understanding

Write the letter of the best choice.

7. Which tool measures distance?
   A. forceps   **C.** meterstick
   B. graduate   **D.** microscope

8. Which of these is a hypothesis?
   F. I wonder how long a cactus can live without water here on a sunny windowsill.
   G. How long can a desert cactus live without water on a sunny windowsill?
   H. This experiment will test how long a desert cactus can live without water on a sunny windowsill.
   J. A cactus will live without water for a month on a sunny windowsill, since it can survive in a desert.

9. **MAIN IDEA AND DETAILS** What is the main purpose of the scientific method?
   A. to ask questions
   B. to share information
   C. to test ideas
   D. to plan an experiment

10. In the scientific method, which of these do you do first?
    F. draw conclusions
    G. ask questions
    H. communicate
    J. hypothesize

11. Which of these is an observation?
    A. The plant needs more water.
    B. The plant wilted on the third day.
    C. The plant will need water daily.
    D. The plant will not live in a desert.

12. Which prediction for recycling in 2010 is based on the graph?

Waste Recycled

F. The rate will increase a little.
G. The rate will decrease.
H. The rate will not increase or decrease.
J. The rate will decrease a lot.

13. Which tool measures volume?
A. hand lens
C. scale
B. measuring cup
D. ruler

14. Which inquiry skill is based on identifying things that are alike?
F. classify
H. predict
G. infer
J. use numbers

15. Which of these is a possible inference based on seeing a bird eat seeds?
A. The bird eats only seeds.
B. The bird has a thick beak.
C. The bird doesn't eat meat.
D. The males are quieter.

16. MAIN IDEA AND DETAILS Which of these is not an inquiry skill?
F. infer
G. communicate
H. scale
J. classify/order

Inquiry Skills

17. A model is not the real thing, so why do scientists **use a model**?

18. Which tool or tools would you use to **measure** and **compare** the mass of a cup of fresh water and a cup of salt water?

Critical Thinking

19. A scientist repeats another scientist's experiment but gets different results. What are possible causes?

20. You want to find out how water temperature affects the movement of goldfish.
Part A Write a hypothesis for your investigation.
Part B Identify the variables you will control in your experiment and the variable you will change.

UNIT

Earth and Space Sciences

 The chapters and features in this unit address these Grade Level Indicators from the Ohio Academic Content Standards for Science.

Chapter 1 The Water Cycle and Weather

ES-1 Explain that air surrounds us, takes up space, moves around us as wind, and may be measured using barometric pressure.

ES-2 Identify how water exists in the air in different forms.

ES-3 Investigate how water changes from one state to another.

ES-4 Describe weather by quantities such as temperature, wind direction, wind speed, precipitation and barometric pressure.

ES-5 Record local weather information on a calendar or map and describe changes over a period of time.

ES-6 Trace how weather patterns move from west to east in the U.S.

ES-7 Describe the weather which accompanies cumulus, cumulonimbus, cirrus and stratus clouds.

Chapter 2 Changes to Earth's Surface

ES-1 Describe how wind, water and ice shape and reshape Earth's land surface.

ES-2 Describe how freezing, thawing and plant growth reshape the land surface by causing the weathering of rock.

ES-3 Describe evidence of changes on Earth's surface in terms of slow processes and rapid processes.

Unit A Ohio Expeditions

The investigations and experiences in this unit also address many of the Grade Level Indicators for standards in Science and Technology, Scientific Inquiry, and Scientific Ways of Knowing.

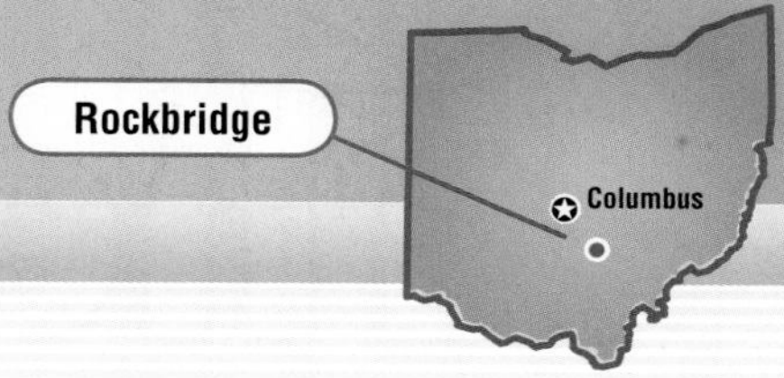

TO: 2wise@hspscience.com
FROM: Raccoon@hspscience.com
RE: Rockbridge Nature Preserve

Dear Mark,

Yesterday, I went with my family to Rockbridge Nature Preserve. I saw the largest natural landbridge in Ohio. It was amazing! Millions of years ago, our state was covered by a warm sea. Can you believe that? The sea drained and the sedimentary rock was exposed to erosion. Rain, wind, and groundwater carved a crevice into the stone. The bridge looks like an arch and is over 100 feet long. You've got to see it!

Rock on, dude!
Jason

Experiment!

The weather changes from day to day and from season to season. A rainy day can help fight a forest fire, but a drought can make forest fires more likely. Can you use the clouds to predict the weather? Is there a pattern of changes that goes with certain clouds? Plan and conduct an investigation to find out.

1 The Water Cycle

Lesson 1 **What Is the Water Cycle?**

Lesson 2 **How Is the Water Cycle Related to Weather?**

Lesson 3 **How Do Land Features Affect the Water Cycle?**

Lesson 4 **How Can Weather Be Predicted?**

Vocabulary

water cycle
precipitation
evaporation
condensation
rain
sleet
snow
hail
tornado
hurricane

sea breeze
land breeze
rain shadow
air mass
cold front
warm front
barometer
anemometer

What do **YOU** wonder?

Each spring as the weather warms, snow and
ice in the Yukon begin to melt. The snow and ice
turn into millions of gallons of moving water.
Where do you think this water goes?

What Is the Water Cycle?

Fast Fact

Got Water? Almost all of Earth's water is in the oceans. In fact, more than 97 percent of Earth's water is ocean water! In the Investigate, you'll find out what ocean water is like.

From Salt Water to Fresh Water

Materials
- spoon
- salt
- 500 ml of warm water
- cotton swabs
- small glass jar
- large bowl
- plastic wrap
- large rubber band
- small ball
- masking tape

Procedure

1. Stir two spoonfuls of salt into the warm water. Dip a cotton swab into the mixture. Touch the swab to your tongue. **Record** what you **observe**. CAUTION: **Throw the swab away. Do not share swabs.**

2. Put the jar in the center of the bowl. Pour the salt water into the bowl. Be careful not to get any salt water in the jar.

3. Put plastic wrap over the bowl. The wrap should not touch the jar. Use the rubber band to hold the wrap in place.

4. Put the ball on the wrap over the jar. Make sure the wrap doesn't touch the jar.

5. Mark the level of the salt water with a piece of tape on the outside of the bowl. Put the bowl in a sunny spot for one day.

6. Remove the wrap and the ball. Use clean swabs to taste the water in the jar and in the bowl. **Record** what you **observe**.

Step 2

Step 4

Draw Conclusions

1. What did you **observe** during the investigation?

2. **Inquiry Skill** Scientists **infer** based on what they **observe**. What can you infer is a source of fresh water for Earth?

Investigate Further

What would happen if you left the bowl and jar in the sun for several days? Write a hypothesis. Test it!

SI-2 Describe patterns/infer; **SI-3** Design and conduct simple investigations; **SK-2** Record results/data

31

Reading in Science

 ES-2 Identify atmospheric water; **ES-3** Investigate water changes;
PS-1 Identify physical changes; **PS-4** Explain states of matter

VOCABULARY
water cycle p. 32
precipitation p. 32
evaporation p. 34
condensation p. 35

SCIENCE CONCEPTS
► what processes make up the water cycle
► how a raindrop is formed

 READING FOCUS SKILL
SEQUENCE Look for the order in which events of the water cycle occur.

The Water Cycle

As you're on the way home from school, it suddenly starts raining. Where did the rain come from? When it reaches the ground, where will it go?

Water is constantly moving through the environment. Water moves from the surface of Earth to the air and then back to Earth's surface again in a never-ending process called the **water cycle**.

Energy from the sun drives the water cycle. When the sun's energy warms water on Earth's surface, the water changes from a liquid to a gas.

The gas form of water, called water vapor, goes into the air. If the water vapor cools, it becomes liquid water again and falls back to Earth. Water that falls back to Earth is called **precipitation** (pree•sip•uh•TAY•shuhn). Precipitation can be rain, snow, sleet, or hail. Rain is liquid water. Snow, sleet, and hail are frozen water. Energy from the sun changes precipitation to water vapor once again. This continues the water cycle.

 SEQUENCE What steps must take place in order for ocean water to become rain?

A cloud forms when water vapor cools. The water vapor becomes liquid again in a process known as condensation. The liquid water in clouds is in the form of tiny droplets that can stay up in the air.

When the sun warms the surface of water, the water changes to water vapor, a gas. The gas then becomes part of the air.

In the clouds, water droplets can bump into each other and join to make larger droplets. Soon the droplets become heavy and fall to Earth as precipitation.

Some precipitation soaks into the ground. Precipitation can also run over the ground and flow into streams, rivers, lakes, and eventually the ocean.

Parts of the Water Cycle

It's a hot day. To cool off, you take a swim. When you get out of the water, you dry yourself with a towel. You leave the towel in the sunlight while you play with your friends. When you come back, the towel is dry. Where did the water in the towel go?

The water evaporated. **Evaporation** (ee•vap•uh•RAY•shuhn) is the process by which a liquid changes into a gas. A large amount of water evaporates from Earth's oceans, lakes, and rivers every day. But water also evaporates from the soil, from puddles, and even from your skin as you sweat.

Water vapor mixes with other gases in the air. When the wind blows, air moves. The water vapor moves with the air. Sometimes the water vapor can move very long distances. It can also move high up into the air.

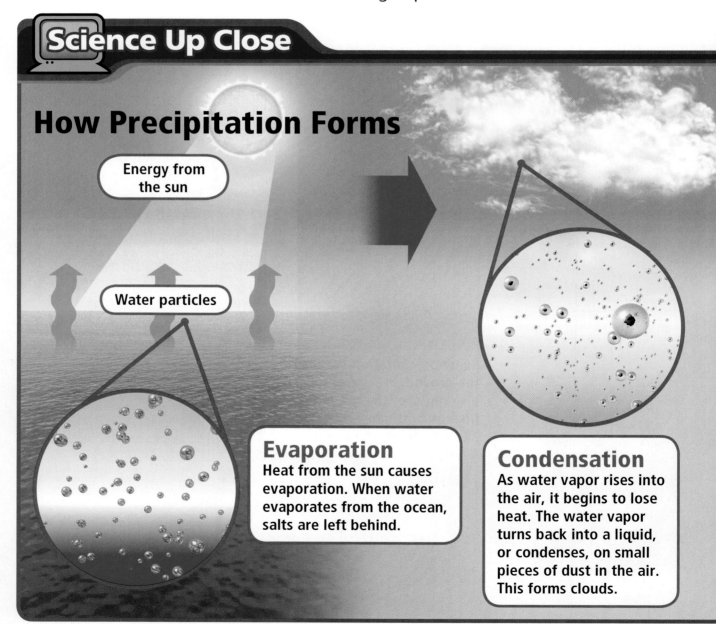

Science Up Close

How Precipitation Forms

Energy from the sun

Water particles

Evaporation
Heat from the sun causes evaporation. When water evaporates from the ocean, salts are left behind.

Condensation
As water vapor rises into the air, it begins to lose heat. The water vapor turns back into a liquid, or condenses, on small pieces of dust in the air. This forms clouds.

When the water vapor moves up in the air, it becomes cooler. If the water vapor cools enough, condensation (kahn•duhn•SAY•shuhn) happens. **Condensation** is the process by which a gas changes into a liquid. Have you ever seen water dripping from an air conditioner? The dripping water is from water vapor that condensed as it cooled.

Air has many small bits of dust in it. When water vapor cools, it condenses on dust particles. The condensed water and dust particles form clouds. Inside clouds, tiny droplets of water can join to make larger droplets. These droplets can join to make even larger, heavier droplets. When the droplets become too heavy to stay in the air, they fall to Earth as precipitation. The type of precipitation that falls depends on the temperature of the air around it.

 SEQUENCE **Heat causes a piece of ice to melt. What will happen next?**

For more links and activities, go to **www.hspscience.com**

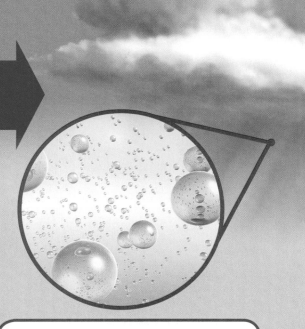

Precipitation
Inside clouds, small water droplets join to form larger droplets. In time, these larger droplets become raindrops that fall to Earth. The water in raindrops is fresh water.

Insta-Lab

Forms of Water
Fill a glass with ice water. Fill another glass with room-temperature water. Observe the glasses for at least five minutes. Describe any changes you see. What property differed between the glasses? What process occurred on the outside of one glass? Why did this process occur? Can you control the process? Try it.

Groundwater and Runoff

When rain falls on land, some of it soaks into the soil. Plants use much of this water. Also, some of it evaporates back into the air. But not all of the water in soil evaporates or is used by plants.

Some of the water that goes into soil moves deeper into the ground. The water deep in the ground moves down until it gets to solid rock. Because the water cannot move through the rock, it begins to collect underground. After a while, a lot of collected water forms a body of groundwater.

Many people rely on groundwater for their drinking water. They dig wells to reach the groundwater. Then they pump the water up to the surface.

Rain that is not soaked up by the soil becomes runoff. The runoff flows into creeks and streams, which flow into rivers. Large rivers, such as the Mississippi River and the Columbia River, flow into even larger bodies of water.

 SEQUENCE In what sequence of events does groundwater form?

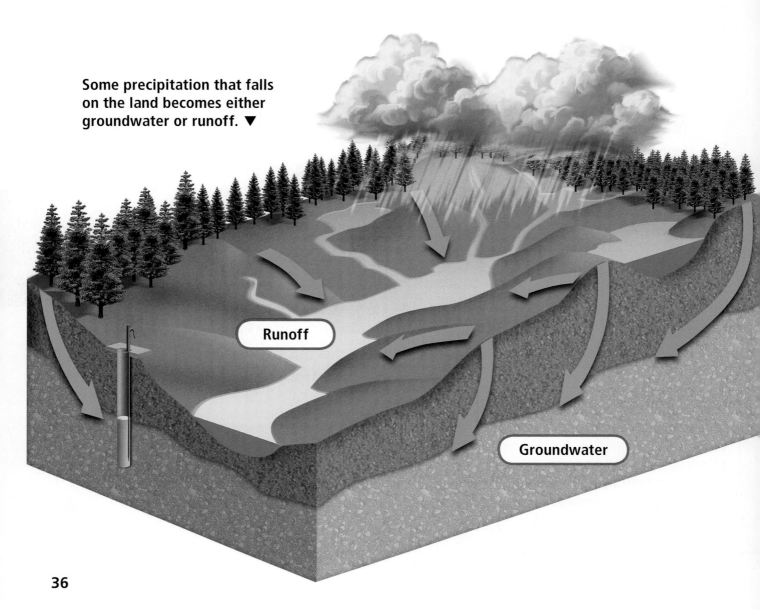

Some precipitation that falls on the land becomes either groundwater or runoff. ▼

Runoff

Groundwater

Focus Skill

1. SEQUENCE Draw and complete each graphic organizer.

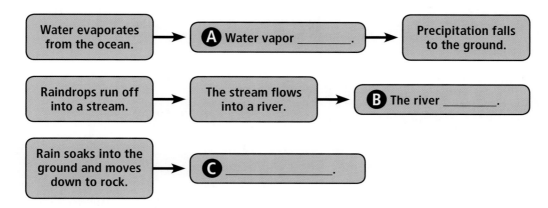

| Water evaporates from the ocean. | → | **A** Water vapor _____. | → | Precipitation falls to the ground. |

| Raindrops run off into a stream. | → | The stream flows into a river. | → | **B** The river _____. |

| Rain soaks into the ground and moves down to rock. | → | **C** _____. |

2. SUMMARIZE Draw a diagram that summarizes this lesson.

3. DRAW CONCLUSIONS Will pond water evaporate faster on a warm, sunny day or on a warm, cloudy day? Explain.

4. VOCABULARY Write one sentence that uses all the vocabulary terms from the lesson.

Test Prep

5. Critical Thinking Most rainwater comes from the ocean, but rainwater is not salty. Why not?

6. Which of the following happens when water vapor cools?

A. condensation   **C.** heating

B. evaporation   **D.** vaporization

Links

Writing

Persuasive Writing
Less than 3 percent of Earth's water is fresh. Write a **speech** that explains to people why it's important to protect Earth's freshwater resources. Present your speech to the class.

Math

Make a Circle Graph
Earth is known as "the water planet." Find out how much of Earth's surface is covered by water. Make a circle graph that shows this information.

Social Studies

Where Is Water?
Find a world map. Make a list of all the major bodies of water you see. Research one of the bodies of water, and report on it. Include information such as how the body of water formed.

 For more links and activities, go to www.hspscience.com

How Is the Water Cycle Related to Weather?

Fast Fact

When It Rains, It Pours Floods cause billions of dollars of damage to property every year. It takes only 60 centimeters (2 ft) of moving floodwater to sweep away a car. Higher waters sweep away trees, bridges, and even buildings! In the Investigate, you'll model a flood.

Modeling a Flood

Materials
- aluminum baking pan
- soil
- plastic gloves
- toothpick
- plastic bag
- water
- beaker

Procedure

1. Half-fill the aluminum baking pan with soil. Always wear gloves when handling any type of soil. Make a path in the soil to form a "river channel" that runs through the center of the pan. Build up some small hills around the river channel. Press the soil in place.

2. Use the toothpick to poke several holes in the bottom of the plastic bag.

3. Measure 150 mL of water in the beaker. Have one partner hold the plastic bag over the pan while the other partner slowly pours the water into the bag. Let the water drip over the pan to model a rainy day. Record what you observe.

4. Repeat Step 3 several times until the pan becomes three-fourths full of water.

Step 1

Step 3

Draw Conclusions

1. What happened to the soil in the pan after the first "rainy day"? What happened after the last "rainy day"?

2. **Inquiry Skill** Scientists often gather, record, and interpret data to understand how things work. Interpret what you observed and recorded about your model. What do you think causes floods?

Investigate Further

Would the results be the same if there were several days between rainfalls? Plan and conduct a simple investigation to find out.

Reading in Science

VOCABULARY
rain p. 40
sleet p. 40
snow p. 41
hail p. 41
tornado p. 42
hurricane p. 42

SCIENCE CONCEPTS
▶ what are some kinds of precipitation
▶ what causes different kinds of weather

READING FOCUS SKILL
CAUSE AND EFFECT Look for the causes of certain types of weather.

| cause | → | effect |

Kinds of Precipitation

You may think of precipitation as bad weather. After all, rain keeps you from playing outdoors. It can even cause floods. Hail can damage cars and homes. Sleet can make roads dangerous. Snow can pile up on driveways and on sidewalks. However, all of these kinds of precipitation are simply part of the water cycle.

What causes different kinds of precipitation? Most water on Earth, such as ocean water, is liquid. You learned in Lesson 1 that if water is heated enough, it becomes water vapor, a gas. If water is cooled enough, it freezes.

Rain, the most common kind of precipitation, is liquid water. Rain falls if the temperature is higher than 0°C (32°F). **Sleet** is frozen rain. Sleet is

Kinds of Precipitation

Kind	Cause
Rain	Water vapor condenses in air.
Snow	Water vapor turns into ice crystals instead of a liquid.
Sleet	Falling rain passes through a layer of freezing-cold air and turns into ice.
Hail	Rain freezes and then falls through a warmer pocket of air. The frozen rain is coated with liquid water and then carried back up to a cold pocket of air, where the liquid coating also freezes.

RAIN
Rain is liquid precipitation. Tiny raindrops are called drizzle. Heavy rain can cause floods.

caused when rain falls through a layer of freezing-cold air. This turns the rain into ice pellets. **Snow** is made of ice crystals. Snow is caused when the air temperature is so cold that water vapor turns directly into ice. **Hail** is round pieces of ice. Hail is caused when rain freezes and then falls to a warmer part of the air. Raindrops coat the frozen rain before it is carried back up to a colder part of the air by wind. The new liquid coating then freezes also. This happens over and over until the hail is too heavy and it falls to the ground.

 CAUSE AND EFFECT What causes rain to become sleet?

SNOW
Snow is made of ice crystals. The crystals, which have many different shapes, form high in the air.

▲ **SLEET**
Sleet is made up of frozen raindrops. Sleet forms when rain falls through a pocket of cold air.

▲ **HAIL**
Hail can be as small as a pea or as large as a grapefruit. The size of a piece of hail depends on how many times it is carried up and down in a storm cloud.

Severe Storms

Heat from the sun provides the energy for the water cycle. This same energy causes severe storms.

One type of severe storm is a thunderstorm. Thunderstorms are storms with lightning, strong winds, and heavy rain. Sometimes tornadoes form during thunderstorms. A **tornado** is a fast-spinning spiral of wind that stretches from the clouds of a thunderstorm to the ground. Tornadoes can have wind speeds greater than 400 kilometers (250 mi) per hour! Every year, there are about 800–1000 tornadoes in the United States.

Another kind of severe storm is a hurricane. A **hurricane** is a large storm with wind speeds of 119 kilometers (74 mi) per hour or more. Hurricanes form

▲ **The United States has more tornadoes per year than any other country in the world.**

Blizzards are severe snowstorms that can last for hours. Blizzards have strong winds, blowing snow, and very low air temperatures. ▼

42

Hurricanes are categorized by their wind speed. Does a hurricane's wind speed relate to the amount of damage it causes?

Hurricane Strength

Category (Wind Speed)	Hurricane	Cost of Damage
5 (over 155 mph)	Hurricane Andrew, 1992	$34.1 billion
4 (131–155 mph)	Hurricane Charley, 2004	$14 billion
3 (111–130 mph)	Hurricane Betsy, 1965	$9 billion
2 (96–110 mph)	Hurricane Floyd, 1999	$4.9 billion
1 (74–95 mph)	Hurricane Agnes, 1972	$9.1 billion

over warm areas of oceans. These storms can last for weeks out at sea. But when a hurricane moves over land, it no longer gets energy from the warm water. It soon becomes weaker.

The winds of a hurricane spin around the calm center of the storm, called the eye. Rain, waves, and "storm surge," a huge bulge of water pushed onto the land by the storm, can cause flooding.

 CAUSE AND EFFECT What causes flooding during a hurricane?

Insta-Lab

Tornado in a Bottle

Tape a washer over the mouth of a clear plastic bottle. Fill the bottle three-fourths full of water. Tape a second clear plastic bottle upside down on top of the first bottle. Turn the bottles over and swirl the top bottle around quickly. What do you observe?

Weather Safety

Severe storms are dangerous. Injuries can be caused by downed power lines and trees. Floods can occur. It's important to keep yourself safe during severe weather. One way to stay safe is to follow safety rules in your community. Local radio or TV stations will tell you if a severe storm is approaching your area.

There are also other ways of warning people about severe weather. For example, some areas have weather sirens that are turned on when people detect a severe storm. Some sirens can even detect nearby tornadoes on their own and warn people in the area.

When there is a severe storm, stay inside a building unless officials tell you to leave. Sometimes people are asked to leave an area before a storm strikes. If that happens, people will follow a safe route away from the area.

 CAUSE AND EFFECT How might a severe storm affect you?

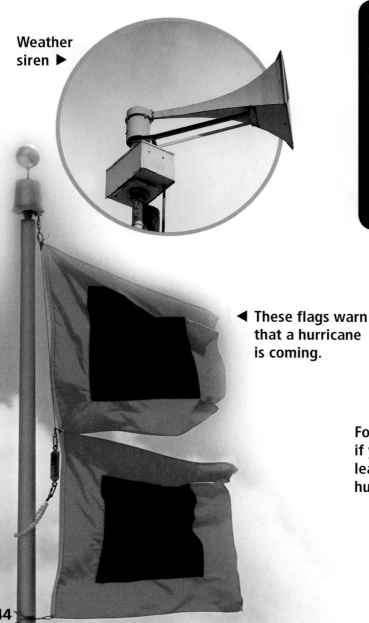

Weather siren ▶

◀ These flags warn that a hurricane is coming.

▲ Watch TV during severe weather to get directions about what to do.

Follow signs like these if you are asked to leave an area when a hurricane is coming. ▶

1. CAUSE AND EFFECT Draw and complete each graphic organizer.

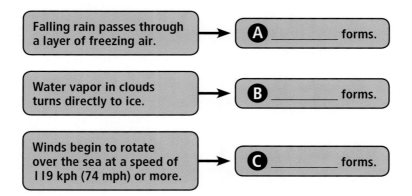

Falling rain passes through a layer of freezing air.	→	**A** _____ forms.
Water vapor in clouds turns directly to ice.	→	**B** _____ forms.
Winds begin to rotate over the sea at a speed of 119 kph (74 mph) or more.	→	**C** _____ forms.

2. SUMMARIZE Summarize this lesson by describing what causes each of these kinds of weather: rain, sleet, snow, hail, tornado, hurricane.

3. DRAW CONCLUSIONS What affects the kind of precipitation that will fall?

4. VOCABULARY Write a weather report that uses at least four of the vocabulary terms that come from this lesson.

Test Prep

5. Critical Thinking Explain how weather is related to the water cycle.

6. Which of the following is **not** a kind of precipitation?
A. air **C.** rain
B. hail **D.** sleet

Links

Writing

Narrative Writing
Suppose that you're a drop of water in a cloud. Write a **story** that describes what you experience as you travel through the water cycle.

Math

Measure Temperature
Measure the outdoor temperature. Based on that temperature, what kind of precipitation is most likely to fall now in your area?

Health

Weather and Health
Make a booklet that shows what to do to stay safe in severe weather such as tornadoes, thunderstorms, and hurricanes.

 For more links and activities, go to **www.hspscience.com**

How Do Land Features Affect the Water Cycle?

Fast Fact

Thunderstorms in a Row When cold air over the ocean meets warm air over the land, squall lines can form. A squall line is a long line of moving thunderstorms. Squall lines can stretch across the land for hundreds of kilometers! In the Investigate, you'll observe how land and water heat up.

Heating Land and Water

Materials
- 2 small plastic or foam cups
- dark soil or sand
- water
- 2 thermometers
- plastic gloves
- stopwatch
- light source with 100-W bulb or greater

Procedure

1. Fill one cup with dark soil or sand. Fill the second cup with water. Place a thermometer upright in each cup.

2. Time one minute, using the stopwatch. Then measure and record the temperatures of the two cups.

3. Remove the thermometer after every measurement. Place the cups under the light. Make sure that the two cups get the same amount of light.

4. After the cups have been under the light for 5 minutes, measure and record their temperatures. Do this four times in all. Then turn the lamp off.

5. Time 5 minutes, and then measure and record the temperatures of the cups. Do this three times in all.

Step 3

Step 4

Draw Conclusions

1. Describe how the soil and water heated differently. How did they cool differently?

2. **Inquiry Skill** Scientists use what they observe to form a hypothesis. Use your observations from this investigation to hypothesize how the weather on Earth would be different if Earth's surface were mostly land instead of mostly water.

Investigate Further

Does wet soil heat differently from dry soil? Conduct an experiment to find out.

Reading in Science

VOCABULARY
sea breeze p. 48
land breeze p. 48
rain shadow p. 50

SCIENCE CONCEPTS
► how temperature affects the water cycle
► how landforms affect the water cycle

 READING FOCUS SKILL
CAUSE AND EFFECT Look for ways that landforms affect the water cycle.

| cause | → | effect |

Sea Breezes and Land Breezes

Have you ever been to the beach on a hot day? It might be so hot that your feet burn when you walk on the sand. But when you go into the water, you quickly cool off. That's because the water is cooler than the sand.

Land heats up much more quickly than water. Land also cools down more quickly than water. Because of this, the temperature of the air over land is almost always different from the temperature of the air over nearby water. During the day, the air over water is cooler than the air over land. The hot air over a beach is pushed upward by the cool air moving in from over the water. This causes a sea breeze. A **sea breeze** is a breeze moving from the water to the land. During the night, the land becomes cooler than the water. This causes a land breeze. A **land breeze** is a breeze moving from the land to the water.

 CAUSE AND EFFECT What causes a land breeze?

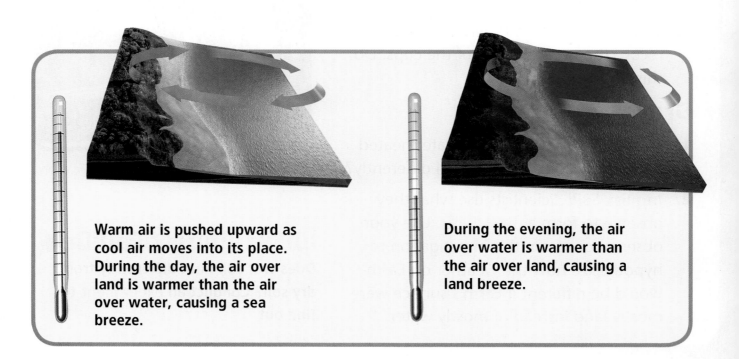

Warm air is pushed upward as cool air moves into its place. During the day, the air over land is warmer than the air over water, causing a sea breeze.

During the evening, the air over water is warmer than the air over land, causing a land breeze.

48

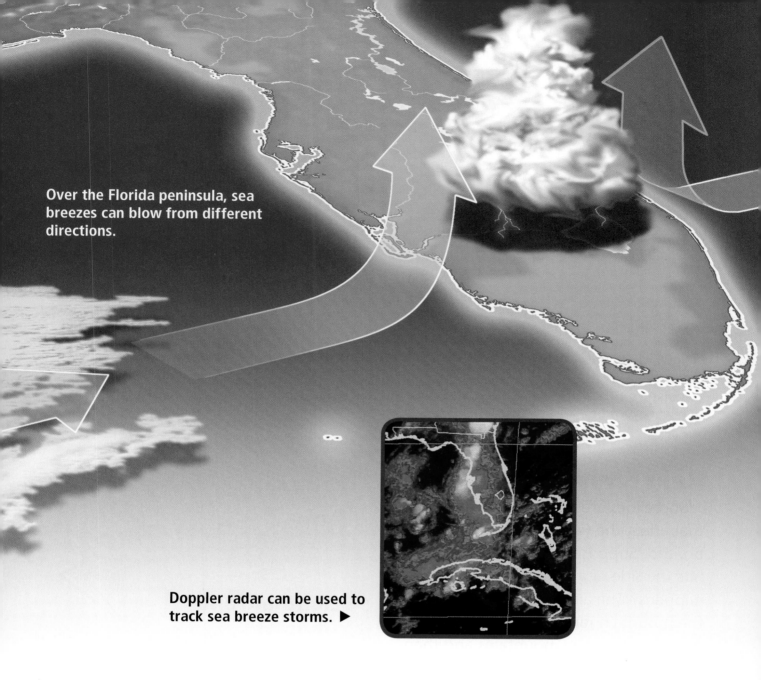

Over the Florida peninsula, sea breezes can blow from different directions.

Doppler radar can be used to track sea breeze storms. ▶

Sea Breeze Storms

You learned in Lesson 1 that when water vapor cools, it condenses to form precipitation. Sometimes, cool sea breezes push clouds toward the shore. The clouds can then produce storms over the land. These storms are called sea breeze storms.

Over the Florida peninsula, for example, sea breezes can come in from both the east and the west. A peninsula is a piece of land that is almost completely surrounded by water. The collision of the two sea breezes causes the air to become unstable. If the two bodies of air have a lot of water vapor, a very strong sea breeze storm can happen over the center of the peninsula. This type of sea breeze storm happens often in Florida during the summer.

 CAUSE AND EFFECT What causes a sea breeze storm?

WET SIDE
As air is pushed upward, it cools and releases its moisture.

DRY SIDE
As the cool air moves downward, it warms and dries out while spreading over land.

Rain Shadows

Shorelines are not the only landforms that affect the water cycle. Mountains do, too. Suppose a moving body of air hits the side of a mountain range. What happens? The air can't move through the mountain range. Instead, it's pushed up one side of the mountains and then over them. As the air moves up on one side, it cools. The water vapor in the cooler air condenses and brings rain to that side. By the time the air reaches the other side of the mountains, the air is dry. So, it doesn't rain on the other side. This causes a rain shadow. A **rain shadow** is the area on the far side of a mountain range that gets little or no rain or cloud cover.

 CAUSE AND EFFECT What is the effect of a rain shadow?

Lightning and Thunder

The next time a thunderstorm approaches your area, watch for lightning. When you see the lightning, start counting "one-Mississippi, two-Mississippi," and so on. When you hear the thunder, stop counting. For every three seconds you count, the thunderstorm is about 1 kilometer from where you are. How far away is the thunderstorm when you first hear the thunder? After five minutes?

Focus Skill

1. CAUSE AND EFFECT Draw and complete the graphic organizers.

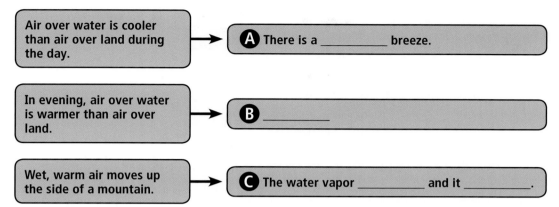

Air over water is cooler than air over land during the day. → **A** There is a _____ breeze.

In evening, air over water is warmer than air over land. → **B** _____

Wet, warm air moves up the side of a mountain. → **C** The water vapor _____ and it _____.

2. SUMMARIZE Write a paragraph summarizing the lesson. Start with this sentence: *The water cycle is affected by landforms.*

3. DRAW CONCLUSIONS Will sea breeze storms happen more often in warm places or cool places? Explain.

4. VOCABULARY Explain the difference between a land breeze and a sea breeze.

Test Prep

5. Critical Thinking Explain why a mountain may be green on one side and desert-like on the other.

6. How does warm air move?
- **A.** It falls.
- **B.** It is pushed upward.
- **C.** It spins.
- **D.** It stays still.

Links

Writing

Expository Writing

Suppose you're an early explorer of a mountain range that has a rain shadow. Write a **journal** describing your explorations of the range.

Math

Solve Problems

A sea breeze storm is moving across Florida from the northeast to the southwest at 23 km/hr. How long does the storm take to reach Tampa if it started above Orlando, which is 137 km away?

Physical Education

Water Sports

Many water sports, such as sailing, make use of sea breezes. Choose a sport that uses sea breezes, and write a simple how-to guide for this sport.

 For more links and activities, go to **www.hspscience.com**

How Can Weather Be Predicted ?

Fast Fact

A Winter Wonderland Ice storms deposit massive amounts of ice over everything. In fact, during a severe ice storm, about 45,000 kilograms (99,000 lb) of ice can pile up on a 15-meter (50-ft) pine tree! In the Investigate, you'll make and use a weather instrument that helps people predict storms and other weather.

Making a Barometer

Materials
- scissors
- safety goggles
- large round balloon
- plastic jar
- large rubber band
- tape
- wooden craft stick
- large index card
- ruler

Procedure

1 CAUTION: **Wear safety goggles. Be careful when using the scissors.** Use the scissors to cut the neck off the balloon.

2 Have your partner hold the jar while you stretch the balloon over the open end. Secure the balloon with the rubber band.

3 Tape the craft stick to the top of the balloon. More than half of the craft stick should stretch out from the jar's edge.

4 On the blank side of an index card, draw a line and label it *Day 1.* Tape the card to a wall. The line should be at the same height as the stick. Next to the line, record the current weather.

5 Air pressure is the force of air pressing down on Earth. Record the air pressure by marking the position of the stick on the index card for four days. Label the marks *Days 2–5.* Also record the weather. Measure distances between the marks.

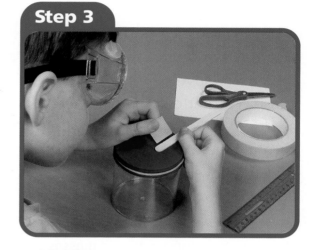
Step 3

Step 4

Draw Conclusions

1. How did the air pressure change? What might cause changes in air pressure?

2. **Inquiry Skill** Scientists use instruments to measure weather data. Infer how a barometer works.

Investigate Further

Track changes in air pressure and weather for five more days. What can you infer is the relationship between air pressure and type of weather?

ES-1 Explain air pressure; **ES-5** Record local weather information; **SI-2** Describe patterns/infer; **SK-2** Record results/data

53

VOCABULARY
air mass p. 54
cold front p. 56
warm front p. 56
barometer p. 60
anemometer p. 60

SCIENCE CONCEPTS
▶ what makes an air mass
▶ how to read a weather map

 READING FOCUS SKILL
CAUSE AND EFFECT Look for the causes of changes in weather.

cause	→	effect

Air Masses

Have you ever wondered why the weather can be sunny one day and rainy the next? Movements of air masses cause weather changes. An **air mass** is a large body of air. All of the air in an air mass has a similar temperature and moisture level. Moisture level means the amount of water that is in air.

The map shows where the air masses that affect North America form. Cool air masses are in blue. Warm air masses are in red. ▼

The temperature and moisture level of an air mass depend on where the air mass formed. Air masses that form over land are dry. Air masses that form over water have a lot of moisture in them. In the United States, cold air masses come from the north. Warm air masses come from the south.

The temperature and moisture level of an air mass affect the kind of weather the air mass brings. Cold, wet air masses can bring snow to an area. But cold, dry air masses can bring cool weather

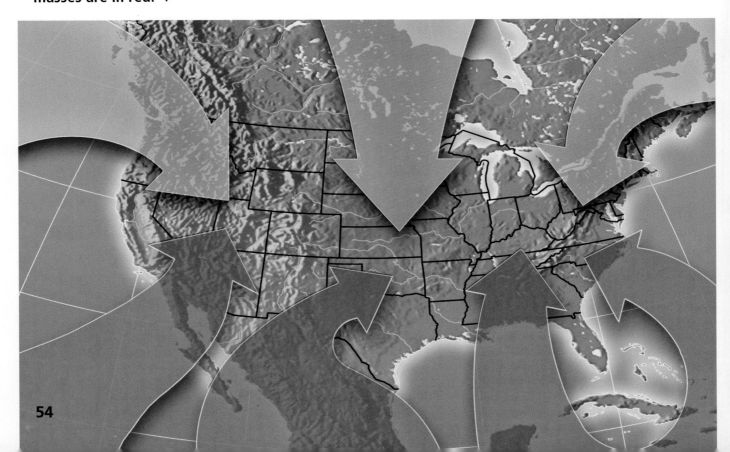

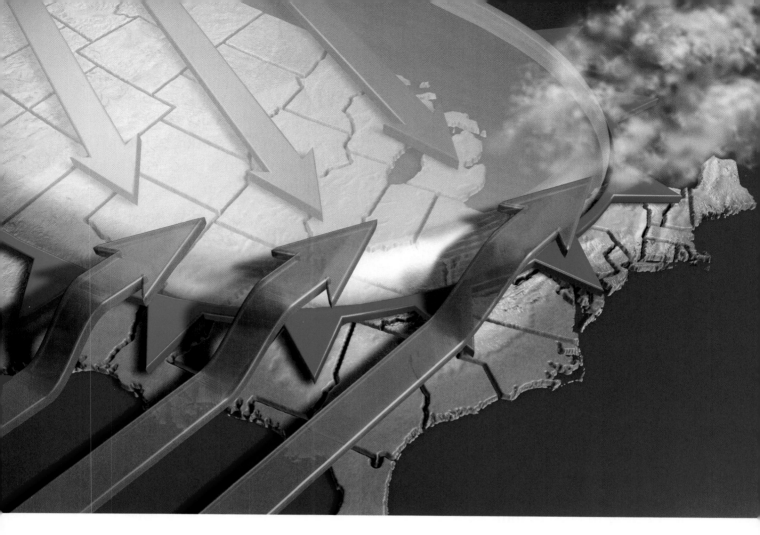

▲ Air masses do not mix very much with each other. Instead, they stay separate as they move.

with little or no precipitation. Warm air masses with a lot of moisture usually bring precipitation. But warm, dry masses can bring warm weather with little or no precipitation.

As air masses move, they tend to stay separate from each other. That's because warm air is lighter than cold air. When they come in contact with each other, warm air masses are pushed upward and cold air masses sink.

 CAUSE AND EFFECT What causes the weather to change?

Making an Air Mass

Fill a cup halfway with ice cubes. Wait five minutes. With one hand, pour chilled water into the cup. Hold the other hand over the cup as you pour the water. What do you feel? If the air you felt were an air mass, how would you describe it?

Fronts

When air masses move, they come into contact with other air masses. The border between one air mass and another is called a front. Most storms happen at fronts.

There are two main types of fronts: cold fronts and warm fronts. A **cold front** forms where a cold air mass moves under a warm air mass. This causes the warm air mass to move upward. As the warm air mass moves up, it begins to cool. Remember that water vapor condenses when it cools. The condensing water vapor in the upward-moving air mass forms clouds. It might begin to rain along the front. Thunderstorms will often develop. Also, the air temperature will become cooler as the cold air mass moves forward.

A **warm front** forms where warm air moves over cold air. The warm air slides up over the cold air as it moves forward. Warm fronts generally move slowly. Because of this, warm fronts bring steady rain instead of thunderstorms. Warm fronts are then followed by clear, warm weather as the warm air mass moves over the area.

Fronts do not always move. A front that stays in one place for many days is called a stationary front. Stationary fronts happen when the two air masses along a front do not have enough energy to move. The weather along a stationary front is often cloudy and wet. This kind of front can leave many inches of snow or cause flooding rains.

For this reason, stationary fronts can be dangerous.

Different kinds of fronts move differently. As a result, they cause different kinds of clouds to form. The types of clouds in an area can help you predict the weather.

 CAUSE AND EFFECT **What are the effects of a cold front?**

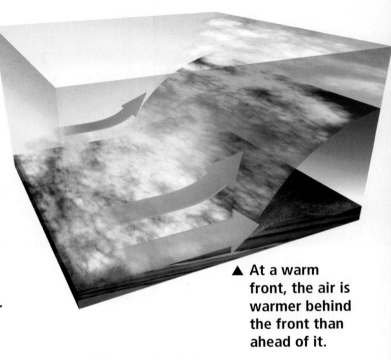

▲ At a warm front, the air is warmer behind the front than ahead of it.

At a cold front, the air is colder behind the front than ahead of it. ▼

◄ STRATUS CLOUDS
Stratus clouds often occur along warm fronts.

Stratus clouds can develop into nimbostratus clouds. Nimbostratus clouds bring light rain or snow showers. ►

◄ CUMULUS CLOUDS
Cumulus clouds are common on clear, warm days.

Cumulus (KYOO•myuh•luhs) clouds can develop into cumulonimbus, or thunderstorm, clouds. ►

CIRRUS CLOUDS
Cirrus (SIR•uhs) clouds usually indicate cooler, fair weather.

Weather Maps

Have you ever used a street map to find a friend's house? Have you ever used a trail map while hiking? Another kind of map you can use is a weather map. A weather map helps you know what the weather is like in an area.

Weather maps use symbols to show the weather. A sun symbol means it is sunny in the area. A symbol of a cloud with rain means it is raining in the area.

Fronts are also shown on weather maps. The symbol for a warm front is a red line with half circles along it. A blue line with triangles shows a cold front.

Many weather maps show temperatures. Sometimes the temperatures are written on a map. In the United States, temperatures are given in degrees Fahrenheit. Almost all other countries give temperatures in degrees Celsius. When temperatures are not written on a weather map, they may be shown using colors. If an area is warm, it is colored red (very hot), orange (warm), or yellow (mild). If an

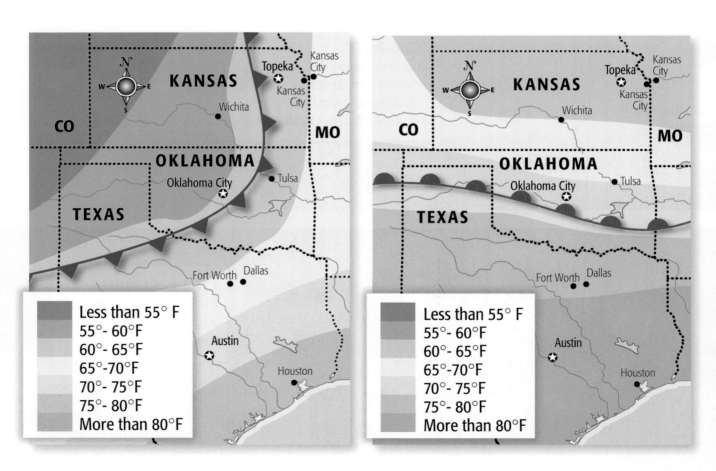

▲ A line with triangles is the symbol for a cold front. The triangles point in the direction of movement.

▲ A line with half circles is the symbol for a warm front. The half circles point in the direction the front is moving.

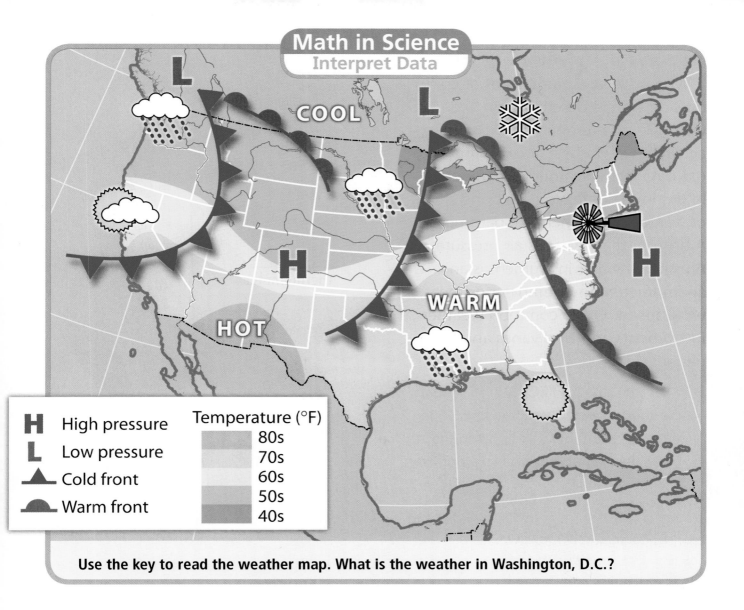

L

COOL

L

H

HOT

WARM

H

	High pressure	Temperature (°F)	
H			80s
L	Low pressure		70s
▲	Cold front		60s
⌒	Warm front		50s
			40s

Use the key to read the weather map. What is the weather in Washington, D.C.?

area is cold, it is colored green (cool) or blue (very cold).

Other information you may see on a weather map includes wind speed and direction, air pressure, and the highest and lowest temperatures in an area for the day.

Where does all the information on a weather map come from? Weather information is collected at thousands of weather stations across the country. A weather station is a place that has many different instruments for measuring weather. The information from the weather stations is reported to the National Weather Service (NWS). The NWS then studies the weather data from all the weather stations. Each day, the NWS makes weather maps based on the information collected at all the weather stations.

 CAUSE AND EFFECT How would the above weather map look if a warm front were moving through Florida?

Measuring Weather

When you say that it is hot or cold outside, you're describing one part of weather—the temperature. The most accurate way to describe weather is to use data from weather instruments. In the Investigate, you built one kind of weather instrument—a barometer. A **barometer** measures air pressure. Another weather instrument is an anemometer. An **anemometer** measures wind speed. Other common weather instruments are wind vanes and rain gauges.

Focus Skill **CAUSE AND EFFECT** While reading a thermometer, you notice that the temperature has fallen throughout the day. What might be causing this?

This school weather station collects data for students. The data is shared with other schools. ▶

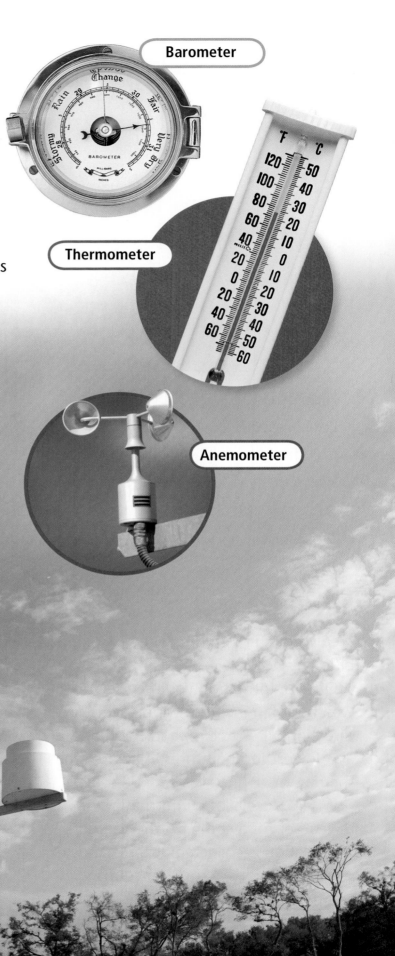

Barometer

Thermometer

Anemometer

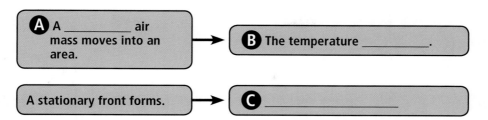

Focus Skill

1. CAUSE AND EFFECT Copy and complete the following graphic organizer.

A A _____ air mass moves into an area. → **B** The temperature _____.

A stationary front forms. → **C** _____

2. SUMMARIZE Write a paragraph explaining how air masses, fronts, and the water cycle are related.

3. DRAW CONCLUSIONS Why might it have been more difficult to predict weather years ago?

4. VOCABULARY Use each vocabulary term from the lesson in a sentence.

Test Prep

5. Critical Thinking You hear on the radio that a cold front is headed toward your town. What type of weather can you expect?

6. Which of the following instruments measures wind speed?

A. anemometer   **C.** rain gauge

B. barometer   **D.** thermometer

Links

Writing

Narrative Writing

Use what you have learned in this chapter to write a short **poem** about weather and the water cycle. Use these terms in your poem: *air mass, front, rain, clouds.*

Math (9÷3)

Subtract Decimals

Suppose you record a rainfall of 0.3 cm in a rain gauge in the morning. You don't empty the gauge. In the afternoon, the gauge reads 1.5 cm. How much rain fell in the afternoon?

Language Arts

Be a Weather Forecaster

Make up a weather map of your state. Present your forecast to the class. Be sure to use the correct vocabulary for the weather you are describing.

 For more links and activities, go to www.hspscience.com

INTO THE EYE OF THE STORM

Hurricane Charley occurred in August 2004. Normally, during such a deadly storm, many people run, drive, or fly away as fast and as far as possible. One flight crew working for the National Weather Service, however, flew into (yes, into) the storm. Called Hurricane Hunters, they actually flew a plane into the center of Charley.

Hurricanes are powerful, whirling storms that form over warm oceans and cause torrential rains and heavy winds. The eye of a hurricane is the calm center of the storm. The eye has little wind and few clouds. Swirling around the eye are heavy winds.

Hurricane Hunters fly directly into the eye of a hurricane—not above it. The reason is that a hurricane can extend more than 50,000 feet high, and the planes can fly only as high as 30,000 feet.

Hurricanes are rated on a scale of 1 to 5. The ratings are based on a storm's wind speed and potential for destruction.		
CATEGORY 1	74 to 95 miles per hour (mph) Minor damage to trees and shrubs; minor flooding	
CATEGORY 2	96 to 110 mph Some trees and signs blown down; some flooding; no major damage to buildings; some evacuations	
CATEGORY 3	111 to 130 mph Some large trees and signs destroyed; some damage to small buildings; some evacuations	
CATEGORY 4	131 to 155 mph Extreme damage to buildings; major beach erosion; evacuations up to 2 miles from shore	
CATEGORY 5	Greater than 155 mph Severe damage to buildings; some small buildings knocked down; evacuations up to 10 miles from shore	

A Hurricane Hunter drops a tube into the eye of a storm.

As their plane "punched through" the eye wall of Charley, crew members experienced a rocky ride. The eye wall is a solid ring of thunderstorms around the eye. The strongest winds and heaviest rains are located here.

The plane contained equipment that records weather. In the eye of the storm, Hurricane Hunters released small tubes attached to parachutes. Each tube was about the size of a can of tennis balls. The tubes sent information about wind speed, power, and moisture back to the crew.

Accurate Forecasting

As part of their job, Hurricane Hunters help forecasters rate storms. Hurricanes are rated on a scale of 1 to 5.

A storm's rating is based on wind speed and potential for damage. Before hitting land, Charley was a Category-4 storm.

Charley packed winds of up to 230 km (145 mi) per hour by the time it hit land. The storm first walloped Jamaica and Cuba before slamming into Florida.

Hurricane Charley left about a million Florida households without electricity. The storm destroyed or severely damaged at least 16,000 homes and left thousands of residents without running water.

THINK ABOUT IT

1. Why is it important that forecasters accurately predict the path of a hurricane?
2. How do you think hurricanes can cause flooding on land?

Find out more! Log on to **www.hspscience.com**

Saving the Earth

Earth Day encourages kids around the world to take action. From cleaning up local parks to testing local water, kids help the Earth on Earth Day, which is on April 22.

But eleven-year-old Michaela Piersanti from New Haven, Connecticut, thinks the environment needs to be protected all year long, not just on Earth Day.

Although the event is important to millions of kids like Michaela, more needs to be done. "We need to keep the Earth clean," Michaela said. "If we pollute, it can make animals sick and possibly kill them."

Water for Life

A big part of Earth Day is making people aware of water pollution. In fact, the theme of a recent Earth Day was "Water for Life."

That theme was chosen because more than 1 billion people around the world do not have clean drinking water. Water gets polluted from sewage, factories, and chemicals. Pollution harms the plants and animals that live in the water. It also makes drinking water unsafe.

Quick and Easy Project

Make a Rain Gauge

Materials
- 1-L clear plastic bottle
- scissors
- plastic ruler
- masking tape

Procedure

1. **CAUTION:** Be careful when using scissors. Remove the cap from the bottle, and ask an adult to cut the top off the bottle.
2. Tape the ruler to the outside of the bottle. The zero mark should be at the bottom of the bottle.
3. Turn the bottle top over so that it will act like a funnel, and put it inside the bottle's upper part.
4. Put the rain gauge out in the open, but away from any roof edges or trees.
5. After it rains, measure the rainfall and empty the bottle.

Draw Conclusions
How much rainfall did you measure? How does measuring rainfall help you describe weather?

Design Your Own Investigation

Weather and the Seasons

How does weather in your area change from season to season? Design an investigation in which you use weather instruments to measure weather over the course of a year. Record data regularly. Take measurements such as average daily temperature, wind speed and direction, and amount of precipitation. Use your data to compare the different seasons. Draw graphs that show how weather in your area changes over the year.

ES-5 Record local weather information; **SI-1** Select appropriate tools; **SI-3** Design and conduct simple investigations

65

Review and Test Preparation

Vocabulary Review

Use the terms below to complete the sentences. The page numbers tell you where to look in the chapter if you need help.

water cycle p. 32

precipitation p. 32

evaporation
p. 34

condensation
p. 35

hurricane p. 42

land breeze
p. 48

air mass p. 54

warm front
p. 56

barometer
p. 60

anemometer
p. 60

1. A breeze moving from the land to the sea is a _____.

2. A large storm with high wind speeds that forms over warm oceans is called a _____.

3. Air pressure is measured with a _____.

4. A gas changes to a liquid during the process of _____.

5. A large body of air is called an _____.

6. Water that falls to Earth from the air is known as _____.

7. A liquid changes to a gas during the process of _____.

8. Warm air pushes forward and moves over cold air along a _____.

9. Wind speed is measured with an _____.

10. The movement of water through the environment is known as the _____.

Check Understanding

Write the letter of the best choice.

11. In the water cycle, what must happen before water condenses in clouds?
    A. Water dissolves salt.
    B. Water evaporates.
    C. Water falls as precipitation.
    D. Water vapor changes to a gas.

12. Look at the diagram below. What is shown?

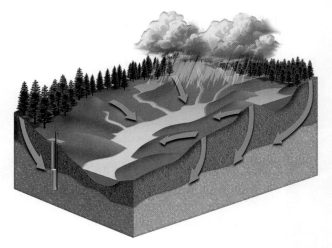

    F. evaporation
    G. groundwater formation
    H. precipitation
    J. sea breeze

13. What type of precipitation is shown in the picture?

A. hail   **C.** sleet
B. rain   **D.** snow

14. Landforms such as mountains affect the water cycle.

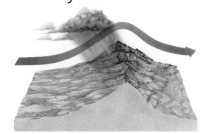

What is it called when one side of a mountain is left dry?

F. a land breeze   **H.** a sea breeze
G. a rain shadow   **J.** a tornado

15. There is a stationary front over Centerville. What kind of weather is Centerville most likely having?
A. a few hours of drizzly rain
B. a few hours of thunderstorms
C. clear weather
D. several days of rain or snow

16. How would an air mass that forms over the Gulf of Mexico most likely be described?
F. cold and dry
G. cold and moist
H. warm and dry
J. warm and moist

Inquiry Skills

17. You **observe** clouds forming on a warm, sunny day. What can you **infer** is happening in the atmosphere? What may happen later in the day?

18. Suppose you plan to **measure** weather conditions over the next week. What will you measure and what equipment will help you?

Critical Thinking

19. Look at the weather map below. Describe the weather in Miami.

20. Tonya watches the weather report every day for a week. Each day, the average temperature is the same and the air pressure doesn't change.
Part A Explain what might be happening to cause the weather in Tonya's town.
Part B How would the weather change if a warm front came through the area?

Chapter 2

Changes to Earth's Surface

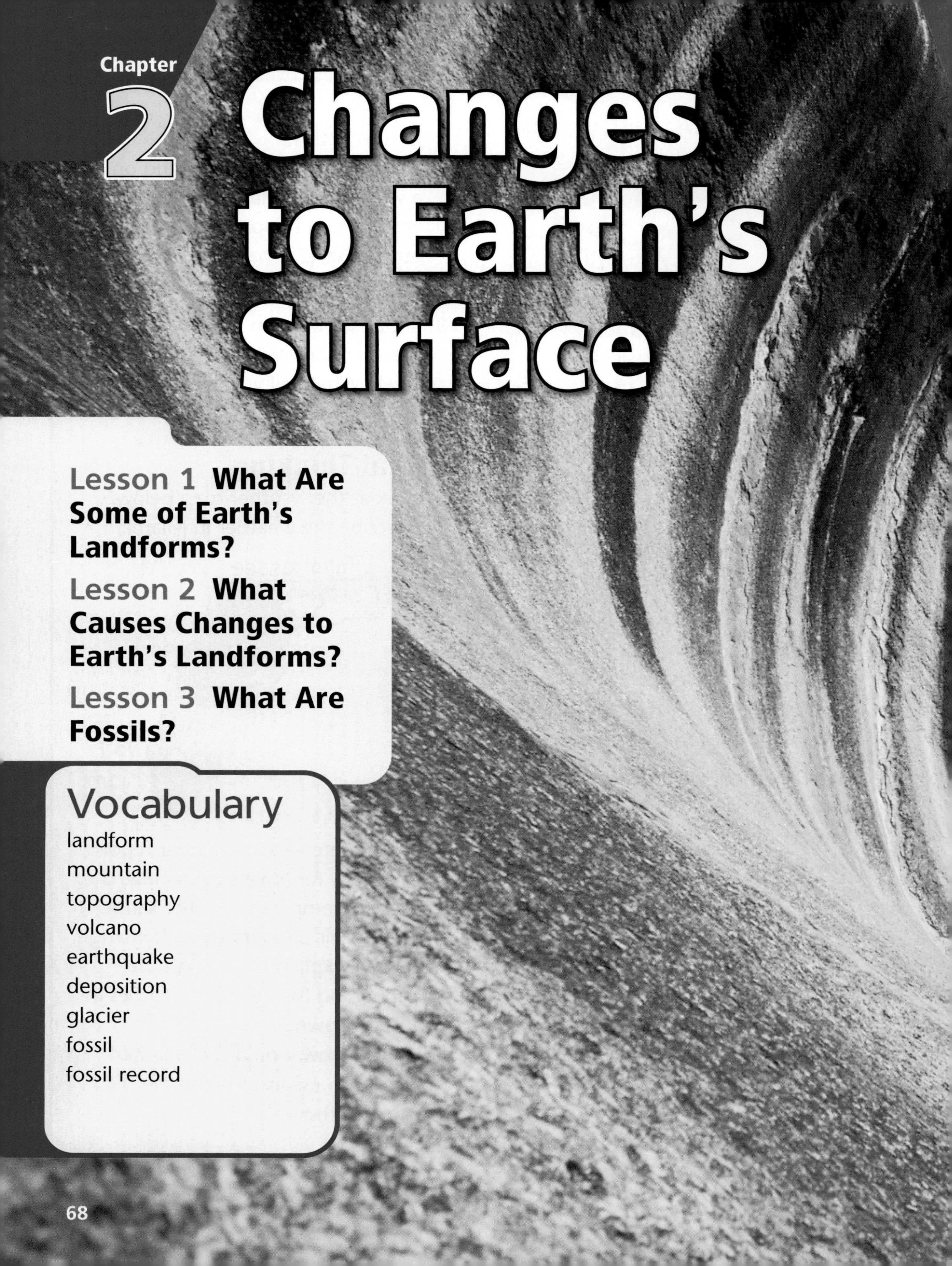

Lesson 1 What Are Some of Earth's Landforms?

Lesson 2 What Causes Changes to Earth's Landforms?

Lesson 3 What Are Fossils?

Vocabulary

landform
mountain
topography
volcano
earthquake
deposition
glacier
fossil
fossil record

What do **YOU** wonder?

This formation, near Hyden, Australia, looks like a tumbling wave. But what is it? From what material do you think it is made? How do you think it formed?

What Are Some of Earth's Landforms?

Fast Fact

Deep Valley Water from melting glaciers cut through Earth's crust to form the Upper St. Croix River gorge in Wisconsin about 10,000 years ago. In the Investigate, you will choose a natural landform and make a model of it.

Make a Landform Model

Materials
- **paper**
- **pencil**
- **modeling clay**
- **heavy cardboard**

Procedure

1. Look for a landform in your area. It might be a mountain, hill, dune, valley, plateau, canyon, or cliff.

2. Observe the landform's shape and size. Sketch the landform on a sheet of paper.

3. Get a piece of modeling clay from your teacher. Place it on a sheet of cardboard.

4. Use clay and your sketch of the landform to make a model.

Step 2

Draw Conclusions

1. Which type of landform did you make a model of with the clay?

2. Predict how the landform might change in the future. What might cause the change?

3. **Inquiry Skill** Scientists often observe objects in nature and then use models to understand them better. How did observing the model help you understand the landform you chose?

Step 4

Investigate Further

Use the information on a topographic map to make a model of one of the landforms shown on the map.

SI-2 Describe patterns/infer; **SI-3** Design and construct simple investigations

VOCABULARY
landform p. 72
mountain p. 72
topography p. 74

SCIENCE CONCEPTS
▶ what major landforms are
▶ how some landforms form

 READING FOCUS SKILL
COMPARE AND CONTRAST
Look for ways that landforms differ.

| alike | — | different |

Mountains and Hills

Earth's surface looks flat from space. However, it is wrinkled, cracked, and folded into many landforms. A **landform** is a natural feature on Earth's surface.

Mountains are some of Earth's most spectacular landforms. A **mountain** is an area that is higher than the land around it. Mountains are usually at least 500 meters (1,600 ft) tall. Hills look like mountains, but they are smaller.

Mountains form in many ways. Some mountains are volcanoes. Other mountains form when forces bend and fold Earth's crust. Blocks of Earth's crust can also get pushed upward to form mountains. It can take millions of years for a chain, or group, of mountains to form.

 COMPARE AND CONTRAST How are **mountains and hills different?**

▼ The temperature of the air decreases as you move up a mountain. Snow and ice always cover the tops of the highest mountains.

▼ These hills are green because of plentiful rainfall. Hills in dry areas can be bare and rocky.

This wide, green valley is in Scotland. It's wide floor and gently sloping sides are different from those of a canyon.

Palo Duro Canyon is 193 kilometers (120 mi) long, as much as 32 kilometers (20 mi) wide, and more than 240 meters (800 ft) deep.

Valleys and Canyons

You have learned that mountains are highlands. There are also lowland areas called valleys. A *valley* is lower area with higher land around it. Valleys stretch between mountains and between hills.

The bottom of a valley is its floor, and its sides are its walls. There are different kinds of valleys. A canyon is a valley with steep walls. Some canyons are so deep and narrow that sunlight barely reaches the floor. Other canyons, like the one shown here, are wide and open.

Rivers or glaciers form most valleys. The moving water or ice cuts through rock and soil. Erosion from rainfall moves soil and rock from valley walls. Some of this rock and soil settles on valley floors. The floors of many valleys have fertile soil that is excellent for farming.

 COMPARE AND CONTRAST How are a valley and a canyon alike?

Plains and Plateaus

Some parts of Earth's surface are mostly flat. These large, flat landforms are called plains. A plain can have a gently rolling surface. It can even have a slight slope. Plains don't have highlands or deep valleys.

Some plains are inland and others are along coasts. A plain that slopes toward the sea along a coast is a coastal plain.

Sometimes rivers overflow their banks, causing floods. When the floods go down, soil and sediment are left behind. This soil helps form plains called floodplains.

A *plateau* (pla•TOH) is also a flat area, but it is higher than the land around it. The edges of plateaus can form steep cliffs. As plateaus erode, they can become other landforms. A much smaller landform with the shape of a plateau is a mesa (MAY•suh). A smaller mesa is a butte (BYOOT). These landforms sometimes make unusual topography (tuh•PAHG•ruh•fee). **Topography** is the shape of landforms in an area. A topographic map shows landforms.

 COMPARE AND CONTRAST How are plateaus and plains alike?

▼ Many farms are located on plains. This wide plain in Asia has rich soil.

This plateau is in Australia. Weathering and erosion are wearing away parts of it.

Deltas can look like different things from space. Some deltas resemble fans or triangles, while other deltas might resemble a bird's foot.

Deltas and Dunes

Deltas and dunes look very different, but both are formed by the movement of sand and sediment.

Deltas form at the ends of rivers. Fast-moving rivers carry away bits of soil and rock. When a river enters a lake or an ocean, it slows down. When this happens, the water can't carry as much material. It drops most of the rock and soil where it meets the lake or ocean, forming a delta.

Dunes form in dry areas or along sandy coasts. They form where wind carries sand. As the wind flows over rocks or other barriers, its speed slows. The wind drops the sand around the object. Over time, a dune forms.

 COMPARE AND CONTRAST What is different about the way deltas and dunes form?

The dunes of White Sands, New Mexico, are made of the mineral gypsum. The highest dunes are about 18 meters (60 ft) tall.

Islands

Every *island* is a body of land surrounded by water. Islands differ in the way they form. Some were once linked to a mainland. When the sea level rose thousands of years ago, water covered the land that formed the link. The British Isles formed this way.

Other islands are the tops of volcanoes that have been built up from the sea floor. Alaska's Aleutian Islands formed this way. Barrier islands are thin, sandy islands that build up along coasts. Barrier islands form where waves deposit sand near the shore.

Coral islands form from the remains of tiny sea animals. The remains form huge structures of limestone in the sea. There are many coral islands in the Pacific Ocean.

 COMPARE AND CONTRAST How are coral islands different from all other types of islands?

Insta-Lab

Make an Island

Build a hill out of clay. Place it in the middle of an aluminum pan. Pour water into the pan until only the top is above water. How is your model like the islands shown on this page?

This view from the air shows a chain, or group, of islands.

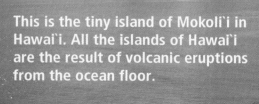

This is the tiny island of Mokoli`i in Hawai`i. All the islands of Hawai`i are the result of volcanic eruptions from the ocean floor.

Focus Skill

1. COMPARE AND CONTRAST Copy and fill in the graphic organizer below.

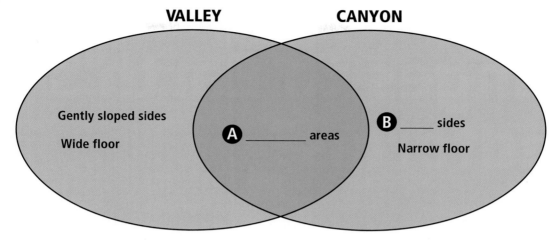

VALLEY

CANYON

Gently sloped sides

Wide floor

A _____ areas

B _____ sides

Narrow floor

2. SUMMARIZE Write one or two sentences to summarize the lesson.

3. DRAW CONCLUSIONS How might a mountain become a plain over a long time?

4. VOCABULARY Write a definition of one of the vocabulary terms. Use your own words.

Test Prep

5. Critical Thinking You want to start a farm. Should you choose land on a mountain or in a valley? Explain your answer.

6. Which of these landforms is all or partly flat?

A. hill   **C.** dune

B. plateau   **D.** mountain

Links

Writing

Expository Writing

Choose an important landform outside the United States. Write an **explanation** of how it formed. Share your explanation with classmates.

Math

Organize Data

Look in an encyclopedia to find the world's five largest islands. Arrange them in a table in order from the largest to the smallest.

Social Studies

Use a Map

Locate two major landforms on a map of the United States. They can be a mountain, valley, canyon, plateau, plain, delta, or island. Write a one-sentence caption to identify each landform.

 For more links and activities, go to www.hspscience.com

What Causes Changes to Earth's Landforms?

Fast Fact

Rocky Coast These tall rocks along the Australian coast are sea stacks. They are all that is left of a rocky cliff that was pounded to pieces by ocean waves. In the Investigate, you will find out about the forces that shape volcanoes.

Volcanic Eruptions

Materials
- 2-liter plastic bottle
- small piece of modeling clay
- aluminum pie plate
- puffed rice cereal
- funnel
- air pump

Procedure

1. Ask your teacher to make a hole near the bottom of a bottle. Stick the bottom of the bottle to a pie plate with clay.

2. Use a funnel to add cereal to the bottle until it is one-fourth full.

3. Attach an air pump to the hole in the bottle. Make sure the nozzle points down. Put a piece of clay around the hole to make it airtight.

4. Pump air into the bottle. Observe what happens.

Draw Conclusions

1. What happened to the cereal when you pumped air into the bottle?

2. Predict how you could model a very large eruption.

3. Inquiry Skill Scientists often make models to help them understand things that happen in nature. How does the bottle model an erupting volcano?

Step 2

Step 3

Investigate Further

Make models using fine sand and gravel to test this hypothesis: A volcano that forms from thick lava is steeper.

Reading in Science

ES-8 Describe how Earth changes; **ES-9** Describe agents of weathering; **ES-10** Describe rapid/slow Earth changes

VOCABULARY
volcano p. 82
earthquake p. 82
deposition p. 84
glacier p. 85

SCIENCE CONCEPTS
▶ characteristics of Earth's structure
▶ what forces change Earth's surface

 READING FOCUS SKILL
CAUSE AND EFFECT Look for causes of changes to Earth's surface.

| cause | → | effect |

Layers of Earth

Every minute of every day, you are on Earth's surface. If you could cut open Earth and look inside, you would find the four layers shown in the diagram below.

Earth's thin outer layer is the crust. The crust includes the land that makes up the continents as well as the land under the oceans.

The mantle is the rock layer below the crust. Deep below Earth's surface, the temperature rises. The upper parts of the mantle are so hot that the rock can flow. In some places the rock is melted to form *magma*.

At Earth's center is the core. The core is made mostly of iron and nickel. The outer core is liquid. The inner core is solid. The inner core is almost as hot as the surface of the sun. It is solid because there is so much pressure on it.

Earth's crust and upper mantle are broken into large slabs of rock called plates. The plates move on a layer of the mantle that can flow like taffy.

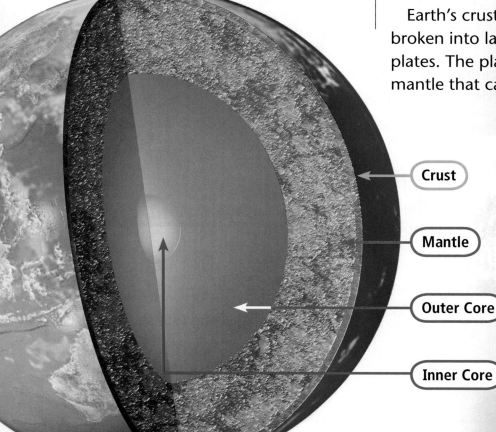

Crust

Mantle

Outer Core

Inner Core

The crust is Earth's thinnest layer. It is solid rock. The crust sits on top of the mantle, which is Earth's thickest layer. Earth's core is mostly metal, and it's very hot. Temperatures in the core reach as high as 5000°C (9000°F).

You can't see the movements of these plates. The plates move only a few centimeters per year. Over a long time, this movement leads to the formation of different landforms.

Plates move in several ways. Some move toward each other. When two land plates meet, the edges crush and fold as one is pushed down under the other, forming mountain chains. Where a land plate and an ocean plate or two ocean plates meet, islands made of volcanic mountains can result.

Some plates travel away from each other. Large cracks can form where the two plates are moving apart. Magma from the mantle oozes up through these cracks. It hardens and makes new crust. Often this happens in the oceans.

Plates can also slide past each other. Where this happens, huge cracks appear at Earth's surface.

 CAUSE AND EFFECT What landform can form where two land plates collide?

Insta-Lab

How Mountains Grow

Place both hands flat on a table, with the fingertips facing each other. Keep moving your hands toward each other until your fingertips are pushing against each other. What happens to your fingers? How does this model mountain formation?

▼ **The Himalayas are Earth's highest mountain chain.**

The Himalayas began to form when the Indian plate and the Asian plate pushed into each other.

Volcanoes and Earthquakes

On the morning of May 18, 1980, the volcano Mount St. Helens, in the state of Washington, erupted. This major eruption threw ash 19 kilometers (12 miles) into the air. The lava, ash, rock, and hot gases that shoot out of volcanoes change the land. Hot rock and gas from Mount St. Helens covered the land, filled in streams, and destroyed forests around the volcano. Since 1980 there have been many small eruptions of Mount St. Helens.

A **volcano** is a mountain that forms as lava flows through a crack onto Earth's surface. There are different types of volcanoes. One type is *composite volcanoes.* They are made of layers of lava, rock, and ash. They can have steep peaks and are usually explosive when they erupt. Hawai`i has *shield volcanoes.* These huge mountains erupt slowly, and lava flows steadily down their gently sloping sides. *Cinder cone volcanoes* are small and have steep sides. They shoot chunks of rock into the air and down their slopes.

Movement between two plates can cause earthquakes. An **earthquake** is the shaking of Earth's surface caused by movement of rock in the crust.

When two ocean plates push together, one plate is forced under the other. In the process, the upper plate melts and forms magma. This magma rises and forms volcanoes.

The base of this Indonesian volcano is on the sea floor.

Strike-Slip Fault

A seismogram shows the movement of Earth's surface during an earthquake. ▶

At a strike-slip fault, slabs of rock slide past each other. Movement at the fault can rip apart roads, bridges, pipelines, and other structures. ▼

Most earthquakes occur along faults. A *fault* is a break in the crust, where rock moves. Sometimes this rock sticks. After some time, it may move forward suddenly. The movement sends out waves of energy that move through the crust. This energy causes shaking, rolling, and cracking in the crust and in Earth's surface.

 CAUSE AND EFFECT What is the cause of most earthquakes?

▲ The motion of an earthquake tore this California highway into several pieces.

Rivers

Rivers are found all over Earth. Although they aren't as dramatic as volcanoes or earthquakes, rivers can cause big changes to Earth's surface. Rivers just take longer to affect the land around them.

Rivers flow through valleys. The shape of a valley depends on the way the river runs through it. In steep areas, rivers move quickly. The rushing water cuts into the soil and rock. These valleys are narrow and V-shaped.

As a river gets older, its valley becomes less steep. The floor of the river becomes more level. The valley walls become farther apart. As a result, older rivers often have wide valleys with flat floors. They flow through the valleys in wide curves.

As rivers flow, they carry soil and rock. As a river moves, deposition occurs. In **deposition** (dep•uh•ZISH•uhn), rivers drop bits of rock and soil along the way. The slower a river moves, the more deposition occurs. River deposition builds landforms such as deltas and floodplains.

 CAUSE AND EFFECT What causes deposition to increase?

Rivers on wide plains flow in large curves like these.

Rivers that flow down steep slopes can cut deep valleys.

Math in Science
Interpret Data

Longest Rivers in the World
In the United States, the longest river is the Missouri, which is 4087 km (2540 mi) long. There are other rivers in the world that are longer. How much longer are each of these rivers than the Missouri?

River	Location	Length
Nile	Africa	6700 km (4163 mi)
Amazon	South America	6430 (4000 mi)
Yangtze	China	6300 km (3900 mi)
Huang He	China	5464 km (3395 mi)
Amur	Asia	4413 km (2742 mi)

Cracks appear in this glacier as it flows slowly down a mountain valley. Glaciers may move as little as a few centimeters or as much as several meters per day.

Fiords form where the sea has flooded valleys formed by glaciers.

Glaciers

In some places, snowfall is high and temperature is low. Sometimes more snow falls in winter than melts in summer. The snow piles up year after year. As it thickens, it turns to ice. If the mass of ice starts to move downhill, it becomes a glacier. A **glacier** (GLAY•sher) is a large, moving mass of ice.

There are two main types of glaciers—alpine glaciers and ice sheets. Alpine glaciers flow down mountain valleys. The ice scrapes the floor and sides of the valley as it moves. The glacier widens the valley, giving it a U shape. *Fiords* (FYAWRDZ) form where these valleys reach the coast. Ice sheets are huge glaciers that cover large areas, such as Antarctica and Greenland.

Thousands of years ago, ice sheets covered much of Earth. As these ice sheets moved over the land, they shaped many landforms people see today.

 CAUSE AND EFFECT What causes glaciers to form?

Wind and Waves

You have seen trees bend and move on a windy day. Wind can also affect the way Earth's surface looks. In dry areas and along sandy coasts, soil is dry and loose. There aren't many plants. Wind lifts particles and carries them.

Wind slams sand into rocky surfaces. The wind-blown sand makes pits and grooves in rock. Wind also carries sand and deposits it in dunes, as you learned in Lesson 1.

Waves break down rocky cliffs. As the cliffs crumble, they move farther inland. Structures such as stone arches and pillars are left behind. As the sea moves inland, the structures are left offshore.

Waves also change the shape of sandy coastlines. They remove sand from some areas and deposit it in other places. This erosion and deposition of sand creates beaches, sand bars, and barrier islands along the shore.

CAUSE AND EFFECT What conditions are needed for wind erosion?

▼ The pounding of waves carved this sea arch. The hole formed when water wore away rock at the center of a solid formation sticking out into the sea.

Erosion from a flood has washed away the soil under this house. It will soon topple into the river below.

1. CAUSE AND EFFECT Copy and fill in the graphic organizer below.

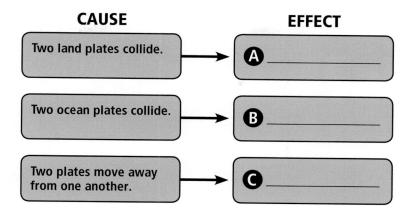

CAUSE   EFFECT

Two land plates collide. → Ⓐ _____

Two ocean plates collide. → Ⓑ _____

Two plates move away from one another. → Ⓒ _____

2. SUMMARIZE Briefly describe the cause and effect of an earthquake.

3. DRAW CONCLUSIONS Which do you think has a greater effect on landforms—wind or water? Why?

4. VOCABULARY Make a crossword puzzle, using the vocabulary terms from Lessons 1 and 2.

Test Prep

5. Critical Thinking What evidence of wave erosion might be seen in landforms along the shore?

6. What is magma?
   A. hot gases   **C.** melted rock
   B. hard rock   **D.** hot metals

Links

Writing

Descriptive Writing
Write a **report** that describes the journey of a piece of rock that erupts from a volcano. Follow the rock from the mantle until it shoots out of the volcano onto Earth's surface.

Math

Make a Bar Graph
Use an encyclopedia to identify the world's five most deadly earthquakes during the past 100 years. Use the number of people who died as the measure. Make a bar graph to compare the earthquakes.

Art

Illustration
Read in a science book or an encyclopedia about a major earthquake or volcanic eruption. Make a drawing that shows some part of what happened. Write a caption to describe it.

 For more links and activities, go to **www.hspscience.com**

Lesson 3

What Are Fossils?

Fast Fact

Big Shell Ammonites were animals similar to squids with shells. They lived millions of years ago. The largest ammonite fossil found so far has a shell almost 2 meters ($6\frac{1}{2}$ ft) across. In the Investigate, you will model another type of fossil.

88

Sets of Animal Tracks

Materials
- poster board
- markers, crayons, or colored pencils
- animal footprint stamps
- ink pad

Procedure

Step 1

1. Old animal tracks, or fossil footprints, are one thing that helps scientists learn about animals from the past. Draw a picture of an area where you might find animal tracks, such as a riverbank or a sandy beach.

2. Each person in your group should choose a different animal. Using an ink pad and stamps or other materials, mark the animal's tracks on the poster board. Keep a record of which animal made tracks first, second, third, and so on.

Step 2

3. Trade finished poster boards with another group. Figure out the order in which the other group's tracks were made. Record your conclusions in an ordered list. Give reasons for the order you choose.

Draw Conclusions

1. Did all the animals move in the same way? How could you tell what kind of animal made the tracks?

2. **Inquiry Skill** Scientists often observe an ecosystem at different times of day to see animals that are out at different times. Predict which tracks you might see if the picture showed tracks of night animals.

Investigate Further

Make animal tracks on a sheet of paper. Have a classmate infer from the tracks how the animal moves. Does it slither, walk, or jump?

VOCABULARY
fossil p. 90
fossil record p. 92

SCIENCE CONCEPTS
▶ what fossils are and how they form
▶ what the fossil record is

Focus Skill **READING FOCUS SKILL**
SEQUENCE Look for the steps in the formation of fossils.

Fossils

Have you ever seen a movie about dinosaurs? The movie probably showed how dinosaurs looked, how they moved, and what they ate. Dinosaurs became extinct millions of years ago. That was long before there were people on Earth. So, how do people today know so much about dinosaurs?

People today know about many plants and animals of the past because of fossils. A **fossil** is the remains or traces of an organism that lived long ago.

Most fossils form in sedimentary rock. First, sediment covers an organism. Then, the sediment hardens into rock, preserving the fossil shape. The soft parts of organisms break down quickly and decay. Because of this, most fossils

Molds and casts, like those of this trilobite, are common fossil types.

Mold and Cast Formation

❶ Sediment covers a clam. The soft parts of the clam decay.

❷ Its shell leaves a clam-shaped hole in the sedimentary rock that forms. This is a fossil *mold.*

❸ The mold fills with minerals. They form a rock *cast* in the shape of the clam inside the rock.

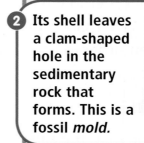

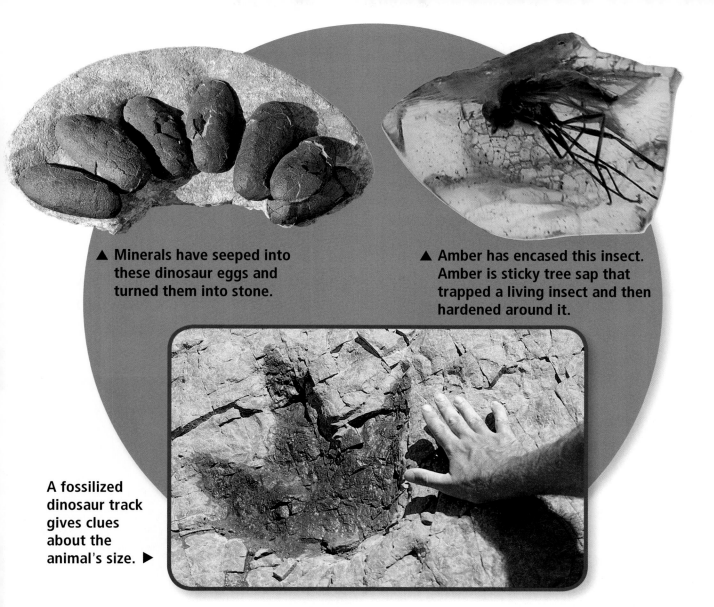

▲ Minerals have seeped into these dinosaur eggs and turned them into stone.

▲ Amber has encased this insect. Amber is sticky tree sap that trapped a living insect and then hardened around it.

A fossilized dinosaur track gives clues about the animal's size. ▶

are formed from only the hard parts of living things, such as shells, bones, and teeth. The numbered diagram shows the steps of forming a mold and cast fossil.

There are other kinds of fossils. When minerals fill the cells of once-living things, a different kind of fossil forms. Petrified wood is an example. It is the wood of a tree that has been replaced by rock. The Petrified Forest, in Arizona, has thousands of stone logs that were trees millions of years ago.

Another type of fossil is a trace fossil. It doesn't show how a whole plant or animal looked, but it tells something about it. A fossil footprint is a trace fossil that helps tell about an animal's size or how it moved. Fossils of animal droppings show what an animal ate.

Some fossils are the remains of whole animals. They were trapped in ice or tree sap that hardened. Scientists have found woolly mammoths preserved in ice in Siberia. These animals died long ago. People know about them because of fossil evidence.

 SEQUENCE How do a mold and a cast form?

Fossil Record

Earth is about 4.5 billion years old. People have lived on Earth for a very small part of that time. Scientists have found clues about Earth's past by using fossils as a record of ancient times. The **fossil record** is the information about Earth's history that is contained in fossils. It's the main source of clues about Earth's past life and environment.

Because of the fossil record, we know about animals that lived and died long, long ago. Dinosaurs and trilobites are examples of such animals. No one has ever seen a living one. We know about them because people have found and studied their fossils.

The fossil record also shows how some species changed over time. Mammoths lived during the last Ice Age. At that time, ice sheets covered much of Earth. The Ice Age ended, and the mammoths died out. Other animals much like elephants continued to live. It is likely that elephants of today are related to some of these animals.

▼ Sediment covered the reef, and it became fossilized over millions of years.

Millions of years ago, this reef was home to corals and many other sea animals. ▶

Scientists study reef fossils to find out about animals that lived in oceans and on reefs long ago.

▲ A dinosaur laid these eggs millions of years ago.

The eggs have become part of the fossil record. The size and number of eggs tell scientists about the dinosaur that laid them. ▶

The fossil record helps scientists learn how Earth's environment has changed over time. Today, palm trees live in warm areas. Scientists have found fossils of palm trees in Wyoming, where it's too cold for palms to grow today. From this evidence, scientists infer that the climate there must have been much warmer in the past.

Scientists have also found fossils of sea animals in Kansas. Today, Kansas is far from any ocean. Scientists have inferred that a shallow sea covered parts of Kansas long ago.

 SEQUENCE What does the fossil record tell us about climate change in Wyoming?

Insta-Lab

Fossil Hunt
Get a cupful of soil from outside. Examine it closely with a hand lens. Describe what you see. Can you see any evidence of fossils? Why or why not?

Geologic Time Scale

Many living things have lived and died out during Earth's long history. Scientists use the *geologic time scale* to understand better what was living during each part of this history.

The scale has several divisions. The table here shows the four eras of the time scale. Each era is millions of years long. In the middle of the Paleozoic (pay•lee•uh•ᴢᴏʜ•ik) Era, there were more fish than any other life form. In the next era, the dinosaurs became the most common vertebrate.

Why is the geologic time scale divided the way it is? The scale shows the way life has changed over time. The fossil record shows that animals died out at certain times during Earth's history. Scientists use these times to mark when eras start and end. For example, trilobites were common at the start of the Paleozoic Era. They died out about 248 million years ago. That marks the end of the Paleozoic Era and the start of the next era. Dinosaurs became extinct about 65 million years ago. That time marks the end of the Mesozoic Era and the start of the present era.

 SEQUENCE What are the four main eras of the geologic time scale, from earliest to the present?

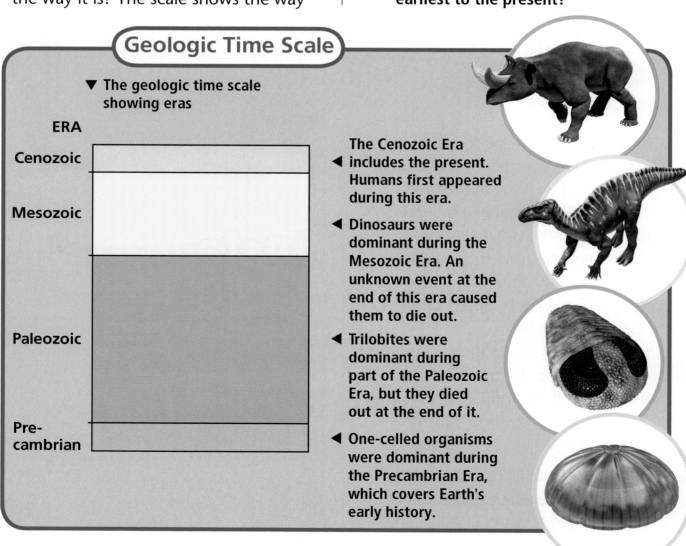

Geologic Time Scale

▼ The geologic time scale showing eras

ERA
Cenozoic
Mesozoic
Paleozoic
Pre-cambrian

The Cenozoic Era ◄ includes the present. Humans first appeared during this era.

◄ Dinosaurs were dominant during the Mesozoic Era. An unknown event at the end of this era caused them to die out.

◄ Trilobites were dominant during part of the Paleozoic Era, but they died out at the end of it.

◄ One-celled organisms were dominant during the Precambrian Era, which covers Earth's early history.

1. SEQUENCE Copy and fill in the graphic organizer below.

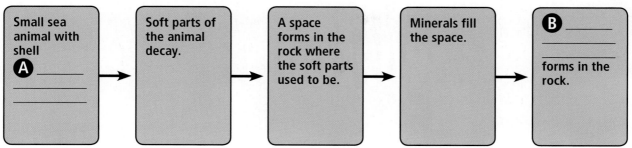

| Small sea animal with shell **A** _____ _____ | → | Soft parts of the animal decay. | → | A space forms in the rock where the soft parts used to be. | → | Minerals fill the space. | → | **B** _____ _____ forms in the rock. |

2. SUMMARIZE Write a brief summary of this lesson. Begin with the sentence *Fossils hold clues to Earth's past.*

3. DRAW CONCLUSIONS Are fossils being formed today? Explain.

4. VOCABULARY Use each of the lesson's vocabulary terms in a sentence.

Test Prep

5. Critical Thinking In which type of rock are you most likely to find a fossil? Why?

6. Which kind of fossil is a dinosaur footprint?

   A. tar pit fossil   **C.** petrified fossil
   B. cast fossil   **D.** trace fossil

Writing

Narrative Writing

Suppose you are hiking near a cliff. You see a large bone trapped in rock. Write a **story** that describes the animal whose fossil you found. Tell how you think it lived and how the fossil formed.

Math

Compare Two Whole Numbers

Ammonites were like squids with shells. Use an encyclopedia to find the size of squids today. Compare their size with the size of the largest ammonite.

Social Studies

Make a Brochure

Research a place in the United States where people can see fossils. It could be a national park, a museum, or another type of area. Design a brochure that encourages people to visit it. Share it with the class.

 For more links and activities, go to www.hspscience.com

WIPEOUT!
Splash

Research by Simon Day, of University College London, United Kingdom, indicates history's biggest tsunami might be caused by a future eruption of the Cumbre Vieja (COOM•bray vee•AY•ha) volcano. Cumbre Vieja is on the island of La Palma in the Canary Islands, a group of islands in the Atlantic Ocean off the northwest coast of Africa.

Day predicts that a volcanic eruption could cause a giant landslide on the unstable western side of the volcano, plopping a trillion tons of rock into the Atlantic. A tsunami caused by such a big landslide would travel a long distance at great speed.

Coastal Terrors

The landslide's impact would produce swells, large waves that radiate from their source until they hit land. Out at sea, the swells are harmless and virtually undetectable. As they approach land, however, they become monstrous. In shallow water the swells bunch up and gain height. Coming ashore, a tsunami pummels coastal cities and shores with destructive force.

Danger, Danger

Simon Day and wave expert Steven Ward, of the University of California, recently used a computer model to calculate the possible impact of a Cumbre Vieja tsunami. Their calculations indicate the danger zones lie north, west, and south of the Canaries.

Danger Zones
A tsunami triggered by a giant Cumbre Vieja landslide would travel north, west, and south of the Canaries and pummel coastal areas in Africa, South America, and North America.

On Africa's Western Sahara shore, waves would reach heights of 100 meters (328 feet)—higher than a 30-story building!

The scientists calculate that waves on the north coast of Brazil would be more than 40 meters (131 feet) high. Florida and the Caribbean would be walloped with waves 50 meters (164 feet) high, hours after a powerful landslide from Cumbre Vieja.

THINK ABOUT IT

1. What changes to Earth's surface may cause tsunamis?
2. How is technology used to study tsunamis?

TSUNAMI OF 2004

- On December 26, 2004, an earthquake at the bottom of the Indian Ocean triggered a tsunami. The wave destroyed coastal areas from Thailand in Asia to Somalia in Africa.
- More than 250,000 people died from the tsunami and earthquake, and millions were left homeless.
- This tsunami was one of the deadliest natural disasters in history.

Find out more! Log on to
www.hspscience.com

WATCHING A VOLCANO

People use telescopes most often to study the planets or stars. But Michael Ballard is using a telescope to look at Earth. He is looking at a special type of Earth landform—a volcano. A volcano is an opening in Earth's crust from which hot lava and steam erupt.

Michael is studying a volcano named Mount St. Helens, in the state of Washington. He is watching the volcano as steam erupts from its top. In 1980, the top of Mount St. Helens blew off in a huge eruption.

Since then, the volcano has had a few small eruptions but nothing like the one in 1980. Recently, Mount St. Helens became active again, sending smoke and steam many kilometers up into the sky. Michael continues to watch the volcano for activity like this with his telescope.

Quick and Easy Project

Making Seismic Waves

Materials
- goggles
- apron
- 9" × 13" cake pan
- water
- food coloring
- spoon
- 2 foam blocks
- sandpaper
- masking tape

Procedure

1. **CAUTION: Put on the goggles and apron.** Pour water into the cake pan to a depth of 1 cm. Add a few drops of food coloring. Mix with the spoon.
2. Tape sandpaper to one long, thin side of each foam block. Put the blocks in the water. Push them together so the sandpaper sides touch.
3. Quickly slide the two blocks along each other in opposite directions. Observe what happens to the water.

Draw Conclusions
What happens if you move the blocks more slowly? Describe how this model is similar to moving plates in an earthquake.

Design Your Own Investigation

How Do Rivers Change the Land?

You know that rivers can change Earth's surface. Some rivers flow down steep slopes. Other rivers flow over flat land. Design an investigation to see how the slope of the land determines how a river changes Earth's surface. Decide what materials to use to model the river and its banks. How will you change the slope of your model? How does the slope of a river affect the way it changes Earth's surface?

ES-8 Describe how Earth changes; **ES-10** Describe rapid/slow Earth changes; **SI-5** Design and conduct simple investigations

2 Review and Test Preparation

Vocabulary Review

Use the terms below to complete the sentences. The page numbers tell you where to look in the chapter if you need help.

landform p. 72   **earthquake** p. 82

mountain p. 72   **deposition** p. 84

topography p. 74   **glacier** p. 85

volcano p. 82   **fossil** p. 90

1. A mountain that forms as lava flows through a crack onto Earth's surface is a _____.

2. When rivers slow down, they drop sediment in a process called _____.

3. Any natural shape on Earth's surface is a _____.

4. The traces or remains of an organism that lived long ago are a _____.

5. The shape of the landforms in an area is _____.

6. The shaking of Earth's surface caused by movement of rock in the crust is an _____.

7. An area that is higher than the land around it is a _____.

8. A huge, moving mass of ice is a _____.

Check Understanding

Write the letter of the best choice.

9. **COMPARE AND CONTRAST** Which pair of landforms are most alike?
   A. plain/plateau   C. valley/fault
   B. canyon/mesa   D. butte/mountain

10. **CAUSE AND EFFECT** Which of these landforms are formed by deposition?
    F. mountains   H. deltas
    G. valleys   J. plateaus

11. Which is the name of the layer of Earth indicated by X?

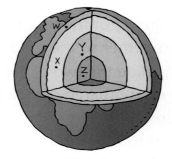

    A. inner core   C. outer core
    B. crust   D. mantle

12. Which thing happens where two land plates push against each other?
    F. valleys form
    G. mountains form
    H. islands form
    J. new sea floor forms

13. Which thing is happening where these two plates meet?

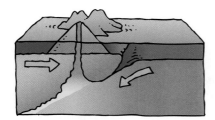

  A. The sea floor is spreading apart.
  B. An undersea canyon has formed.
  C. Volcanic islands are forming.
  D. The coast is eroding.

14. Which of these does **not** come from an erupting volcano?
  F. ice   **H.** lava
  G. gases   **J.** ashes

15. Which of these changes to land does an earthquake cause?
  A. Soil is deposited.
  B. River valleys become wider.
  C. Rocks split in Earth's crust.
  D. Lava covers the surface.

16. Which kind of fossil is illustrated by this picture?

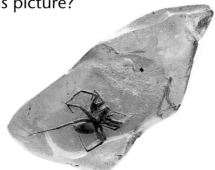

  F. amber fossil   **H.** fossil cast
  G. trace fossil   **J.** petrified wood

Inquiry Skills

17. Why is it useful to **use a model** to study processes such as stream and river deposition?

18. What would be the importance of being able to **predict** when a volcano might erupt?

Critical Thinking

19. You discover a fossil in the bottom layer of a canyon wall. You identify the fossil as an animal that lived between 250 and 230 million years ago. What information can this fossil give you about the area where the canyon is located?

20.

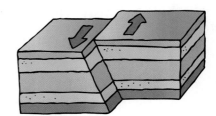

Part A Describe what is happening in the diagram. How is the event changing Earth's surface in the area right around it?

Part B How could this affect Earth's surface several kilometers away?

Kelleys Island

Columbus

Glacial Grooves

Hang on to your hat, and hop on the ferry to Kelleys Island. There you will see a great example of the power of nature. What you will see are glacial grooves. These grooves are deep cuts into the rock. The cuts were made by the movement of glaciers thousands of years ago.

Kelleys Island is the largest island on the American side of Lake Erie. Its landmass is about 10 square kilometers (4 sq mi). The island is a few miles south of the Canadian border. You can take a ferry to reach the island.

Glacial Grooves State Memorial

Fossils and More

When you get to the island you can walk around and see the largest site of glacial grooves in the entire world. Long ago, thick sheets of ice flowed down from the north. These were glaciers. The glaciers were so huge that they cut grooves into the rock. When the glaciers melted, the grooves were left behind.

Along with the glacial grooves, you can find fossils that are about 400 million years old. By cutting the grooves, the glaciers gave us a view of an even more distant past. Kelleys Island is so important that it is now a National Natural Landmark.

Exposing the limestone at Kelleys Island allowed these ancient fossils to be found

Think and Do

I. SCIENCE AND TECHNOLOGY Suppose it took 12,000 years for a glacier to cut a field of glacial grooves. A modern tractor might have ten times more power. How long would it take the tractor to cut the same grooves?

2. SCIENTIFIC THINKING Fences have been put up to protect the glacial grooves at Kelleys Island. The grooves are thousands of years old. Why do you think they need protection now?

ES-8 Describe how Earth changes; ES-9 Describe agents of weathering; ES-10 Describe rapid/slow Earth changes

Serpent Mound

There is a mystery in Adams County, Ohio. In fact, there are two. There is a strange mound built by people. And there is a natural mystery, too.

The mound is shaped like a snake. It is in the Serpent Mound State Memorial, overlooking the Brush Creek Valley. Experts say the mound was built by an ancient native culture. No one knows why the mound was built.

The Serpent Mound is made of clay and rock. It is about 0.4 kilometer (0.25 mi) long and looks like an uncoiling serpent. The soil covering the rock is about 1.5 meters (5 ft) high. Over the years, the mound has changed shape due to changes in the land.

Serpent Mound

A Natural Mystery

The land around Serpent Mound is also mysterious. The rocks in an 8-kilometer (5-mi) area around the site are broken and folded. This is very unusual in Ohio. Experts say the mound was built on a crypto-explosion site. *Crypto* means "unknown." The word tells us that an unknown force changed the land. Some experts say it was a meteor. Others say that it was an underground explosion. Experts keep studying the land to learn what really happened.

Think and Do

1. **SCIENCE AND TECHNOLOGY** Imagine you have a chance to visit Serpent Mound. You want to study the crypto-explosion structure. What tools do you think would be useful? Make a list.

2. **SCIENTIFIC THINKING** No one knows why Serpent Mound was built. Still, most experts think it had some purpose. Is this enough to call the mound technology? Write a paragraph to explain your answer.

Lake Erie

Columbus

Shoreline Erosion

Lake Erie is one of Ohio's greatest natural resources. It's one of the Great Lakes. Its shoreline in Ohio runs 502 km (312 mi) long. You can find clay bluffs along its eastern shoreline. On the western shore, you can visit beaches of sand and clay.

This area is in trouble. The shoreline is wearing away. This is called erosion. Nature causes some erosion. Beaches are worn down by wind and water, but people can add to the problem. Some build barriers to prevent erosion on their beach. Doing that may save one beach, but it keeps sand away from other beaches. That makes erosion worse on the other beaches.

Beach along Lake Erie

Bluffs along Lake Erie

Protection Needed

Why is erosion a problem? For one thing, it leaves less land for beaches. That means less room for fun. Local animals and plants have less room, too. And when the beaches wear away, the water comes too close to houses and other buildings. That can lead to property damage.

Some parts of the Lake Erie shore are already state parks and nature preserves. The rest of the shore is owned by people who want to live or work near the beach. Some conservation groups have suggested buying the shore from individuals. These groups would give it to the state. Then, the Ohio government would be able to protect the land and manage erosion.

A section of Ohio's shoreline along Lake Erie has eroded several hundred meters since 1876.

Area of photo

OHIO

Erosion caused a bluff to collapse, damaging this building.

Think and Do

 I. SCIENCE AND TECHNOLOGY Suppose you are managing conservation at a beach. You know that waves carry sand from another beach to your beach. You can see that a wall has been built in the water between the two beaches. What will happen? Write a letter to the manager at the other beach, explaining what you think and requesting action to fix the problem.

 2. SCIENTIFIC THINKING Erosion is often a natural process. Why do some people want to stop it? List three reasons. Is stopping erosion a good idea or a bad idea? Explain.

ES-8 Describe how Earth changes; **ES-9** Describe agents of weathering; **ES-10** Describe rapid/slow Earth changes; **ST-1** Explain how technology improves lives

How Did the Glacial Grooves Begin?

Materials

About $\frac{1}{2}$ kg of soft clay

Flat surface to use as a work table

Small ruler

Small objects, like coins, shells,
buttons, plastic animals or insects

Procedure

1. Build the clay into a hill. Then, using your hands, scoop out a portion from the middle.

2. Use the edge of your ruler to scrape grooves into the depression.

3. Take each small object and push it into the clay depression. When you remove the objects, you'll have fossil imprints.

Draw Conclusions

1. What happened to the grooves when you left the fossil imprints?

2. What would happen if you placed the objects in the clay first and then made the grooves?

3. How does this model explain the formation of the glacial grooves? How does it provide us with a window to our prehistoric past?

ES-8 Describe how Earth changes; **ES-9** Describe agents of weathering;
ES-10 Describe rapid/slow Earth changes; **SI-4** Control variables

How Did the Shoreline Along Lake Erie Change?

Materials
Aluminum tray
Sand
Container or bowl
  15-30 cm tall
Water
Pitcher
250-mL measuring
  cup
30-cm ruler

Procedure
1. Pack the sand into the container. Then invert the container onto the tray. You have just made a sand dune.

2. Measure and record the height of your sand dune.

3. Pour a few drops of water onto the sand dune.

4. Measure and record the height of your dune.

5. Measure 125 mL of water. Pour the water on your sand dune.

6. Measure and record the height of your sand dune.

Draw Conclusions
1. Compare the three heights of the sand dune. How much of a change did you see? If you continued pouring water on your sand dune, what do you predict would happen?

2. From this model, how can you explain the erosion of shoreline? How do forces, like falling water, change an object?

3. To prevent the shoreline from eroding, what needs to take place? What problems might this cause elsewhere?

ES-8 Describe how Earth changes; **ES-9** Describe agents of weathering; **ES-10** Describe rapid/slow Earth changes; **SI-4** Control variables

109

Life Sciences

 The chapters and features in this unit address these Grade Level Indicators from the Ohio Academic Content Standards for Science.

Chapter ## Plants

LS-1	Compare the life cycles of different plants including germination, maturity, reproduction and death.
LS-2	Relate plant structures to their specific functions (e.g., growth, survival and reproduction).
LS-3	Classify common plants according to their characteristics (e.g., tree leaves, flowers, seeds, roots and stems).
LS-4	Observe and explore that fossils provide evidence about plants that lived long ago and the nature of the environment at that time.

Chapter ## Ecosystems and Energy

LS-5	Describe how organisms interact with one another in various ways (e.g., many plants depend on animals for carrying pollen or dispersing seeds).

Unit B Ohio Expeditions

The investigations and experiences in this unit also address many of the Grade Level Indicators for standards in Science and Technology, Scientific Inquiry, and Scientific Ways of Knowing.

TO: Katie@hspscience.com

FROM: Jamaal@hspscience.com

RE: Reynoldsburg Tomato Festival

Dear Katie,

You won't believe what a good time I had at the Tomato Festival in Reynoldsburg. I know it sounds crazy, but it was fun! They had a contest for the largest tomato. You should have seen the one that won. It was huge! There was a Tomato Queen and a Tomato Princess. The Tomato Festival honors Alexander W. Livingston. He loved tomatoes. He grew them all his life. People in Ohio say he grew the first tomato that tasted good. All this fuss over tomatoes—can you believe it?

"Seed" you later...
Jamaal

Experiment!

Living things respond to certain factors in their environments. A plant's roots grow toward the ground because they respond to gravity. Another environmental factor that plants respond to is light. How do plants respond to light? For example, will plants grow toward a light source? Plan and conduct an experiment to find out.

Plants

Lesson 1 What Are Some Plant Types?

Lesson 2 How Do Plants Grow?

Lesson 3 How Do Plants Reproduce?

Lesson 4 How Do Plants of the Past Compare with Those of Today?

Vocabulary

classify
vascular
nonvascular
vascular tissue
xylem
phloem
photosynthesis
spore
gymnosperm
angiosperm
germinate
fossil
extinction

What do YOU wonder?

The azaleas you see in this picture are flowering plants that grow naturally in woodlands. How many different kinds of flowering plants do you think there are in the world?

113

What Are Some Plant Types?

Fast Fact

Pretty But Smelly Don't bother to sniff this flower! It smells like rotting meat. The Rafflesia is not like other flowers. It does not have visible roots, and it is very large—up to one meter across. In the Investigate, you will practice classifying.

Classifying Beans

Materials • bag of mixed beans

Procedure

1. Pour the beans from the bag, and observe them carefully.

2. Make a list of the characteristics, or qualities, that you observe about the beans. Use all of these characteristics to classify, or sort, the beans into as many different groups as possible.

3. Draw a table like the one shown. In it, record the characteristics of each group of beans. Draw a picture of one bean from each group. Give the group a name. Then write a short description of the bean's characteristics.

Draw Conclusions

1. Compare your results with the results of your classmates. How many different ways did your class find to classify the beans?

2. What characteristics did you use to classify the beans? What characteristics did your classmates use?

3. **Inquiry Skill** Scientists classify living things to show how they're similar and how they're different. Why do you think it's important for all scientists to use the same characteristics to classify living things?

Step 2

Picture of Bean	Name of Group	Characteristics of Bean

Investigate Further

Classify **a different set of objects, such as shells. How is your classification system like the one you used for the beans? How is it different?**

SI-2 Describe patterns/infer; SK-3 Explain discrepancies

VOCABULARY
classify p. 116
vascular p. 120
nonvascular p. 120

SCIENCE CONCEPTS
- ▶ how plants are classified
- ▶ what the characteristics are of vascular and nonvascular plants

 READING FOCUS SKILL
COMPARE AND CONTRAST
Look for similarities and differences in plants.

| alike | — | different |

Classification

There are about 270,000 kinds of plants in the world. That is too many to study in one group. In order to compare and contrast plants, scientists classify them. When you **classify**, you group things that are alike.

A coin machine can be used to divide coins into groups. It uses size to divide them into dollars, half-dollars, quarters, dimes, nickels, and pennies. Is this the only way that you can classify coins?

Coins have symbols on them that tell where they were made. They also have dates of the year when they were made. Each state has a different quarter with its own picture on the back.

Just as coins have main groups and many ways to compare them, so do plants. In this lesson, you will learn about many ways to compare plants.

 COMPARE AND CONTRAST How are coins and plants the same?

◀ A coin-sorting machine is used to divide coins into groups by their size.

▲ You probably already know that the pine, the palm, and the buckeye are all trees. Did you know that bamboo and wheat are grasses?

Trees and Grasses

What kinds of plants do you see when you look out of the window? The very tall plants that you see are probably trees. Trees are tall, woody plants. How are trees different fom each other? The buckeye tree has broad, fan-like leaves that are green in the spring, and then change color and fall to the ground in the autumn. Trees like the buckeye are called deciduous trees. The pine tree has narrow, needle-like leaves that are green all year. Trees with needles are called evergreens. Palm trees have fronds that look like many leaves joined together.

What are the plants that cover much of the ground that you see? These are called grasses. Grasses have narrow leaves and are usually much shorter than trees. The grass that is used for lawns is called turf. Turf is very short. Wheat is a taller type of grass.

Is bamboo a tree or a grass? Bamboo is a grass that can grow as tall as a tree.

 COMPARE AND CONTRAST How are trees and grasses alike?

▼ Turf

Stems and Branches

In what other ways can you classify plants? You can look at their stems and branches, the structures that grow from the plant.

Most plants have stems. There are soft stems and woody stems.

Soft stems are usually green and flexible. Leaves and flowers grow out of soft stems. Soft stems are covered with a thin skin and don't usually get very big.

When they are thick, they are usually used for storing water.

Woody stems are covered in bark, and won't bend the way soft stems do. They can have scars where twigs and fruit have dropped off. Woody stems can grow to be very thick.

Branches grow in different ways. Some trees have trunks that grow straight up, with branches growing out of the trunks. Pine trees grow like this.

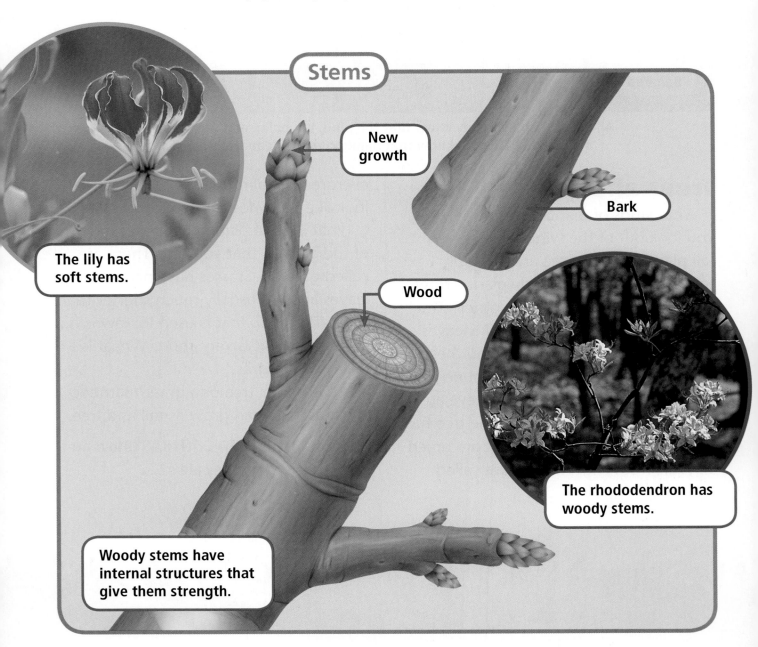

Stems

The lily has soft stems.

New growth

Bark

Wood

Woody stems have internal structures that give them strength.

The rhododendron has woody stems.

The barberry has branches that grow in a zigzag style.

The oak tree has many smaller branches that grow out of the large branches.

The pine tree has many branches that grow out of the trunk.

But some trees, like the oak tree in the picture, grow different kinds of branches. They grow large branches out of their main trunk, and then many smaller branches grow out of those.

Other trees, and some other plants, grow branches a third way. Their branches grow out of each other in a zigzag pattern. Trees with these kinds of branches don't have trunks.

 COMPARE AND CONTRAST How are soft stems different from woody stems?

How Are Plants Used?

Make a list of plants that you know about, and then classify them by how they are used. Is the plant used for food, for decoration, for construction, or for something else?

Transport in Plants

In order to survive, all plants must have a way to transport food and water to different parts of the plant. Vascular plants do this with tubes. The word **vascular** means "having vessels." When you look closely at a leaf, you can see tiny lines that look like the veins under your skin. These lines are tubes, or vessels, that vascular plants use to transport food and water.

Nonvascular means "without vessels." Nonvascular plants do not have tubes to move water and food around the plant. These plants absorb water directly, like sponges. When these plants are dry, they look like dried sponges. Because they don't have tubes, nonvascular plants grow close to the ground. That way they can quickly and easily absorb water from their surroundings.

 COMPARE AND CONTRAST Why must nonvascular plants grow close to the ground?

Vascular plants have tubes that look like the veins in your body.

Water and nutrients travel up the stem to the rest of the plant.

Nonvascular plants soak up water like a sponge.

Water and nutrients are absorbed by roots.

1. COMPARE AND CONTRAST Copy and complete this chart.

Plant Types	Alike	Different
Trees and Grasses	Both have leaves. **A** _____	Grasses are shorter. **B** _____
Stems and Branches	Both support plants. **C** _____	Branches grow in 3 different ways. **D** _____

2. SUMMARIZE Use the chart to help you summarize the lesson.

3. DRAW CONCLUSIONS What would happen to a vascular plant if you cut it off at ground level and placed it in a bowl of water?

4. VOCABULARY Use vocabulary terms and other science terms to describe vascular and nonvascular plants.

Test Prep

5. Critical Thinking What kind of transport do trees use? Why?

6. Which statement is true?
- **A.** All grasses are short.
- **B.** All plants have woody stems.
- **C.** All plants move water with tubes.
- **D.** All trees have branches.

Links

Writing

Narrative Writing
Write a **story** for a school newspaper about a strange plant you have found. Describe what it looks like, where it is growing, and whether it is vascular or nonvascular.

Math

Measure a Tree
Your friend, who is four feet tall, stands next to a tree. You back away from the tree until your friend is as big as your thumb. The tree is 10 thumbs tall. About how tall is the tree in feet?

Social Studies

Draw Plant Pictures
Draw pictures of several kinds of plants to illustrate a children's book about plants. Choose at least one flowering plant.

 For more links and activities, go to **www.hspscience.com**

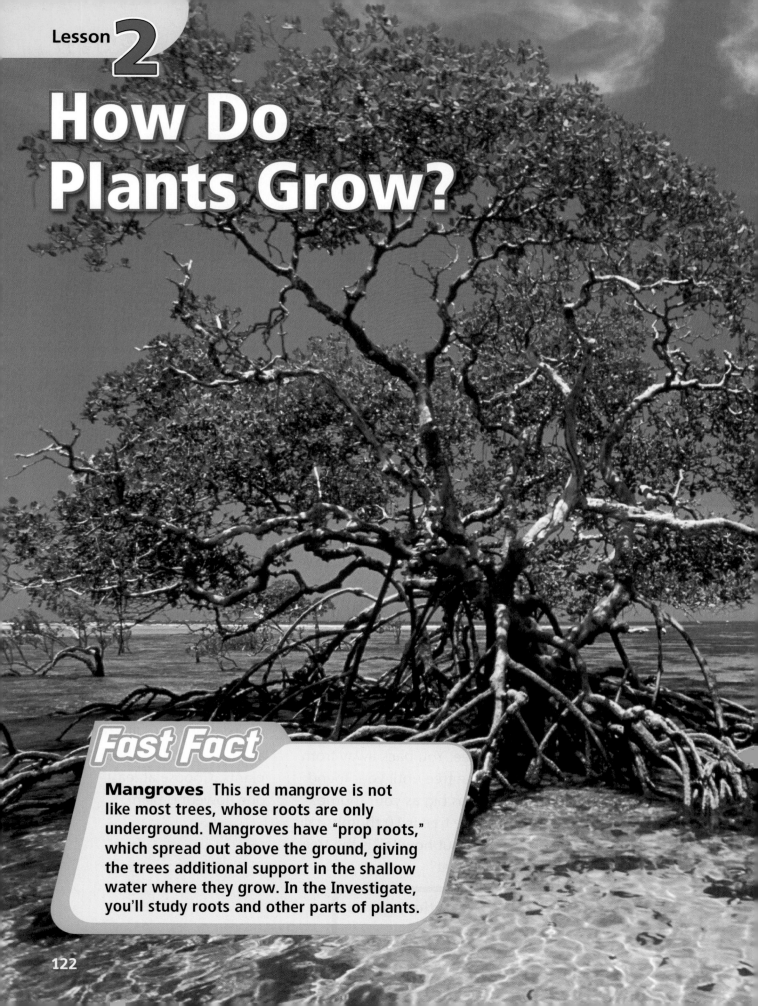

How Do Plants Grow?

Fast Fact

Mangroves This red mangrove is not like most trees, whose roots are only underground. Mangroves have "prop roots," which spread out above the ground, giving the trees additional support in the shallow water where they grow. In the Investigate, you'll study roots and other parts of plants.

Vascular Plant Parts

Materials • potted plant • newspaper • ruler • hand lens

Procedure

1 Hold the potted plant upside down over the newspaper. Tap the pot gently until the plant comes out. Shake the soil from the roots so you can see them clearly.

2 Observe the leaves of the plant. Measure and calculate their average length and width. Use the hand lens to observe the leaves more closely. Record your observations.

3 Observe the stem. Use the hand lens to see it in more detail. Does it bend? Does it have branches? Record your observations.

4 Observe the roots. Notice their shape. Measure and calculate their average length. Use the hand lens to observe them more closely. Record your observations.

5 Make a drawing of the plant. Label all the parts.

6 Put the soil and the plant back into the pot, and water the plant lightly.

Step 2

Step 4

Draw Conclusions

1. What did you observe about each part of the plant?

2. **Inquiry Skill** What can you infer about the functions of roots, stems, and leaves?

Investigate Further

Look at a carrot that has its leaves attached. Compare it to the potted plant. Draw a picture of a carrot growing in soil.

SI-1 Select appropriate tools; **SI-6** Communicate instructions/data; **SK-2** Record results/data

VOCABULARY
vascular tissue p. 125
xylem p. 125
phloem p. 125
photosynthesis p. 128

SCIENCE CONCEPTS
▶ how nonvascular plants get water and nutrients
▶ how the parts of vascular plants function

READING FOCUS SKILL

MAIN IDEA AND DETAILS
Look for plant structures and how they function.

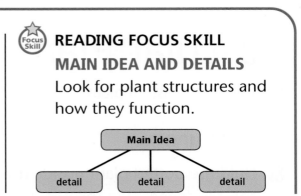

Nonvascular and Vascular Plants

Have you ever seen a rock or log covered with a moist, velvety green plant? What you've seen isn't really one plant, but many tiny moss plants.

Mosses are *nonvascular plants*. Non-vascular plants don't have true roots, but they are anchored by small, rootlike structures. They have parts that look like stems, but these aren't true stems. And they have small, leaflike structures that make food. But these aren't true leaves because they don't have veins.

Nonvascular plants don't have any tissue for carrying materials throughout the plant.

Nonvascular plants absorb water and nutrients from their surroundings. Water in the plants carries food and nutrients directly from cell to cell. Because of this, the plants cannot grow very tall. With their small size, they can absorb enough water to carry materials throughout the plants. When there is not enough water, a nonvascular plant such as moss quickly dries out and turns brown. When it rains, many mosses turn green again.

If you look at moss with a hand lens, you can see individual moss plants. The plants grow close to a surface, allowing all their cells to receive water and nutrients. ▶

Mosses grow on rocks, on trees, and in other places where they can absorb nutrients and moisture.

Trees, like the one shown here, are more complex than mosses. Trees belong to the group called *vascular plants,* which contain vascular tissue. **Vascular tissue** supports plants and carries water and food. Roots, stems, and leaves all contain vascular tissue.

There are two types of vascular tissue. **Xylem** (ZY•luhm) carries water and nutrients from roots to other parts of a plant. **Phloem** (FLOH•em) carries food from leaves to the rest of the plant. With these tissues, vascular plants are not dependent on water moving to nearby cells only, as in mosses.

Vascular plants vary more than non-vascular plants. They include tiny duckweed (a fraction of an inch long) and giant redwood trees. They also include cacti that grow in deserts, with little water, and orchids that grow in damp rain forests.

 MAIN IDEA AND DETAILS What does each type of vascular tissue do?

Xylem cells in the trunk of a tree transport water. Phloem cells, just under the bark, transport food. Each year, new layers of xylem and phloem cells grow. You can tell the age of a tree by counting the rings of xylem.

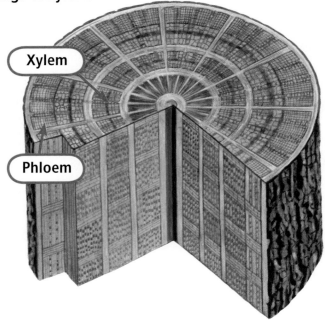

Xylem

Phloem

Xylem

Cross section of a root

Phloem

Fibrous roots spread out and absorb water near the surface.

Taproots anchor plants firmly and can absorb water from deep in the ground. ▶

Roots and Stems

Roots absorb water and nutrients from the soil. In the Investigate, when you looked at the roots of the potted plant, you may have noticed the tiny hairs covering them. Root hairs absorb water and nutrients. Xylem cells take the water and nutrients from the root hairs and move them to the stem.

Roots are a plant's anchor and are adapted to the environment and the needs of the plant. A taproot is one large, strong root that pushes deep into the soil. It anchors the plant firmly. Some taproots also store food. The plants use the stored food when they make flowers and fruits. Some taproots store so much food that people use them for food, too.

Carrots and beets are examples of plants with large taproots.

Other plants have fibrous roots. Fibrous roots are thin and branching,

Water Movement

Break several toothpicks in the middle, but make sure the halves remain connected. Arrange the toothpicks as shown. Wet the center of the pile with several drops of water, and observe the result. Explain how the result relates to water moving through plant stems.

and they form a mat below the surface of the ground. They spread out and absorb water from a large area. The mat of roots holds the plant in the soil and keeps the soil from washing away. Grasses are often used to hold the soil because they have many fibrous roots.

Some roots grow above the ground and help hold a plant upright. The mangrove tree you saw earlier is one such plant. Corn is another. Roots that grow above the ground are known as prop roots.

Like roots, stems carry water and nutrients. Stems act as pipelines for transporting water and nutrients between roots and leaves. In a stem, as in larger roots, vascular tissue is gathered into bundles. In some plants, the bundles are scattered all through the stem. In trees and many other flowering plants, the bundles are arranged in a ring. You can see these rings in the enlarged view at the right.

Stems also provide support. They usually grow from the ground and hold the leaves up in the sunlight. Trees and other tall plants have woody stems. In plants without woody stems, water pressure holds the stems upright. A droopy stem is a clue that a plant might need water. Some plants, such as cacti, store water and food in fleshy stems.

New plants can grow from some stems. For example, strawberry plants have stems called runners, which grow sideways. New plants grow from the runners.

 MAIN IDEA AND DETAILS What functions do roots perform?

Tall trees have strong trunks and branches. ▶

The interior of a tree trunk is heartwood, filled with xylem cells. The cells provide support but no longer carry water.

Leaves

Just from looking at a leaf, you'd never know that it's manufacturing food. But leaves do make food—by a process called **photosynthesis**. This process uses light energy, carbon dioxide, and water to make sugar.

Photosynthesis takes place inside chloroplasts in leaf cells. Chloroplasts contain a green pigment that absorbs sunlight. Leaves get the carbon dioxide for photosynthesis from the air. Xylem cells in leaf veins bring in water from the soil. Phloem cells in the veins carry the sugar from photosynthesis throughout the plant. Oxygen, a waste product, goes into the air. You will learn more about photosynthesis in another chapter.

The outer layer of cells in a leaf is the *epidermis.* It protects the leaf from damage. Many leaves have a waxy coating on the epidermis. The coating helps keep moisture inside the leaf. Some water does escape through tiny holes, called *stomata,* on the underside of the leaf. Stomata open and close, letting carbon dioxide in and oxygen out. Stomata can also close when water is in short supply.

 MAIN IDEA AND DETAILS **What process takes place in the chloroplasts of leaf cells?**

◀ **Most leaves are flat, which helps them easily absorb sunlight. Without sunlight, leaves cannot make food.**

The green color of a leaf comes from chlorophyll, a green pigment found in chloroplasts. Stomata let carbon dioxide into leaves and let oxygen escape. Xylem in leaf veins brings in water, and phloem carries food throughout the plant. ▼

Xylem

Phloem

Stomata

1. **MAIN IDEA AND DETAILS** Draw and complete this graphic organizer about the details of photosynthesis.

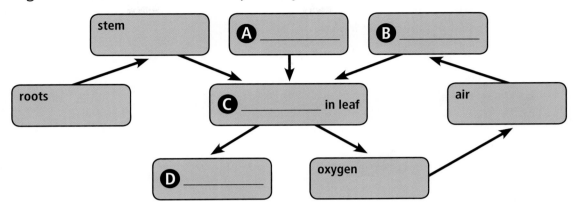

2. SUMMARIZE Use your graphic organizer to write a paragraph explaining photosynthesis.

3. DRAW CONCLUSIONS You get energy from cereal that you eat. From what other sources does food energy come?

4. VOCABULARY Describe two kinds of vascular tissue.

Test Prep

5. Critical Thinking Why is it hard to pull all of a plant out of the ground?

6. Which part of a plant lets oxygen enter the leaf?
   A. root hairs   **C.** stomata
   B. stem   **D.** xylem

Links

Writing

Narrative Writing
Write a **story** about the travels of a water drop from the soil to a leaf. You might also tell what happens to the water after it gets to the leaf.

Math

Solve a Problem
A mature tree produces about 118 kg (260 lb) of oxygen a year; enough for a family of four! About how much oxygen does a person use in a year?

Art

Draw a Picture
Draw a picture of a tree that you would like to sit under. Label the parts of the tree that are used for photosynthesis.

 For more links and activities, go to www.hspscience.com

How Do Plants Reproduce?

Fast Fact

Yoo-hoo! The color, smell, and shape of flowers attract pollinators such as insects. Pollinators help with plant reproduction by transferring sticky pollen between flowers, starting the development of seeds. In the Investigate, you'll observe seeds and other plant parts that help plants reproduce.

Spores and Seeds

Materials
- fern frond
- hand lens
- white paper
- apple
- plastic knife

Procedure

CAUTION: Be careful when handling sharp objects such as knives.

1. Observe the fern frond, or leaf. Look at both sides of the frond, using the hand lens.

2. Hold the frond over a sheet of white paper. Rub the underside of the frond so that the contents of the spots on the frond fall onto the paper.

3. Observe the paper with the hand lens. There should be one or more clusters of small objects on the paper. Notice if there are dustlike particles on the paper. These particles are spores.

4. Observe the apple closely. Use the knife to cut the apple through the middle, vertically. Look at the inside of the apple with the hand lens.

5. Take the seeds out of the apple. Observe them with the hand lens. How many seeds are there? Record all your observations.

Draw Conclusions

1. How do the seeds of an apple compare to the spores of a fern?

2. **Inquiry Skill** Based on your observations, hypothesize about the function of an apple.

Step 2

Step 4

Investigate Further

Dissect a flower such as a lily to observe its parts. Separate the pieces of the flower, and cut open any parts you can.

SI-1 Select appropriate tools; **SK-2** Record results/data

VOCABULARY
spore p. 132
gymnosperm p. 134
angiosperm p. 135
germinate p. 138

SCIENCE CONCEPTS
▶ how simple plants and vascular plants reproduce
▶ how seeds germinate

 READING FOCUS SKILL

COMPARE AND CONTRAST Look for differences in reproductive structures.

```
alike ———— different
```

How Simple Plants Reproduce

Most plants reproduce by means of spores or seeds. When you looked at the fern spores in the Investigate, were you surprised by how tiny they were? A **spore** is a single reproductive cell that can grow into a new plant. Mosses and ferns are two kinds of plants that reproduce by spores.

Remember that mosses are nonvascular plants, while ferns are vascular plants. But the life cycles of ferns and mosses are similar—they both reproduce in two different generations. In one generation, called the *sporophyte generation,* the plants reproduce by spores. In the other generation, called the *gametophyte generation,* the plants reproduce by gametes, male and female cells.

This close-up of moss shows spore stalks growing on the parent plants. The stalks are the sporophytes. The green plants are the gametophytes.

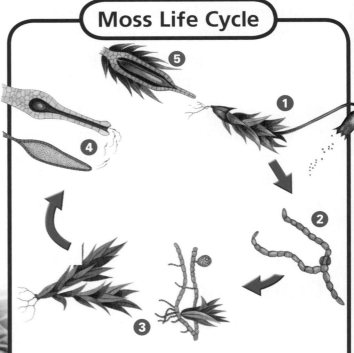

Moss Life Cycle

(1) Spores are released. (2) Gametophytes grow from spores. (3) Structures on female gametophytes produce eggs. Structures on male gametophytes produce sperm. (4) Egg and sperm join. (5) New sporophyte grows.

Although spores can be carried by the wind, the gametophyte generation needs a moist environment to reproduce. Male reproductive cells (gametes), called *sperm,* must swim to the female gametes, called *eggs.* This process is known as *fertilization.* A fertilized egg grows into a sporophyte, a plant that reproduces by spores.

You've probably seen moss growing on rocks or logs. The green plants are the moss gametophytes. Moss sporophytes are tall, thin stalks that grow from the gametophytes.

In ferns the sporophytes are more visible than the gametophytes. You've probably never even seen a fern gametophyte. They are tiny and grow flat on the ground. After fertilization, a fern sporophyte grows from the gametophyte.

In the Investigate, you observed the underside of a fern frond. You saw spore cases in clusters. Airborne spores can be blown far from the plant by a light breeze.

Focus Skill **COMPARE AND CONTRAST** How are fern sporophytes and moss sporophytes different? How are they alike?

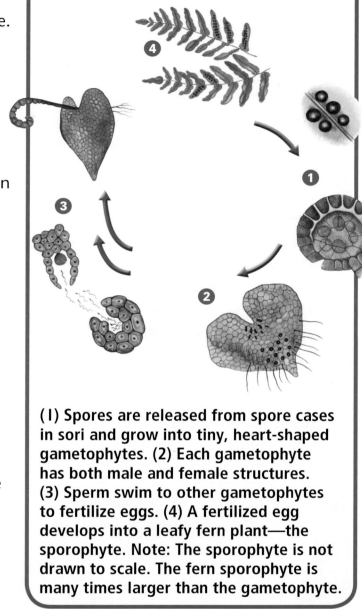

Fern Life Cycle

(1) Spores are released from spore cases in sori and grow into tiny, heart-shaped gametophytes. (2) Each gametophyte has both male and female structures. (3) Sperm swim to other gametophytes to fertilize eggs. (4) A fertilized egg develops into a leafy fern plant—the sporophyte. Note: The sporophyte is not drawn to scale. The fern sporophyte is many times larger than the gametophyte.

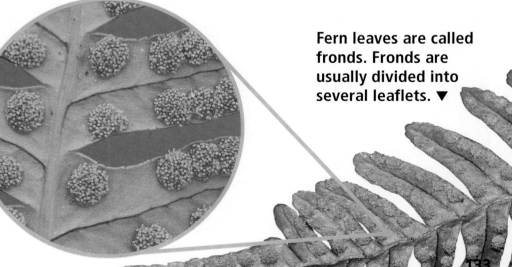

Notice the clusters on the underside of the frond. Each one is filled with hundreds of spores. ▶

Fern leaves are called fronds. Fronds are usually divided into several leaflets. ▼

Seed-Bearing Plants

Have you ever seen a pine tree with cones hanging from its branches? If so, you were looking at a vascular plant that grew from a seed. The cones that you saw probably contained more seeds. Seeds enable plants to grow in many environments. Unlike plants that reproduce by spores, seed plants don't need water for fertilization.

The seeds of pines are considered "naked," because they are protected only by a seed coat. This is in contrast to seeds that are protected inside a fruit. A plant that produces naked seeds is classified as a **gymnosperm**.

You might have seen male pine cones covered with yellow *pollen.* Pollen contains sperm. Female cones are larger and grow high on trees, above the male cones. *Ovules* grow on the scales of female cones. Ovules contain eggs.

Mature male cones release millions of pollen grains. They look like a golden dust cloud as they're blown by the wind. Some pollen settles on ovules. Sperm from the pollen fertilize the eggs, and then seeds develop.

When the seeds are mature, the cone scales separate and the seeds, which have winglike parts, travel on the wind. If a seed lands in a suitable habitat, a new tree begins to grow. Then a new life cycle begins.

Pollen is produced in male cones. Ovules are produced at the bases of the scales in female cones (shown here). After fertilization, seeds develop on the scales. ▼

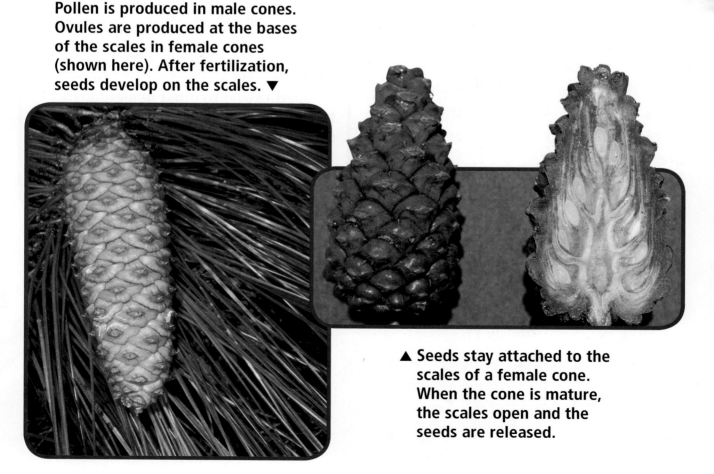

▲ **Seeds stay attached to the scales of a female cone. When the cone is mature, the scales open and the seeds are released.**

▲ When a fruit tree is in bloom, insects go to it and pollinate the flowers. Sperm in the pollen of one flower can fertilize the eggs in other flowers.

Gymnosperms are very different from flowering plants, such as apple trees. Apple trees have flowers instead of cones. Flowers produce seeds inside fruit. A flowering plant, which has seeds protected by a fruit, is classified as an **angiosperm**.

Seed development is more complex in angiosperms. Their protected seeds have made it possible for angiosperms to live in nearly all parts of the world.

 COMPARE AND CONTRAST How are gymnosperm seeds and angiosperm seeds different? How are they alike?

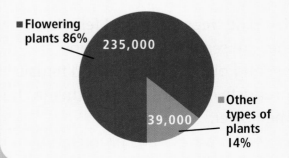

Math in Science
Interpret Data

Numbers of Plant Species
This circle graph shows the number of species of flowering plants compared to the number of all other plant species. From the data, what might you infer about the success of flowering plants compared to other types of plants?

Comparing Types of Plants

■Flowering plants 86% 235,000

■Other types of plants 14%

39,000

Inside a Flower

Look inside a flower to see the parts that work together to make seeds.

Stigma—collects pollen

Anther—makes pollen

Ovary—contains ovules. After fertilization, the ovary develops into a fruit.

Ovules—produce eggs. Eggs are fertilized by sperm from pollen and develop into seeds.

Petals—attract insects for pollination

For more links and activities, go to **www.hspscience.com**

Flowers to Seeds

On pine trees, male and female cones are separate. But in many flowering plants, the male and female reproductive organs are together in the same flower.

Flowers start as buds protected by leaflike sepals. In time, the sepals drop back and the flower petals unfold. The petals are often like advertisements for flowers. They lure animals to the flowers with their colors, making it more likely that the animals will transfer pollen. Many flowers also have attractive scents. Sometimes the scents attract certain animals even though people might think the scents are pretty bad. Flowers also make sugary nectar that attracts and feeds insects and birds.

If you stand in a field of wildflowers, you'll probably see bees going from blossom to blossom. As a bee crawls into a flower to get nectar, pollen sticks to the bee's hairy legs. When the bee goes into another flower, some of the pollen on its legs is left behind.

After fertilization, a tiny plant called an *embryo* develops in the ovule. An embryo has a root and one or two leaves. The ovule wall develops into a protective seed coat, and the ovary becomes the fruit.

Different fruits are specialized in ways that help with seed dispersal, or the spread of seeds. For example, many

Insta-Lab

Cool Beans

Your teacher will give you a lima bean that has been soaking in water. The bean is a seed. Take it out of the water and break it open. Observe it with a hand lens. Hypothesize how the parts of the seed help the plant grow.

fruits can be eaten by animals. The animals then deposit the seeds on the soil.

Focus Skill **COMPARE AND CONTRAST** What are the differences between pollen transfer in a pine tree and in many flowering plants?

Fruits of some seeds are carried by wind. Some have winglike parts. Others, like this dandelion, have structures like little parachutes. ▼

▲ Fruits that attract seed-eating birds are small enough to fit in a beak. Birds can carry seeds far away from the plants that produced them.

Seed Germination

Seeds are adapted so that they **germinate**, or sprout, when conditions are right for growth. A thick, hard seed coat protects the embryo until the seed germinates. Sometimes seeds stay in the ground for several years before conditions are right.

Seed germination is dependent on the needs of the plant. Some seeds germinate when there are enough hours of light. Most need to have warm soil, which happens in the spring. Seeds also need water.

When the time is right, a seed absorbs water and expands. This breaks the seed coat, and the embryo begins growing.

First, the root emerges from the seed and begins to anchor the embryo and take up water. Then, a shoot pushes up.

The leaves of an embryo can't make food as the leaves of a mature plant do. When you opened the seed of a lima bean, you saw structures around the embryo. These structures contain food that provides energy until the plant can make its own food.

When the first leaves emerge from the ground, they turn green, as chlorophyll for photosynthesis is produced. Rapid growth begins, and the embryo becomes a plant seedling.

 COMPARE AND CONTRAST How do the leaves of an embryo differ from the leaves of a mature plant?

A seed with a tiny embryo inside remains in the ground until conditions are right for the seed to germinate.

After the seed coat splits, the embryo root begins to grow into the soil. Now the embryo can get water.

Food in the seed feeds the embryo as the shoot grows up toward the light.

The stem grows, leaves develop, and roots spread in the soil. Now the seedling can make its own food.

Focus Skill

1. COMPARE AND CONTRAST Draw and complete the graphic organizer.

Compare and Contrast				
	New plants grow from	Sperm travel by means of	Eggs are fertilized in	Spores/seeds develop in/on
Mosses	Ⓐ _____	Ⓑ _____	water	Ⓒ _____
Ferns	Ⓓ _____	water	Ⓔ _____	clusters on frond
Gymnosperms	Ⓕ _____	Ⓖ _____	Ⓗ _____	Ⓘ _____
Angiosperms	Ⓙ _____	insects/air	Ⓚ _____	Ⓛ _____

2. SUMMARIZE Use the graphic organizer to write a summary of this lesson, comparing reproduction by spores and reproduction by seeds.

3. DRAW CONCLUSIONS Why do ferns produce so many spores? Why don't flowering plants produce as many seeds?

4. VOCABULARY Provide the terms that complete this sentence:

Gymnosperm is to _____ as _____ is to flower. Think of similar sentences to use in a game.

Test Prep

5. Critical Thinking What time of year would be best for planting bean seeds? Why?

6. In which structure do seeds develop?

   A. anther **C.** pollen grain

   B. ovary   **D.** spore

Links

Writing

Expository Writing

Write a paragraph that **explains** how you use plants every day. Write about both gymnosperms and angiosperms.

Math

Display Data

Read the directions on several seed packets to find out how long it takes for the seeds to germinate. Make a bar graph comparing the germination times of the seeds.

Language Arts

Word Origins

Research the origins of the words for the two seed-plant groups—*gymnosperms* and *angiosperms.* Share your findings with the class.

 For more links and activities, go to www.hspscience.com

How Do Plants of the Past Compare with Those of Today?

Fast Fact

Polished Wood Look closely at this section of a petrified tree trunk. How old do you think it is? Petrified wood is not really wood—it is a fossil made out of minerals! In the Investigate, you will examine other plant parts that turn into fossils.

Comparing Cones and Fruits

Materials
- **lemon leaves**
- **lemon half**
- **conifer needles**
- **conifer cone**
- **hand lens**
- **safety goggles**

Procedure

1 Observe the lemon leaves and conifer needles. Both are leaves with adaptations that help the plants survive.

2 Use a hand lens to observe the leaves. Compare the leaves, and record your observations by drawing the leaves. Write a description of what you observe.

3 Observe the lemon half. Record your observations.

4 CAUTION: **Put on safety goggles.** Carefully break open the cone, and observe the inside. Record your observations.

Draw Conclusions

1. Are lemon trees vascular plants? Are conifers? How can you tell?

2. Lemon trees grow very quickly. Conifers can survive periods when there is little water. Infer how the leaf adaptations you observed help these different plants survive.

3. **Inquiry Skill** Compare the lemon half and the conifer cone. What similarities do you observe?

Step 2

Step 4

Investigate Further

The seeds of conifers are adapted to travel. Formulate a hypothesis about seed adaptations. Design an experiment to test your hypothesis.

VOCABULARY
fossil p. 142
extinction p. 146

SCIENCE CONCEPTS

► how nature produces fossil plants

► about extinct prehistoric plant species

Focus Skill **READING FOCUS SKILL**

COMPARE AND CONTRAST

Compare living plants with fossilized plants.

| alike |——| different |

Plants Without Fruit

Scientists learn a lot about what the world used to be like by studying plants that lived long ago. How do they do this? They study fossils. **Fossils** are the remains of once-living things that have been preserved by being petrified or by leaving different kinds of imprints.

Many of the fossils scientists study come from plants that didn't bear fruit. Scientists can often get a better picture of what these plants were like because they have more of the plants' parts.

The living fern and the fossil fern look very much alike.

Compare the sago palm with this fossil of a frond. They are very similar.

Tree needles can become fossils. Compare the living redwood needles with the fossil of redwood needles.

Scientists think that only a small fraction of prehistoric plants have been preserved as fossils. Many of the fossils that have been found are similar to plants alive today.

One such preserved plant is the fern. Some prehistoric ferns were the size of today's trees. Using fern fossils, scientists can see that even though today's ferns are much smaller, they have the same structures and shapes as prehistoric ferns.

Scientists believe that the modern sago palm is related to prehistoric cycads. Cycad fossils, like fern fossils, are similar to plants alive today. Although cycads resemble palms, they are not true palms. True palms are flowering plants that have fruit. Cycads have cones.

Scientists have linked modern conifer trees, or trees that have cones, with prehistoric conifer trees. Scientists have found fossils of petrified conifer trunks and fossil imprints of leaves. These fossils were found in areas that are now in an arctic environment—cold and icy. This shows that these areas were warmer when the trees lived there. The change in climate probably helped preserve the fossils.

 COMPARE AND CONTRAST How are fossils different from living plants?

143

Plants with Fruit

Plant fossils are formed only if the plants are uneaten and don't rot. This means it can be hard to find fossils that include fruit. But when these fossils are found, they can teach scientists many things.

Fossils of water lilies are very common. They are much like lilies today. Lilies are fragile, so changes in environment must happen very quickly to fossilize them. These fossils can tell how prehistoric environments changed.

Fossil records also show that magnolias have survived from prehistoric times. Flower beetles, not

▲ The lily is a fruit-bearing plant that is very common in the fossil record.

Eidothea (eye•DOH•thee•uh), or nightcap oak, was thought to be extinct—until a living tree that was almost identical to known fossils was found. The nightcap oak is an endangered species.

▼ This fossil of magnolia fruit shows that prehistoric magnolia had fruit, just like today's magnolia.

The *Archaefructus sinensis* (ar•kay•FRUK•tuhs sin•EN•sis) plant had thin stems that reached above the surface of the water it grew in. It is the oldest known fruit-bearing plant. It is not like anything living today. ▶

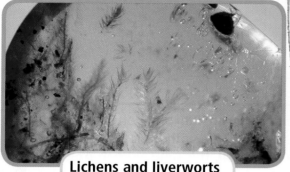

Lichens and liverworts are still around today.

bees or butterflies, pollinate magnolias. Prehistoric flower beetles probably lived at the same time as the prehistoric magnolias.

Small Plant and Plantlike Fossils
Liverworts are plants that have fleshy, rounded bodies. Lichens have stalks that make spores. Lichens are quite different from plants—they are made up of fungi and algae. The fossil record tells us very little about lichens. Scientists believe this is because lichens grow mostly in tundra, mountains, and desert. These environments do not produce many fossils.

 COMPARE AND CONTRAST Why are fossil lilies more common than fossil lichens?

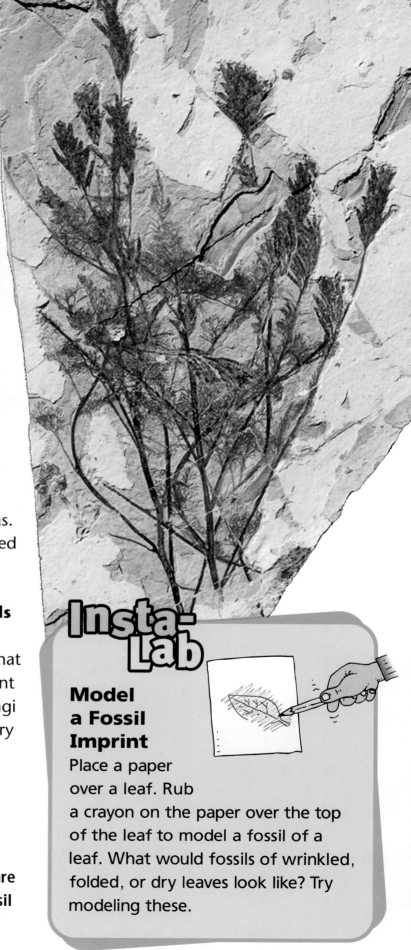

Insta-Lab

Model a Fossil Imprint
Place a paper over a leaf. Rub a crayon on the paper over the top of the leaf to model a fossil of a leaf. What would fossils of wrinkled, folded, or dry leaves look like? Try modeling these.

Extinct Plants

Some prehistoric plants are related to plants that are living today. Other prehistoric plants are not like anything living today. Look at the pictures of fossils on this page. Studying these fossils is the only way we will learn about these plants. This is because these plants became extinct. **Extinction** is when an entire living species dies.

Scientists can use fossils of extinct plants to compare them to plants living today. If they have just one thing in common, this could mean that they are both related to an even older plant that might not yet have been discovered.

COMPARE AND CONTRAST
How do these fossils compare to living plants?

Cordaites, which are extinct, are believed to be related to modern conifers.

Lepidodendron (luh•pih•doh•DEN•druhn), was a giant tree with bark that looked like this fossil. It is now extinct. A variety of ground moss is believed to be one of its living relatives.

▼ *Hymenaea protera* (hy•muhn•AY•uh proh•TAIR•uh) is extinct, but is believed to be related to some modern trees. Much amber is fossilized sap of *Hymenaea protera*.

146

1. COMPARE AND CONTRAST Copy and complete this chart.

Category	Plants		
Plants Without Fruit	**A** _____	redwoods	
	B _____	**C** _____	
		lichens and liverworts	
Plants with Fruit	lilies **D** _____	Eidothea	
Extinct Plants	*Archaefructus sinensis* **E** _____		
	Hymenaea protera **F** _____		

2. SUMMARIZE Use the chart to write a summary of prehistoric plants.

3. DRAW CONCLUSIONS If scientists cannot find a living plant that is like a fossil, what is probably true about the plant that made the fossil?

4. VOCABULARY Use vocabulary words and other science words to describe a lepidodendron.

Test Prep

5. Critical Thinking How would a scientist know if he or she found a prehistoric plant that had fruit?

6. To what prehistoric plants is the sago palm related?

A. ferns   **C.** cycads

B. conifers   **D.** palms

Links

Writing

Expository Writing

Imagine that you are explaining to your friend about plant fossils. Write a short **explanation** of how fossils can be formed.

Math

Identify Place Value

Scientists believe that magnolias have been around for one hundred million years. How do you write the number for this?

Social Studies

Amber

Amber, a gemstone, was first discovered by ancient people. Research to find out how amber was used in the past. Then write a paragraph on one way in which amber was used.

 For more links and activities, go to www.hspscience.com

Farms of the Future

Could you grow a garden in your bathroom? Is it possible to have a farm without soil? It might sound like something from the future, but that kind of growing is happening today. Hydroponics is the growing of plants in nutrient-rich solutions.

Growing in Water

Hydroponic farming has been around for many years. But researchers are now using hydroponics to develop new techniques to grow food quickly and in an environmentally safe way.

With hydroponics, plant roots grow directly in water and are supported by materials such as peat moss, sand, or gravel. Nutrients are added to the water to imitate the nutrients plants would normally get out of soil. Hydroponic plants grow about twice as fast as plants grown in soil.

New Techniques

Today, researchers are finding new ways to use hydroponics. Scientists in New Mexico are showing that hydroponics can work in the desert by growing alfalfa plants. They have shown that less water is needed to grow hydroponic food than to grow the same amount of food in soil. That is important because in many parts of the world, water is hard to find.

Hydroponic flowers

Growing and packing hydroponic lettuce

Hydroponic farming is also helping Florida's beaches. When hurricanes hit Florida, they erode the sand on the beaches. Researchers grow plants called sea oats hydroponically and then transplant the sea oats to beaches. The sea oats trap sand and help restore beaches.

Healthier Growing?

Many researchers and hydroponic farmers believe that hydroponics is the farming method of the future. In addition to saving water, hydroponically farmed fruits and vegetables are more healthful to eat because the plants receive a well-balanced diet in their water.

The nutrient-filled water helps give the fruits and vegetables vitamins and minerals, which are passed on to people who eat them. Fruits and vegetables gro in soil get their nutrients from the land, b pollution and chemicals in the soil can li the amount of nutrients the plants receiv

Think About It

1. How are hydroponic plants and plants grown in soil different?
2. Do you think hydroponic plants might taste different from plants grown in so Why or why not?

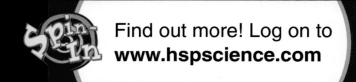

Spin In

Find out more! Log on to
www.hspscience.com

ST-1 Explain how technology improves lives;
ST-2 Explain how technology meets needs

Birds Help Trees

Birds are Khloe Ziff's favorite animals. Khloe became interested in birds when she went to camp at a wildlife rehabilitation center. She learned how birds help the trees and other plants in an ecosystem.

Birds help an ecosystem by spreading seeds. They often drop the seeds they carry in their beaks. The seeds then grow to become plants that feed other animals.

"Hummingbirds get pollen on their feet and carry it to a different flower," said Khloe. This pollinates the flowers. Pollinating flowers makes the flowers develop seeds. The seeds fall to the ground and grow more plants.

You Can Do It!

Materials
- potted plant
- clear fingernail polish
- microscope slide
- microscope

Quick and Easy Project

Leaf Cast

Procedure

1. Paint a 2-cm square of clear fingernail polish on the underside of one leaf. Let the polish dry.
2. Add another layer of polish, and let it dry. Repeat until you have six layers of polish.
3. When the last layer is dry, peel all the polish off the leaf. The polish now contains a cast of the leaf epidermis.
4. Put the dried polish on a microscope slide.
5. Observe the slide with the microscope.

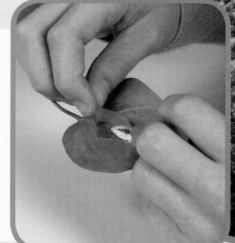

Draw Conclusions

On the cast, you should observe two types of cells. Compare the two types. Explain any differences between them. How are the stomata formed?

Design Your Own Investigation

Sunlight and Chlorophyll

Would plants have green leaves if there were no sunlight? Design an experiment to determine if plants need sunlight to develop chlorophyll. Remember that chlorophyll is the green pigment in leaves. Form a hypothesis, and then design an experiment to see if your hypothesis is correct.

Chapter 3 Review and Test Preparation

Vocabulary Review

Use the terms below to complete the sentences. The page numbers tell you where to look in the chapter if you need help.

classify p. 116
vascular p. 120
xylem p. 125
photosynthesis p. 128
gymnosperm p. 134
angiosperm p. 135
germinate p. 138
fossil p. 142

1. The remains of a once living plant that has been preserved in stone is a _____.

2. A plant with a naked seed is a _____.

3. Water is transported in vascular tissue called _____.

4. When the ground is warm and wet, a seed can sprout, or _____.

5. A plant with flowers and protected seeds is an _____.

6. Plants produce food by _____.

7. When you _____, you group things that are alike.

8. Plants with tubes are called _____ plants.

Check Understanding

9. When soft stems are thick it is often because they are being used to
   A. store water **C.** store seeds
   B. make food **D.** grow leaves

10. Which tissue carries water and nutrients from the roots?
   F. cork **H.** phloem
   G. dogwood **J.** xylem

11. Which of the following is a product of photosynthesis?

   A. carbon dioxide **C.** sugar
   B. nitrogen **D.** water

12. **MAIN IDEA** What kind of plant would have a flower like this?

   F. a moss **H.** a gymnosperm
   G. a liverwort **J.** an angiosperm

13. **COMPARE AND CONTRAST** Kris is allergic to pollen. Which of these plants should she avoid?
   A. fern   **C.** moss
   B. frond   **D.** pine

14. What kind of plant would you choose to attract butterflies to your garden?
   F. angiosperm
   G. fern
   H. gymnosperm
   J. moss

15. What prehistoric plants were probably pollinated by flower beetles?
   A. lilies
   B. lepidodendrons
   C. magnolias
   D. sago palms

16. On a trip through the desert, Tim saw many plants. What kind of roots would you expect to find on a desert plant?
   F. aerial   **H.** prop
   G. fibrous   **J.** tap

Inquiry Skills

17. **Hypothesize** why nonvascular plants are rare in desert areas.

18. Angiosperms from one continent can be found growing on other continents. **Infer** how this can happen.

Critical Thinking

19. If a prehistoric plant is vascular, what parts might you see in a fossil of the plant that you most likely will not see in the fossil of a nonvascular plant?

20. Trees and shrubs benefit people in many ways.
   Part A How can trees reduce the amount of carbon dioxide in the atmosphere?
   Part B What other benefits might there be from planting trees and shrubs?

4 Ecosystems and Energy

Lesson 1 What Are the Parts of an Ecosystem?

Lesson 2 What Factors Influence Ecosystems?

Lesson 3 What Are the Roles of Living Things?

Lesson 4 How Do Living Things Get Energy?

Vocabulary

environment	producer	niche
ecosystem	consumer	food chain
population	herbivore	prey
community	carnivore	predator
biotic	omnivore	food web
abiotic	decomposer	energy pyramid
diversity	habitat	

What do YOU wonder?

This lynx must catch and eat hares and many other small animals in order to live. This hare may provide energy for the lynx. Where do hares get the energy they need to live?

What Are the Parts of an Ecosystem?

Silver Kings The tarpon in this photograph are not yet full-grown! These fish don't become adults until they are between 7 and 13 years old, when they can weigh more than 91 kilograms (200 lb). Tarpon live in salt water, but they can survive in a variety of ecosystems. In the Investigate, you will observe how sunlight affects plants in another ecosystem.

Modeling an Ecosystem

Materials
- gravel
- sand
- soil
- 6 small plants
- water in a spray bottle
- clear plastic wrap
- 2 empty 2-L soda bottles with tops cut off
- 2 rubber bands

Procedure

1. Pour a layer of gravel, a layer of sand, and then a layer of soil into the bottom of each bottle.

2. Plant three plants in each bottle.

3. Spray the plants and the soil with water. Cover the top of each bottle with plastic wrap. If necessary, hold the wrap in place with a rubber band.

4. Put one of the terrariums you just made in a sunny spot. Put the other one in a dark closet or cabinet.

5. After three days, observe each terrarium and record what you see.

Step 2

Step 3

Draw Conclusions

1. What did you observe about each of your ecosystems after three days? What part was missing from one ecosystem?

2. **Inquiry Skill** Scientists often learn more about how things affect one another by **making a model.** What did you learn by making a model and observing how its parts interact?

Investigate Further

What effect does sunlight have on seeds that have just been planted? First, write your hypothesis. Then plan an experiment to see if your hypothesis is supported.

VOCABULARY
environment p. 158
ecosystem p. 158
population p. 160
community p. 162

SCIENCE CONCEPTS
▶ how living and nonliving parts of an ecosystem interact
▶ what populations and communities are

READING FOCUS SKILL

MAIN IDEA AND DETAILS

Look for the parts that make up an ecosystem.

Main Idea		
detail	detail	detail

Ecosystems

Where do you live? You might name your street and town. But you also live in an environment. An **environment** is all the living and nonliving things that surround you. The living things in your environment are people, other animals, and plants. The nonliving things around you include water, air, soil, and weather.

The parts of an environment affect one another in many ways. For example, animals eat plants. The soil affects which plants can live in a place. Clean air and clean water help keep both plants and animals healthy. All the living and nonliving things in an area form an **ecosystem** (EE•koh•sis•tuhm).

An ecosystem can be very small. It might be the space under a rock. That space might be home to insects and tiny plants. You might need a microscope to see some of the things living there.

This prairie smoke plant grows well in the hot, dry climate of prairies and grasslands. ▼

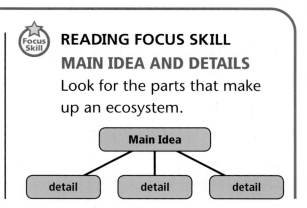

Prairie dogs also live on the prairies and grasslands. ▼

Moose thrive in a coniferous forest ecosystem.

The small ecosystem found under a rock has nonliving parts, too. They include pockets of air and the soil under the rock. You might find a few drops of water or maybe just damp soil. All ecosystems must have at least a little water.

The ecosystem under this rock has a climate. The *climate* in an area is the average weather over many years. Climate includes temperature and rainfall. The climate of an ecosystem depends on where the ecosystem is. If this rock is in Florida, its climate is warm and wet. If the rock is in Maine, its winters are icy.

An ecosystem can also be as large as a forest. A forest can provide many kinds of food and shelter. This ecosystem may include hundreds of kinds of plants and animals. Each organism finds what it needs in the forest.

Like all ecosystems, a forest has nonliving parts. They include water, air, soil, and climate. Later, you will read more about ways living and nonliving parts of an ecosystem affect one another.

 MAIN IDEA AND DETAILS **Name the two parts of an ecosystem, and give two examples of each part.**

This individual water lily is part of a large population of water lilies.

Individuals and Populations

One plant or animal is an *individual.* For example, one blueberry bush is an individual. One honeybee is an individual. One blue jay is an individual. You are an individual.

A group made up of the same kind of individuals living in the same ecosystem is a **population**. A group of blueberry bushes is a population. So is a hive of bees. So are all the blue jays living in one forest. So are all the people living in one city.

Robins might live in the same forest as the blue jays. Robins are a different kind of bird. That makes them a different population.

The members of a population might not live in a group. For example, frogs don't live in families. Still, a number of green tree frogs may live near the same pond. They belong to the same population. Bullfrogs might also live near that pond. They are a different population.

Many animals live in groups. People live in families. How many people are in your family? Wolves live in packs. A pack can have from 3 to 20 wolves. A wolf population may have several packs. The wolf population in Yellowstone National Park includes 19 packs.

Some populations can live in more than one kind of ecosystem. For instance, red-winged blackbirds often live in wetlands, but they are also found in other areas. Red-winged blackbirds can live in different ecosystems. If one ecosystem no longer meets the needs of these birds, they fly to another one.

Some populations can live in only one ecosystem. One such population is the Hine's emerald dragonfly. This insect can live only in certain wetlands. It can't survive in other places. Because this dragonfly can live only in specific places, its total population is very small.

Ecosystems are often named for the main population that lives there. For example, one kind of ecosystem forms where a river flows into the ocean.

There, fresh water mixes with salt water. Many trees can't live in salty water. But mangrove trees have roots that enable them to get rid of the salt in the water. Where many mangrove trees live in a salty ecosystem, the area is called a *mangrove swamp.*

 MAIN IDEA AND DETAILS Name an individual and a population that are not mentioned on these two pages.

Eeek! Oh System!

Work with a partner to list some of the populations in your school ecosystem. Think about the building and the land around it. Then compare lists with other students. Did you list the same populations?

This individual male red-winged blackbird is part of a large population of blackbirds.

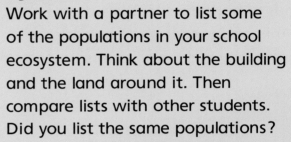

A population of red-winged blackbirds can include several million birds. Some of the birds fly 80 kilometers (50 mi) to find food.

Communities

You live in a community. Other animals and plants do, too. A **community** is all the populations that live in the same place.

Have you visited the Everglades National Park? Many different populations make up this community. The plants include mangrove trees, cypress trees, and saw grass. If you have been to the Everglades, you may also know about the mosquitoes. Did all 43 kinds try to bite you? Did you see all 50 kinds of butterflies that live there?

Animals found in the Everglades community include alligators, bobcats, and raccoons. Bird-watchers like to visit the Everglades. They try to see some of the 350 kinds of land birds and 16 kinds of wading birds that live there.

In some ways, the Everglades is like all communities. The plants and animals there depend on one another. Some animals eat the plants. Other animals eat the plant eaters. The animals help spread the plants' seeds. The plants provide shelter for the animals.

 MAIN IDEA AND DETAILS Name three populations that might be found in a forest community.

▼ Many populations make up the communities in this cold taiga ecosystem. They include evergreen trees, moose, and many kinds of birds.

Focus Skill

1. MAIN IDEA AND DETAILS Draw and complete this graphic organizer.

An ocean ecosystem is made up of living and nonliving things.

 **Living Things**
A _____
_____
_____

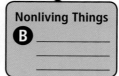 **Nonliving Things**
B _____
_____
_____

2. SUMMARIZE Write a summary of this lesson by using the lesson vocabulary words in a paragraph.

3. DRAW CONCLUSIONS Why do some ecosystems include more living things than other ecosystems?

4. VOCABULARY Use the lesson vocabulary words to create a matching quiz.

Test Prep

5. Critical Thinking How is a population different from a community?

6. Which word describes a group of cows standing together?

A. community   **C.** individual
B. ecosystem   **D.** population

Links

Writing

Expository Writing
You are a scientist planning an ecosystem on the moon. Write **two paragraphs** explaining what this ecosystem should include.

Math

Solve a Problem
The Everglades includes many "rivers of grass." The water in these rivers moves slowly, only 30 meters (100 ft) a day. How many meters would the water move on average in June? In February?

Social Studies

Ecosystems and People
Choose a group of people who live in an ecosystem different from yours. Find out how that ecosystem affects the people. Share what you learn in an oral or written report.

 For more links and activities, go to www.hspscience.com

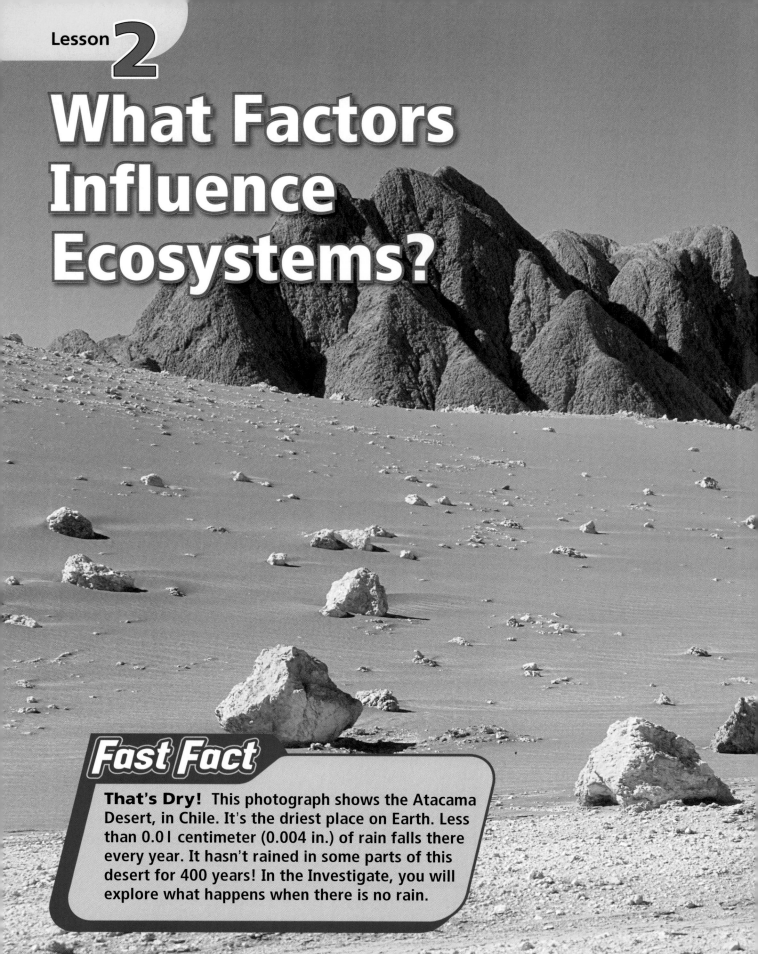

2

What Factors Influence Ecosystems?

Fast Fact

That's Dry! This photograph shows the Atacama Desert, in Chile. It's the driest place on Earth. Less than 0.01 centimeter (0.004 in.) of rain falls there every year. It hasn't rained in some parts of this desert for 400 years! In the Investigate, you will explore what happens when there is no rain.

Observing the Effects of Water

Materials
- 4 identical small plants in clay pots
- water
- large labels

Procedure

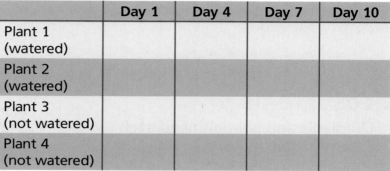

	Day 1	Day 4	Day 7	Day 10
Plant 1 (watered)				
Plant 2 (watered)				
Plant 3 (not watered)				
Plant 4 (not watered)				

1 Use the labels to number the pots 1, 2, 3, and 4. Label pots 1 and 2 *watered*. Label pots 3 and 4 *not watered.*

2 Make a table like the one shown here. Draw a picture of each plant under Day 1.

3 Place all four pots in a sunny window.

4 Water all four pots until the soil is a little moist. Keep the soil of pots 1 and 2 moist during the whole experiment. Don't water pots 3 and 4 again.

5 Wait three days. Then observe and record how each plant looks. Draw a picture of each one under Day 4.

6 Repeat Step 5 twice. Draw pictures of the plants on Days 7 and 10.

Step 4

Draw Conclusions

1. What changes did you observe during this Investigate? What do they tell you?

2. **Inquiry Skill** Scientists compare changes to determine how one thing affects another. How could you compare how fast the soil dries out in a clay pot with how fast it dries out in a plastic pot?

Investigate Further

How does covering a plant with plastic wrap affect the plant's need for water? Write your hypothesis. Then design and carry out an experiment to check your hypothesis.

VOCABULARY
biotic p. 166
abiotic p. 168
diversity p. 172

SCIENCE CONCEPTS
▶ how biotic and abiotic factors affect ecosystems
▶ how climate influences an ecosystem

Focus Skill **READING FOCUS SKILL**
CAUSE AND EFFECT
Look for ways in which factors affect ecosystems.

Living Things Affect Ecosystems

Do plants and animals need each other? Yes, they do! Plants and animals are living parts of an ecosystem. These living parts are **biotic** factors. *Bio* means "life." Biotic factors affect the ecosystem and one another in many ways.

For example, plants provide food for caterpillars, birds, sheep, and other animals. People eat plants every day—at least they should.

Plants also provide shelter for animals. For instance, many insects live in grasses. Squirrels make dens in trees. Your home likely contains wood from trees.

Animals help plants, too. When animals eat one kind of plant, it can't spread and take over all the available space. This gives other kinds of plants room to grow.

A gypsy moth can lay 1000 eggs or more. Most of the eggs hatch into hungry caterpillars like this one. ▶

A healthy tree isn't hurt when a few insects nibble on it.

Gypsy moth caterpillars can eat all the leaves on a tree. Bad weather or an attack by other insects may kill this tree.

Animals help plants in other ways. Animal droppings make the soil richer. Earthworms help loosen the soil. Rich, loose soil helps plants grow.

At the same time, too many plant eaters can be harmful. A herd of hungry deer can eat enough leaves to kill a tree. A huge swarm of locusts can leave a field bare of plants.

You know that animals affect one another. For example, wolves eat rabbits. If the wolf population becomes too large, wolves can wipe out the rabbits. Then the wolves go hungry. Without the rabbits to eat them, the grasses spread.

In this case, an increase in wolves causes a decrease in rabbits. Fewer rabbits causes an increase in plants.

A change in plants can also cause a change in animals. If dry weather or disease kills the grasses, the rabbits starve. Then the wolves go hungry, too. Disease can also kill the living parts of an ecosystem.

Sometimes, a new kind of plant or animal changes an ecosystem. For example, people brought the skunk vine to the United States from Asia in 1897. For a time, they planted it as a crop. Now it grows wild. This smelly vine can grow 9 meters (30 ft) long! It crowds out other plants, and it can even grow underwater.

 CAUSE AND EFFECT
Explain how an increase in plants could affect an ecosystem.

Math in Science
Interpret Data

food supply

number of deer

0   5 years   10 years   15 years   20 years   25 years

What happened to the population of deer as the food supply got smaller?

Tree leaves are a main source of food for deer. It takes 15 to 30 acres of land to provide enough food for one deer.

167

Nonliving Things Affect Ecosystems

Plants and animals are the living parts of an ecosystem. The nonliving parts include sunlight, air, water, and soil. The nonliving parts are **abiotic** factors. They are just as important as the biotic factors.

For example, a change in the water supply can affect all the living things in an ecosystem. Too little rain causes many plants to wilt and die. Animals must find other homes. Some may die.

An ecosystem with rich soil has many plants. Where the soil is poor, few plants grow. Few plants mean few animals in the ecosystem.

Air, water, and soil can contain harmful substances. They can affect all living things. You will learn more about this problem later in the chapter.

 CAUSE AND EFFECT How might a change in the water supply affect a rabbit?

Insta-Lab

Super Soil!
With a partner or a group, compare two different soil samples. How might each soil affect its ecosystem?

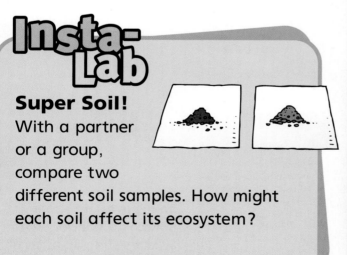

Nonliving Factors
Without the nonliving parts of an ecosystem, there would be no living parts.

Sunlight
Plants need sunlight to produce food. Where trees shade the ground, not many other plants can grow.

Water
Almost all living things need water. Plant roots absorb water, and animals drink it.

Soil
Most plants need soil to grow. The kind of soil in an ecosystem is one of the factors that determines which plants grow there.

For more links and activities, go to
www.hspscience.com

Climate Affects Ecosystems

What is the climate like where you live? Is it warm and sunny, or is it cool and rainy? Maybe it's something in between.

Climate is an abiotic factor. It's a combination of other abiotic factors. Climate includes the amount of rainfall and sunlight in a region. It also includes the repeating patterns of the temperature of the air during the year.

Climate affects the soil. Some climates allow many plants to grow and help dead plants decay. Animals that eat the plants leave behind their droppings. The decaying plants and droppings make the soil richer.

Climate affects the kinds of plants and animals in an ecosystem. For example, warm, wet climates support tropical rain forests. Hot summers and cold winters result in temperate forests.

The frozen tundra suits the hardy caribou. The mosses they eat thrive there. Zebras could not survive in the tundra. They need the mild climate and tender grasses of the savanna.

 CAUSE AND EFFECT What would happen to an ecosystem if its climate changed?

World Climate Zones

This map shows six climate zones around the world.

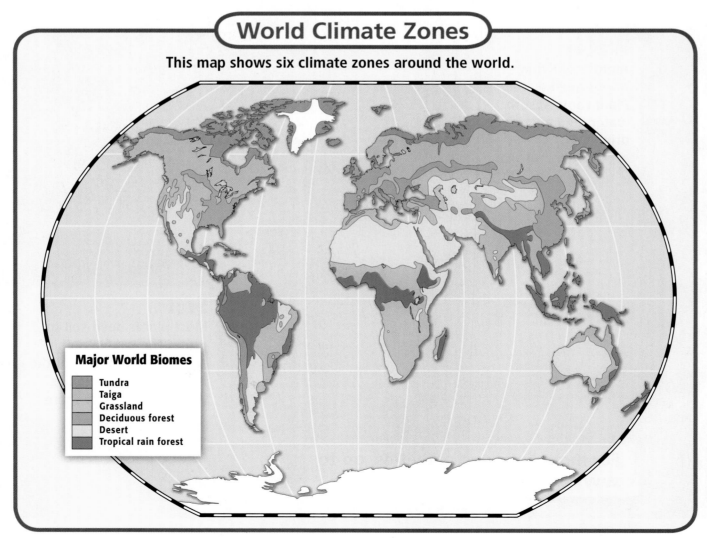

Major World Biomes
- Tundra
- Taiga
- Grassland
- Deciduous forest
- Desert
- Tropical rain forest

Temperate forests have four seasons. The trees, such as oaks and maples, lose their leaves in the fall. This helps them survive the cold winters.

Rain forests receive 2000 to 10,000 millimeters (7 to 33 ft) of rain each year! Tropical rain forests are near the equator. Temperate rain forests are farther north, along some coasts.

The climate in the grassy savanna is nearly the same all year. The temperature stays between 18°C and 22°C (64°F and 72°F).

Deserts get only about 250 millimeters (10 in.) of rain a year. Plants there grow very quickly after a rain. Their seeds can survive for years as they wait for more rain.

The taiga covers more of Earth than any other kind of plant community. The taiga is just south of the tundra and is very cold in winter. Most of its trees are evergreens.

The tundra has the coldest climate: −40°C to 18°C (−40°F to 64°F). *Tundra* means "treeless plain."

There are layers in a rain forest.

The *canopy* is the upper part of the trees. It is home to most rain-forest animals.

Diversity

A rain-forest ecosystem provides many sources of food and shelter. That's why it has the most diversity of all of Earth's ecosystems. **Diversity** refers to the number of different kinds of living things.

In a rain forest, a wide range of plants and animals can find what they need to survive. Many kinds of monkeys live in the treetops. Snakes slip from branch to branch. Bright butterflies flit among the flowers. Frogs of many colors cling to tree trunks. Mushrooms and earthworms hide under decaying leaves. Some rain-forest plants have giant leaves. Other plants can't be seen without using a microscope.

Some ecosystems don't have much diversity. The tundra, for example, is very cold and dry. Much of its soil is frozen. Few living things can survive there.

How much diversity does the ecosystem where you live have?

🟡 **Focus Skill** **CAUSE AND EFFECT** What leads to a diversity of living things in an ecosystem?

The next layer is the cool, dark *understory*. This layer is just right for plants that grow well in shade.

The bottom layer is the *forest floor*, where decaying matter provides food for plants.

172

1. CAUSE AND EFFECT Draw and complete the graphic organizer.

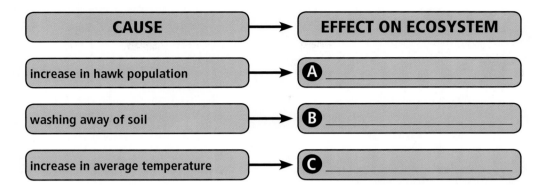

CAUSE		EFFECT ON ECOSYSTEM
increase in hawk population	→	**A** _____
washing away of soil	→	**B** _____
increase in average temperature	→	**C** _____

2. SUMMARIZE Use your completed graphic organizer to write a lesson summary.

3. DRAW CONCLUSIONS Which can exist without the other—biotic factors or abiotic factors? Explain your answer.

4. VOCABULARY Write a quiz-show question for each of the vocabulary words.

Test Prep

5. Critical Thinking How might flooding in their ecosystem affect some robins?

6. Which of these is an abiotic factor in an ecosystem?

A. ant   **C.** earthworm

B. decaying plant   **D.** sand

Links

Writing

Persuasive Writing

Write a **travel brochure** for a climate where few people vacation, such as the tundra or taiga. Tell your readers what interesting things they can see and experience there.

Math   9÷3

Make a Graph

Find the average rainfall in five of the six world climate zones, including your own region. Then make a bar graph that compares the rainfalls.

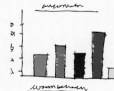

Literature

Learn More

Read a current nonfiction book about one of the world climates, such as the desert. After learning more about that climate, share what you know by making a display or a written report.

 For more links and activities, go to www.hspscience.com

What Are the Roles of Living Things?

Fast Fact

Nothing Fishy About Eating This archer fish is leaping for its prey. It eats insects to get energy for living. Archer fish also hunt by spitting at insects to knock them into the water. Some archer fish are eaten by other animals or die and then decay in the water. In the Investigate, you will find out how decomposers (dee•kuhm•POHZ•erz) help once-living matter decay.

Decomposing Bananas

Materials
- 2 slices of banana
- 2 zip-top plastic bags
- spoon
- package of dry yeast
- marker

Procedure

1. Put a banana slice in each bag.

2. Sprinkle $\frac{2}{3}$ spoonful of dry yeast on one banana slice. Yeast is a decomposer, so use the marker to label this bag *D*.

3. Close both bags. Put the bags in the same place.

4. Check both bags every day for a week. Observe and record the changes you see in each bag.

Draw Conclusions

1. Which banana slice shows more changes? What is the cause of these changes?

2. **Inquiry Skill** Scientists use time relationships to measure progress. How long did it take for your banana slice to begin showing signs of decomposition? How long do you think it would take for your banana slice to completely decompose?

Step 2

Step 4

Investigate Further

What will happen if you put flour, instead of yeast, on one banana slice? Write down your prediction, and then try it.

SI-3 Design and conduct simple investigations;
SI-4 Control variables

175

VOCABULARY
producer p. 176
consumer p. 176
herbivore p. 178
carnivore p. 178
omnivore p. 178
decomposer p. 180

SCIENCE CONCEPTS

▶ how living things use the energy from sunlight

▶ how living things get energy from other living things

READING FOCUS SKILL

MAIN IDEA AND DETAILS
Look for details about the movement of energy among living things.

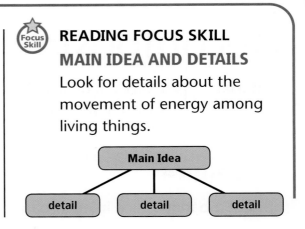

Producers and Consumers

Most living things on Earth get the energy to live from sunlight. Green plants and algae (AL•jee) use energy in sunlight, plus water and carbon dioxide, to make their own food. Any living thing that can make its own food is called a **producer**. Producers can be as small as a tiny moss or as large as a huge redwood tree.

Some animals, such as deer and cattle, get the energy they need to live by eating plants. When these animals eat, the energy stored in the plants moves into the animals' bodies.

Not all animals eat plants. Lions and hawks, for example, get the energy they need by eating other animals.

An animal that eats plants or other animals is called a **consumer**. Consumers can't make their own food, so they must eat other living things.

These plants are using energy in sunlight to produce food. Without sunlight, the plants would die.

Horse

Which animal gets its energy directly from producers? Which one gets its energy from other consumers? Which one gets its energy from both?

Florida panther

Some consumers eat the same kind of food all year. Horses, for example, eat grass during warm weather. During winter, they eat hay, a kind of dried grass.

Other consumers eat different things in different seasons. For example, black bears eat grass in spring. Later on, they might eat birds' eggs. Bears might also dig up tasty roots or eat fish from streams. In fall, bears eat ripe berries.

Florida panthers eat other consumers, but their diet varies. Mostly, panthers consume wild hogs, which are easy for them to catch. Another favorite meal is deer. Panthers also eat rabbits, raccoons, rats, birds, and sometimes, even alligators.

 MAIN IDEA AND DETAILS What is a producer? What is a consumer? Give two examples of each.

Black bear

Kinds of Consumers

Consumers are not all the same. In fact, there are three kinds—herbivores, carnivores, and omnivores.

A **herbivore** is an animal that eats only plants, or producers. Horses are herbivores. So are giraffes, squirrels, and rabbits.

A **carnivore** is an animal that eats only other animals. The Florida panther and the lion are carnivores. A carnivore can be as large as a whale or as small as a frog.

An **omnivore** is an animal that eats both plants and other animals. That is, omnivores eat both producers and other consumers. Bears and hyenas are omnivores. Do any omnivores live in your home?

Producers and all three kinds of consumers can be found living in water. Algae are producers that live in water. They use sunlight to make their own food. Tadpoles, small fish, and other small herbivores eat algae. Larger fish that are carnivores eat the tadpoles. Some animals, including green sea turtles, are omnivores. Green sea turtles eat seaweed, algae, and fish. In fact, algae makes the flesh of the green sea turtle green!

 MAIN IDEA AND DETAILS Name the three kinds of consumers. Give two examples of each.

This diagram shows how kinds of consumers get energy to live.

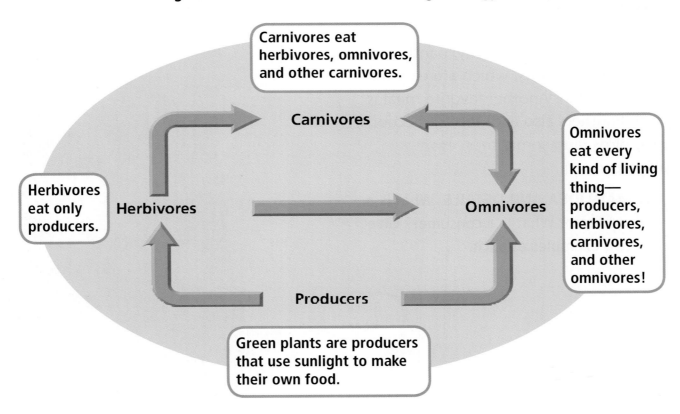

Carnivores eat herbivores, omnivores, and other carnivores.

Herbivores eat only producers.

Omnivores eat every kind of living thing—producers, herbivores, carnivores, and other omnivores!

Green plants are producers that use sunlight to make their own food.

Carnivores

Herbivores

Omnivores

Producers

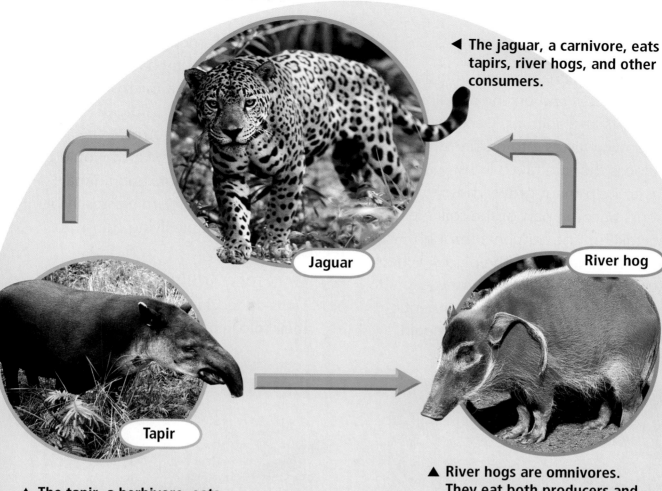

◀ The jaguar, a carnivore, eats tapirs, river hogs, and other consumers.

Jaguar

River hog

Tapir

▲ The tapir, a herbivore, eats only producers. It eats tender buds and twigs.

▲ River hogs are omnivores. They eat both producers and herbivores.

Jungle bush

▲ These plants are producers. They make their own food and provide stored energy for consumers.

Insta-Lab

Who's an Omnivore?

Read the nutrition labels on several food containers.

Think about the source of each kind of food. What does the food's source tell about consumers who eat it?

Decomposers

A **decomposer** is a living thing that feeds on wastes and on the remains of dead plants and animals. Decomposers break down wastes into nutrients, or substances that are taken in by living things to help them grow. These nutrients become part of the soil. Next, plants take up the nutrients through their roots. Animals eat the plants. When plants and animals die, decomposers break down their bodies into nutrients. This cycle is repeated again and again.

Decomposers come in many shapes and sizes. Some are tiny bacteria that you can see only with a microscope. Other decomposers are as big as mushrooms and earthworms.

Without decomposers, Earth would be covered with dead plants and animals. Instead, decomposers turn wastes into nutrients. They enable living things to recycle nutrients.

 MAIN IDEA AND DETAILS Name two kinds of decomposers, and describe their role in nature.

Sow bugs

Sow bugs are related to lobsters. They help plant matter decay faster than it would without them.

Millipede

In the forest, millipedes chew up dead plant material. Like sow bugs, millipedes aren't insects.

Bracket fungus

The bracket fungus is one of a group of fungi (FUN•jy) that includes mushrooms. Bracket fungi often grow on dead tree trunks and help them decay quickly.

Focus Skill

1. MAIN IDEA AND DETAILS Copy and complete this graphic organizer.

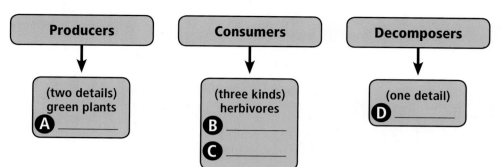

Producers	Consumers	Decomposers
(two details) green plants **A** _____	(three kinds) herbivores **B** _____ **C** _____	(one detail) **D** _____

2. SUMMARIZE Write two sentences that tell what this lesson is mainly about.

3. DRAW CONCLUSIONS How are decomposers consumers?

4. VOCABULARY Construct a crossword puzzle, using this lesson's vocabulary words.

Test Prep

5. Critical Thinking How do eagles depend on sunlight for their energy?

6. Which term describes a hyena?
  A. carnivore
  C. omnivore
  B. herbivore
  D. producer

Links

Writing

Narrative Writing
Write a **science fiction story**. Tell about a time when all the producers on Earth disappear. Describe what happens to the consumers.

Math

Solve a Problem
A shrew eats about $\frac{2}{3}$ of its body weight daily. Suppose a child who weighed 30 kilograms (66 lb) could eat $\frac{2}{3}$ of his or her body weight. How many kilograms of food is that?

Health

Eating Decomposers
Find out what vitamins and minerals are in mushrooms. Find healthful recipes that have mushrooms as one of the ingredients.

 For more links and activities, go to **www.hspscience.com**

How Do Living Things Get Energy?

Make a Food Chain

Materials ● 8 to 10 blank index cards
 ● colored pencils or markers
● reference books about animals

Procedure

1 Choose a place where animals live. Some examples are pine forest, rain forest, desert, wetland, and ocean.

2 On an index card, draw a living thing that lives in the place you have chosen. Draw more living things, one kind on each card. Include large animals, small animals, and producers. Look up information about plants and animals if you need help.

Step 2

3 Put your cards in an order that shows what eats what. You might have more than one set of cards. If one of your animals doesn't fit anywhere, trade cards with someone. You can also draw another animal to link two of your cards. For example, you could draw a rabbit to link a grass card and a hawk card.

Step 3

Draw Conclusions

1. Could the same animal fit into more than one set of cards? Explain your answer.

2. **Inquiry Skill** Scientists communicate their ideas in many ways. What do your cards communicate about the relationships of these living things to one another?

Investigate Further

Draw a series of cards in order, with yourself as the last consumer. Compare your role with the roles of other consumers.

Reading in Science

VOCABULARY
habitat p. 184
niche p. 185
food chain p. 186
prey p. 186
predator p. 186
food web p. 188
energy pyramid p. 190

SCIENCE CONCEPTS
▶ how consumers depend on other living things
▶ how energy moves through food chains and food webs

READING FOCUS SKILL
SEQUENCE Look for the order in which things happen.

Habitats

You probably wouldn't see a heron in a desert or a penguin in a swamp. Animals must live in places that meet their needs. A **habitat** is an environment that meets the needs of a living thing. An insect's habitat can be as small as the space under a rock. A migrating bird's habitat can cross a continent.

Many habitats can overlap. For example, the three living things pictured on this page all live in a desert habitat. This desert habitat meets all their needs. Sagebrush grows well here. Sidewinders and tarantulas find many small consumers to eat.

These living things thrive in the desert habitat, even though it's hot and has little water.

The venomous sidewinder eats mice, rats, lizards, and birds. ▶

Sidewinder

◀ Tarantulas are venomous, too. They eat insects, other spiders, lizards, snakes, frogs, and birds.

Tarantula

Sagebrush can grow where other plants can't. Sheep and cattle often eat sagebrush in the winter. ▶

Sagebrush

Each living thing in a habitat has a role, or **niche** (NICH). The term *niche* describes how a living thing interacts with its habitat. Part of a living thing's niche is how it gets food and shelter. Its niche also includes how it reproduces, cares for its young, and avoids danger. Each animal has body parts that help it carry out its role. For example, a cat's pointed claws and sharp eyes help it catch its food.

Part of the sidewinder's niche is to eat small animals in its habitat. If all these snakes died, the desert would have too many mice, birds, and lizards. These small animals would eat all the available food and would soon starve. The sidewinder's niche helps keep the number of small desert animals in balance.

 SEQUENCE What would happen next if all the sagebrush disappeared from a desert?

Crab

Lion-fish

Anemone

This coral reef habitat has a balance of producers and consumers. Everything in this picture is a consumer.

Food Chains

Living things depend on one another to live. A **food chain** is the movement of food energy in a sequence of living things. Every food chain starts with producers. Some consumers, such as deer, eat these producers. Then the deer are eaten by other consumers, such as mountain lions. Consumers that are eaten are called **prey**. A consumer that eats prey is a **predator**. Prey are what is hunted. Predators are the hunters.

Some animals in a habitat are prey, while other animals are predators. Predators limit the number of prey animals in a habitat. Wolves are predators of antelope. They keep the population of antelope from increasing too much, so the antelope don't eat all of the producers. Predators often compete for the same prey. This limits the number of predators in a habitat.

 SEQUENCE **What would happen next if the number of predators in a habitat increased too much?**

A mangrove swamp is one kind of habitat. Special prop roots hold mangrove trees in the muddy soil. Fresh water and salt water mix in this habitat.

Many organisms live in and around the mangrove roots.

Mullets are fish that can live in fresh water or salt water.

◄ Without hawks, the chipmunk population would get very large. The chipmunks would eat all the acorns and then starve.

Acorns provide energy for the chipmunk, which in turn provides energy for the hawk. ▶

An alligator is just one of the predators in a mangrove swamp. Alligators dig burrows for themselves that also provide shelter for other animals during dry times.

Insta-Lab

Chain of Life

Cut white paper into strips that are 2.5 cm (1 in.) by 12.5 cm (5 in.). On each strip, write the name of a producer or a consumer. Then use glue or tape to combine the strips into paper food chains. Which food chains end with you?

Food Webs

A food chain shows how an animal gets energy from one food source. But food chains can overlap. One kind of producer may be food for different kinds of consumers. Some consumers may eat different kinds of food. For example, hawks eat sparrows, mice, and snakes.

Several food chains that overlap form a **food web**. There are food webs in water habitats, too. For example, herons eat snails, fish, and other birds.

On the next page, you can see an ocean food web. It shows that energy moves from plankton, small producers in the ocean, to small fish. These fish are called *first-level consumers*.

These fish then become prey for bigger fish, called *second-level consumers*. They, in turn, are eaten by the biggest fish and the mammals in the ocean, called *top-level consumers*.

 SEQUENCE What happens after a first-level consumer eats a producer?

Follow several paths in this food web. Begin at the bottom, with a producer, and trace the movement of energy through the web.

Antarctic Ocean Food Web

This food web begins with energy from the sun. The producers are tiny plants called phytoplankton (FYT•oh•plangk•tuhn). They float near the water's surface. Sunlight can't reach deep underwater. No plants grow at the bottom of the ocean. Where would decomposers fit in this food web?

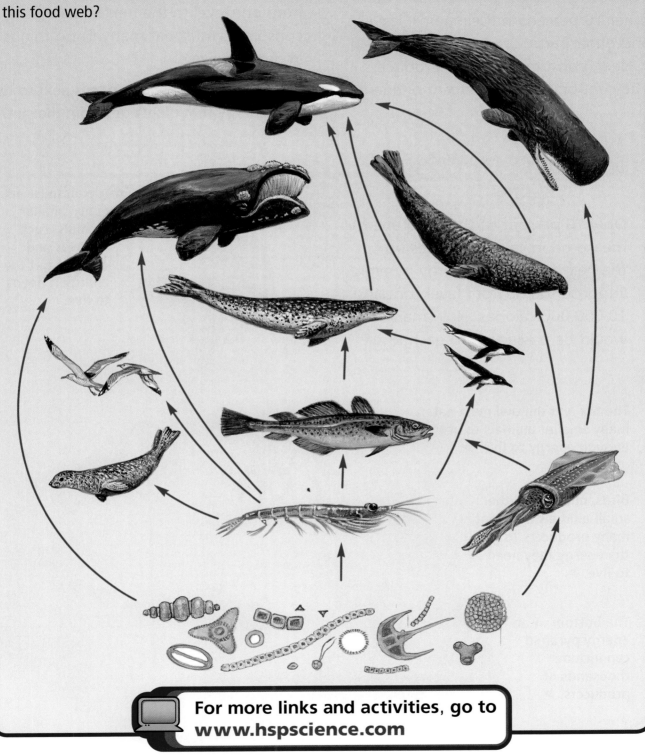

For more links and activities, go to www.hspscience.com

Energy Pyramids

An **energy pyramid** shows how much energy is passed from one living thing to another along a food chain. Producers form the base of the pyramid. They use about 90 percent of the energy they get from the sun to grow. They store the other 10 percent in their stems, leaves, and other parts.

Next, consumers eat the producers. They get only the 10 percent of energy that the plants stored. These consumers use about 90 percent of the energy they get from the producers to grow and then store the other 10 percent in their bodies. That 10 percent is passed on to the consumers that eat them.

You can see how little energy is passed from one level to the next. That's why consumers must eat many living things in order to live.

 SEQUENCE What happens next to the energy that plants get from the sun?

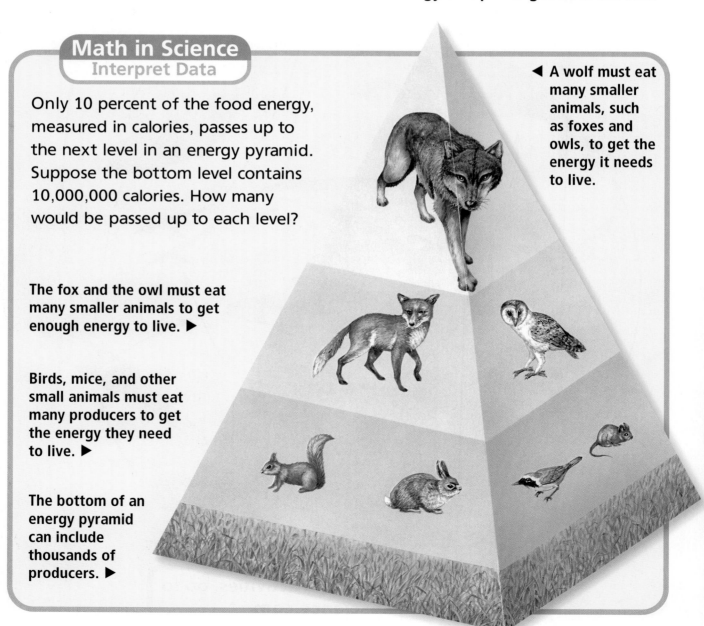

Math in Science
Interpret Data

Only 10 percent of the food energy, measured in calories, passes up to the next level in an energy pyramid. Suppose the bottom level contains 10,000,000 calories. How many would be passed up to each level?

◀ A wolf must eat many smaller animals, such as foxes and owls, to get the energy it needs to live.

The fox and the owl must eat many smaller animals to get enough energy to live. ▶

Birds, mice, and other small animals must eat many producers to get the energy they need to live. ▶

The bottom of an energy pyramid can include thousands of producers. ▶

1. SEQUENCE Copy and complete this graphic organizer. Put the living things in order to create a food chain.

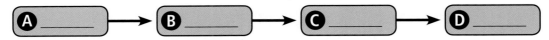

woodpecker   hawk   leaves   insect

A _____ → **B** _____ → **C** _____ → **D** _____

2. SUMMARIZE Write a summary of this lesson by using the lesson vocabulary terms in a paragraph.

3. DRAW CONCLUSIONS How are predators good for prey?

4. VOCABULARY Use the vocabulary terms to make a quiz. Then trade quizzes with a partner.

Test Prep

5. Critical Thinking How would the death of all of one kind of consumer affect a food web?

6. Which of these best shows why deer must eat grass all day long?
  A. diagram   **C.** food chain
  B. energy pyramid   **D.** food web

Links

Writing

Expository Writing
Write a **description** of ways humans might affect a food web and what would then change. For example, people might clear trees for a housing development or feed the deer in a park.

Math

Solve a Problem
Producers in a field have stored 20,000 calories. Herbivores get 2000 calories by eating the producers. How much energy is available to the next level of the energy pyramid?

Art

Food Chains
Choose any art medium, such as watercolor, charcoal, collage, or torn paper, to show the living things in a food web. (You don't have to show them eating one another!)

For more links and activities, go to
www.hspscience.com

AQUARIUS
An Underwater Lab With A View

Many kids share their bedrooms with brothers or sisters. Sharing a room can be a pain. Six scientists know it! They squeezed into a small underwater laboratory to study a coral reef. They worked and slept in the tiny space for ten days.

"I've been on missions where people snored," said Celia Smith, who led the mission in October. "You just kind of kick their bunk and try to get to sleep before they do."

This buoy supplies the *Aquarius* with fresh air and electricity.

▲ An aquanaut peers through a window in the *Aquarius* as another aquanaut swims around the laboratory.

The underwater lab is called *Aquarius*. It looks like a little yellow submarine.

The *Aquarius* was placed near the Florida Keys National Marine Sanctuary, a protected area of the ocean. Each year, several teams of scientists have lived in *Aquarius* for up to ten days at a time. The scientists who live and work in *Aquarius* are called aquanauts (AH•kwuh•nawtz). The aquanauts study the nearby coral reef and the creatures that live in it.

A Room with a View

The latest team to visit *Aquarius* says the best part of living there is the view. They can see colorful fish swimming in the nearby reef. Smith said it's hard to tell, though, whether the aquanauts are watching the fish or the fish are watching the aquanauts.

The aquanauts spend as much time as they can on the reef studying sea life.

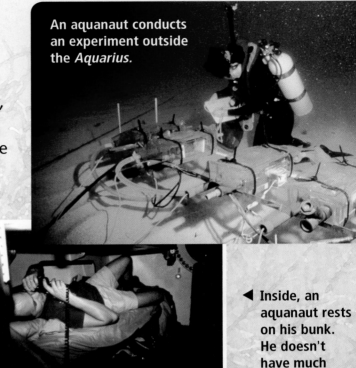
An aquanaut conducts an experiment outside the *Aquarius*.

◄ Inside, an aquanaut rests on his bunk. He doesn't have much room.

They can spend up to nine hours at one time outside the laboratory.

Smith likes to remind people that humans have barely begun to explore the oceans and need to learn more about life in the deep. "The really important thing for us to realize is how much we don't know about the oceans," she said.

THINK ABOUT IT

1. How might living underwater help scientists learn more about a coral reef ecosystem?
2. What might be the best thing about living underwater? What might be the worst thing?

IN THE DEEP

Aquarius is located about 19 meters (63 ft) deep in the ocean. It has sleeping space for six, a bathroom, a trash compactor, and computer stations.

Electrical cables and tubes connect the *Aquarius* to a buoy on the ocean's surface. The tubes carry fresh air to the *Aquarius*, and the cables supply electricity.

The work the aquanauts are doing is expected to help NASA. NASA scientists say that living and working on the *Aquarius* is similar to what it will be like to live and work in a space station. They hope to better prepare astronauts for space by studying how the aquanauts live and work underwater.

Spin In Find out more! Log on to **www.hspscience.com**

ST-3 Describe design process; **SK-3** Explain importance of record keeping

Meet a Young CONSERVATIONIST

Fourth grader Blake Wichtowski told people at last year's Kids' Summit that wild blue lupine flowers would help the endangered Karner blue butterfly. Officials from New York are turning this idea into a reality.

Blue lupine is the only food that Karner caterpillars will eat.

With the help of the Seneca Park Zoo in Rochester and other officials, Blake's fourth grade class and a class at another elementary school will plant seeds for a blue lupine garden near the local airport.

Materials
- plastic funnel
- gravel
- sand
- bowl
- water with some soil and leaves in it

Quick and Easy Project

Getting Out the Dirt

Procedure

1. Fill the bottom of a funnel with gravel. Then add a thick layer of sand.
2. Hold the funnel over a bowl. Pour the "dirty" water into it. The water will run out the bottom of the funnel, into the bowl.
3. Observe the water in the bowl. See if you can find the soil and leaves.

Draw Conclusions

How did your funnel filter affect the dirty water? Where might you find this kind of natural filter? How might soil and other substances get into a water supply?

Design Your Own Investigation

Checking for Air Pollution

Is the air in your school or neighborhood polluted? Air pollution often includes bits of ash and dust. If you smear petroleum jelly on the inside of baby-food jars and put them somewhere for several days, bits of pollution may stick to the jelly. Which areas of your school or neighborhood do you think might have this kind of pollution? Write a hypothesis. Then design an experiment and carry it out to see whether your hypothesis is supported.

SI-3 Design and conduct simple investigations; **SK-1** Distinguish fact from opinion

Review and Test Preparation

Vocabulary Review

Use the terms below to complete the sentences. The page numbers tell you where to look in the chapter if you need help.

producers p. 176   **niche** p. 185
consumer p. 176   **predators** p. 186
omnivore p. 178   **food chain** p. 186
decomposers p. 180   **energy pyramid** p. 190

1. An animal that eats other living things is a _____.

2. Nutrients would be lost without _____.

3. The animals at the top of a food chain are always _____.

4. The kind of food that an animal eats is part of its _____.

5. An animal that eats both producers and other consumers is an _____ .

6. Herbivores and omnivores both eat _____.

7. A food web shows relationships among living things more accurately than a _____.

8. The loss of energy along a food chain is shown in an _____.

Check Understanding

Write the letter of the best choice.

9. All the living things and nonliving things around you are
   A. a population   **C.** an environment
   B. abiotic factors **D.** a niche

10. **MAIN IDEA AND DETAILS** Which term includes herbivores, carnivores, and omnivores?
    F. consumers   **H.** prey
    G. predators   **J.** producers

11. How much energy is used at each level of the energy pyramid and not passed on?
    A. 10 percent   **C.** 80 percent
    B. 20 percent   **D.** 90 percent

12. Which of the following is not an abiotic factor?
    F. rain   **H.** chipmunks
    G. climate   **J.** soil

13. What is shown below?

    A. niche   **C.** habitat
    B. food chain   **D.** food web

14. What are robins, which eat worms and insects?

    F. carnivores   **H.** omnivores

    G. herbivores   **J.** prey

15. Antelopes are herbivores. What other term describes them?

    A. omnivores   **C.** prey

    B. predators   **D.** producers

16. MAIN IDEA AND DETAILS A group made up of the same kind of individuals living in the same ecosystem is

    F. a population

    G. an ecosystem

    H. an abiotic factor

    J. a food chain

Inquiry Skills

17. Compare a carnivore and a predator. How are these living things the same? How are they different?

18. While hiking with your family, you follow a trail that leads past many dead plants. Even the trees seem to be dying. The soil is very dry. What can you **infer** is happening to the consumers in this area?

Critical Thinking

19. Which of these could survive without being part of a food chain—a strawberry plant, a chicken, or a dog? Explain your answer.

20. Different types of diagrams are used to show the relationships among living things. Study the diagram below.

Part A Would this diagram be correct if there were two snakes at the top? Explain your answer.

Part B How is this diagram different from a food chain?

Franklin Park Conservatory

At the Franklin Park Conservatory in Columbus you will be able to see, touch, smell, and hear things related to nine different climates. Look for the butterflies when you walk past the different flowers and plants. Butterflies are very important to the plants and other insects at the conservatory.

The butterfly gardens at the conservatory have the plants that butterflies need. A butterfly's life has four stages. In the first stage, a parent butterfly lays its eggs underneath the leaves of a plant. The eggs live on the plant. An egg turns into a caterpillar, also called a larva. This is the second stage. The caterpillar eats the plant's leaves. Then it starts the third stage of life. It turns into a pupa, or chrysalis. A pupa doesn't eat. The plant shelters the pupa as it hangs from a twig among the stems and branches. In the fourth stage, the pupa becomes a butterfly.

Franklin Park
Conservatory

Butterflies and Flowers

There are many kinds of flowering plants at the conservatory. That's good news for butterflies. Butterflies need all kinds of plants. Each type of butterfly prefers different types of flowers. Having lots of plants means that all kinds of butterflies can find the plants they need.

Butterflies also help plants survive. Butterflies carry pollen from one flower to another. The pollen helps the plants reproduce.

One of the butterflies you can see at the conservatory

Think and Do

 1. SCIENTIFIC THINKING Draw a picture showing how butterflies and plants help each other survive. Be sure to show the life stages of the butterfly.

 2. SCIENTIFIC THINKING What do you think would happen if one kind of butterfly was removed from the conservatory? What if all of the butterflies were taken away? What would happen to the plants? Write a paragraph to explain your answer.

Cleveland

Columbus

Holden Arboretum

Myrtle S. Holden Wildflower Garden

When you think of plants in Ohio, you might think of the Holden Arboretum. The arboretum is in Cleveland. It is the largest preserve for trees and other plants in the United States. The arboretum holds woodlands, meadows, display gardens, and mountain areas. There are places for plants that live near rivers, lakes, streams, and other wetlands. Wildlife roams among the plants.

You can find many rare Ohio plants here. The Wildflower Garden alone has more than 165 rare Ohio plants. Arboretum workers watch the plants carefully. They work to keep the different types of plants healthy. They also try to help these special plants grow and reproduce. For instance, seeds from the Labrador tea plant were planted in the wildlife bog. New tea plants then grew. These plants are the only ones of their kind that you will see in Ohio.

The arboretum offers tours showing unusual rock formations and rare plant communities.

Labrador Tea Is a Part of History

The Labrador tea is a shrub that grows about 1.2 meters (4 ft) tall. It has special leaves. The edges of the leaves are rolled. Underneath the leaves there is a layer of thick, tan fuzz. The shrub has white flowers that open in the summer. During the Revolutionary War, the leaves were used instead of regular tea leaves to make tea.

The work of the arboretum is important. Rare plants are cared for so that people in the future can enjoy them too.

To protect the plants, only a few people at a time can visit some areas.

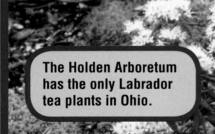

The Holden Arboretum has the only Labrador tea plants in Ohio.

Think and Do

I. SCIENTIFIC THINKING You can find flowers and plants in many places. Why would a visit to the Holden Arboretum be worth the time? Make a list of your reasons.

2. SCIENCE AND TECHNOLOGY Suppose you are helping a plant expert at the Holden Arboretum. She tells you that a new plant will be brought in. Make a list of questions that will help you find the best location for the plant.

 LS-1 Compare plant life cycles; **LS-2** Relate plant structure to function; **LS-5** Describe organism interactions; **SI-1** Communicate instructions/data

The Lakeside Daisy

Marblehead Peninsula

Can you picture rare and beautiful yellow daisies growing in a rock pit? Go to Lakeside Daisy State Nature Preserve. It is on Marblehead Peninsula. This preserve is a 150-year-old quarry. It is a good place for the Lakeside daisy to grow.

The preserve protects the only group of Lakeside daisies in the country. Most plants can't grow in the quarry. But here the daisies are strong.

Lakeside daisies are very rare. They are the only ones of their kind in the United States. They grow in only two other places in the world.

The only Lakeside daisies in North America grow in Ohio.

These rare daisies are found in only two locations outside of Ohio.

Rare and Beautiful

This daisy is one of Ohio's most beautiful wildflowers. It is a perennial. This means that it grows year after year. In early May, its bright flowers can be seen across the quarry. Each plant makes a single flower. All the flowers in the quarry usually bloom at the same time. The flower heads all turn toward the sun. After about a week, the petals of the flowers fade and then they fall. The seeds blow over the rocks. New flowers grow where the seeds fall.

The Lakeside daisy is strong enough to grow where other plants do not. But the daisy survives only because people protect it. The state of Ohio bought the quarry and turned it into a state nature preserve.

The Lakeside daisy grows well on the stone of this former quarry.

Think and Do

 1. SCIENTIFIC THINKING Quarries are very large holes cut into rock. People get stone or rock building materials from them. Why do you think this rare flower grows where other plants don't?

 2. SCIENTIFIC THINKING Suppose you heard of a plan to restore nature to the Lakeside Daisy State Nature Preserve. Write a letter to the people making the plans for the quarry. Tell them if you think restoration is a good or bad idea. Give your reasons.

What Are the Parts of a Flower?

Materials

Flower with visible stamen, such as a tulip

Research materials on the parts of a flower

Cardboard and markers

Procedure

1. In your research materials, find out about these parts of a flower: stamen, sepals, pistil, pollen, ovule, and petals. Find out what each part looks like and what part it plays in pollination of the flower. Pollination is necessary for a new seed to grow.

2. Take your tulip, or other flower, and find as many parts of the flower as you can. You will need to open up the flower.

3. Make a diagram that shows the flower parts you discovered. Write a caption for each part, telling what it does during pollination.

Draw Conclusions

1. Flowers are pollinated by insects. What parts of a flower attract them? How do butterflies and bees move pollen from flower to flower?

2. How could you use this project to predict what would happen to flowers if there were a shortage of pollinating insects?

Do Plants Always Turn Toward the Light?

Materials

Two small milk cartons
Bean seeds
Water
Dirt
Shoe box
Scissors
Ruler

Procedure

1. Plant several seeds in each of the two milk cartons

2. Water the seeds.

3. Cut out a square hole about 2 cm by 2 cm in the side of the shoe box.

4. Put one carton of seeds on a windowsill. Place the other carton of seeds in the box with a hole in it. Keep the lid on the box. Put the box next to the carton already on the windowsill.

5. Keep watering the seeds until they start to grow.

Draw Conclusions

1. Compare the two groups of plants. How are they the same? How are they different?

2. What was different about the way the plants in the two containers were grown? What was the same?

3. From this experiment, do you think that other varieties of plants, besides the Lakeside daisies, grow facing the sun?

 LS-1 Compare plant life cycles; **LS-2** Relate plant structure to function; **LS-5** Describe organism interactions; **SI-1** Select appropriate tools; **SI-3** Design and conduct simple investigations; **SK-2** Record results/data

Physical Sciences

The chapters and features in this unit address these Grade Level Indicators from the Ohio Academic Content Standards for Science.

Chapter 5

Matter and Its Properties

PS-3 Describe objects by the properties of the materials from which they are made and that these properties can be used to separate or sort a group of objects (e.g., paper, glass, plastic and metal).

Chapter 6

Changes in Matter

PS-1 Identify characteristics of a simple physical change (e.g., heating or cooling can change water from one state to another and the change is reversible).

PS-2 Identify characteristics of a simple chemical change. When a new material is made by combining two or more materials, it has chemical properties that are different from the original materials (e.g., burning paper, vinegar and baking soda).

PS-4 Explain that matter has different states (e.g., solid, liquid and gas) and that each state has distinct physical properties.

PS-5 Compare ways the temperature of an object can be changed (e.g., rubbing, heating and bending of metal).

Unit C Ohio Expeditions

The investigations and experiences in this unit also address many of the Grade Level Indicators for standards in Science and Technology, Scientific Inquiry, and Scientific Ways of Knowing.

Wapakoneta

Columbus

TO: Juan@hspscience.com

FROM: Jesse@hspscience.com

RE: Neil Armstrong Air and Space Museum, Wapakoneta

Dear Juan,

Do you remember reading about Neil Armstrong walking on the moon? When he stepped onto its surface, he said it was "One small step for [a] man, one giant leap for mankind."At the Space Museum, I saw all sorts of things and learned how spacesuits protect astronauts. I was even able to see a moon rock. Scientists learned a lot about the moon by studying the properties of moon rocks.

Gotta get ready for takeoff...

Jesse

Experiment!

When sidewalks and roads are covered with ice, people sprinkle salt on the ice to melt it. The salt combines with the ice, forming salt water. The ice melts because salt water freezes at a lower temperature than pure water. What are the freezing points of different liquids? Plan and conduct an experiment to find out.

Lesson 1 How Can Physical Properties Be Used to Identify Matter?

Lesson 2 How Does Matter Change States?

Lesson 3 What Are Mixtures and Solutions?

Vocabular

matter	liquid
mass	gas
volume	mixture
density	solution
state of matter	solubility
solid	suspension

What do YOU wonder?

Doctors use plastic and metal to replace hip joints. Think about a material that could replace bone. What might it be like?

1

How Can Physical Properties Be Used to Identify Matter?

Fast Fact

Amazing Water Density affects floating for liquids and solids. Water is unusual. It's less dense when it is solid ice than when it is liquid water. That's why ice floats on water. No other common material has this property of being denser as a liquid than as a solid. In the Investigate, you will find the densities of three liquids. Amazing water is one of them.

Measuring the Densities of Liquids

Materials
- graduate
- vegetable oil
- balance
- corn syrup
- water

Procedure

1. Make sure the graduate is empty, clean, and dry. Then use the balance to find its mass. Record the mass.

2. Add 10 mL of water to the graduate. Measure and record the mass. Empty the graduate and dry it.

3. Repeat Step 2, using 10 mL of vegetable oil.

4. Repeat Step 2, using 10 mL of corn syrup.

5. Subtract the mass of the empty graduate from each of the masses you measured in Steps 2, 3, and 4. Record each result.

6. To find the densities, divide the mass of each liquid by its volume, 10 mL. Record and compare the densities.

Draw Conclusions

1. Which liquid has the greatest density? Which has the least? Compare the amount of matter in each liquid sample.

2. Inquiry Skill Display data by making a bar graph that shows the density of each liquid you measured.

Step 1

Step 2

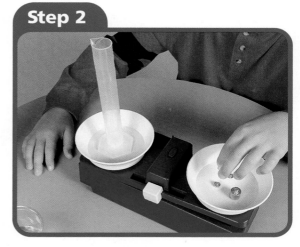

Investigate Further

Tint 10 mL of water red. Pour it into the graduate. Then add 10 mL of corn syrup. Observe what happens. How do you explain your observation?

VOCABULARY

matter p. 212
mass p. 213
volume p. 214
density p. 214

SCIENCE CONCEPTS

► how physical properties can be used to identify substances

► how density can be determined

READING FOCUS SKILL

MAIN IDEA AND DETAILS

Find out how physical properties help identify matter.

Main Idea

detail	detail	detail

Matter

What is matter? Just about everything! Everything that takes up space is **matter**. This includes you, your skateboard, the clothes you're wearing, and the sidewalk under you. Breakfast cereal is matter. Your bowl, your spoon, and the milk you pour on the cereal are all matter, too.

If you can taste, smell, or touch something, it's matter. Even a breeze is matter, because air takes up space. You prove that when you blow up a balloon. The air you blow into the balloon pushes out its sides. The air inside the balloon takes up space.

Some things exist without taking up space, so they are not matter. What is not matter? Heat, light, and ideas are examples of things that are *not* matter. Even though they exist, they don't take up any space.

MAIN IDEA AND DETAILS Define *matter*, and name three examples.

◄ What do you have in common with a skateboard?

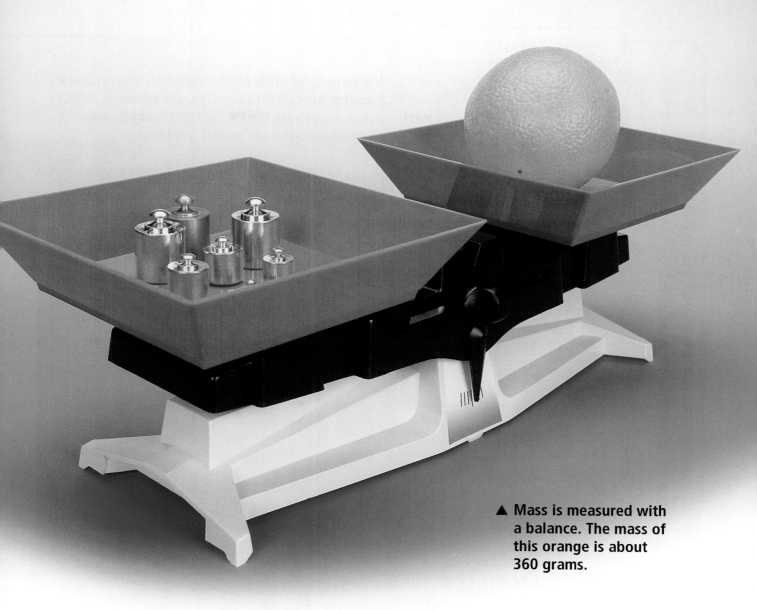

▲ Mass is measured with a balance. The mass of this orange is about 360 grams.

Mass

Matter not only takes up space but also has mass. **Mass** is the amount of matter something contains. A heavy object has more mass than a light object. Finding mass is a way of measuring matter.

All matter is made of tiny particles. You can see them only under the strongest microscopes. In general, the more particles an object has, the more mass it has. The more mass it has, the heavier it is.

A golf ball and a table tennis ball both are made of matter. The balls are about the same size. However, the golf ball is heavier because it has more mass.

The mass of an object is one of its physical properties. A physical property is something you can observe or measure. You can measure mass. Other physical properties include an object's look and texture.

 MAIN IDEA AND DETAILS Define *mass.* **Name one object with a lot of mass and one with little mass.**

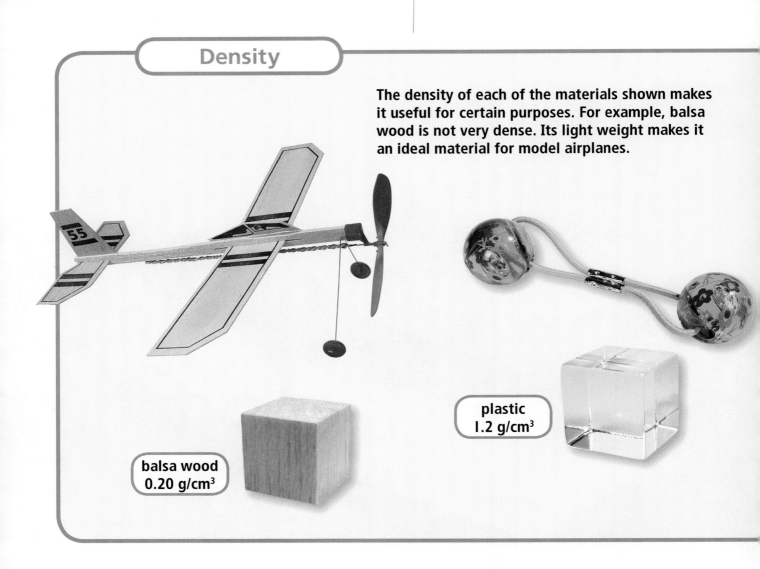

The density of each of the materials shown makes it useful for certain purposes. For example, balsa wood is not very dense. Its light weight makes it an ideal material for model airplanes.

plastic
1.2 g/cm³

balsa wood
0.20 g/cm³

Volume and Density

Volume is the amount of space that matter takes up. Some objects, such as a blown-up balloon, have little mass (few particles). Yet a balloon takes up a lot of space. A marble has more mass but takes up little space. How can we show this relationship between mass and space?

The answer is density. **Density** is the amount of matter in an object compared to the space it takes up. In the Investigate, you measured density. You divided the masses of three liquids by their volumes. Each liquid had the

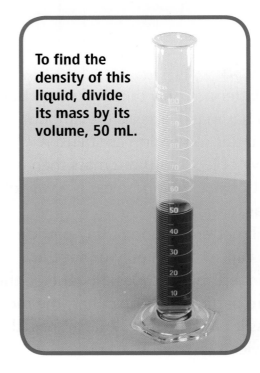

To find the density of this liquid, divide its mass by its volume, 50 mL.

aluminum
2.7 g/cm³

brass
8.5 g/cm³

copper
8.9 g/cm³

same volume but a slightly different mass. This explains why each liquid had a different density.

You can find the density of a solid object by dividing its mass by its volume. For example, a certain wooden block has a mass of 20 grams. Its volume is 10 cubic centimeters (**cm³**). When you divide its mass by its volume, the answer is 2 grams per cubic centimeter. So, the block has a density of 2 grams per cubic centimeter.

 MAIN IDEA AND DETAILS How are mass and density different?

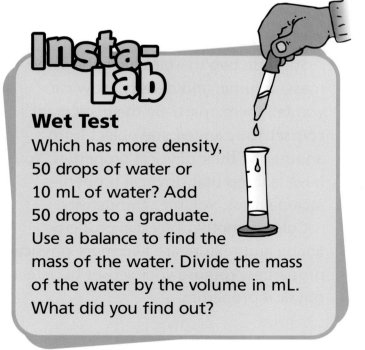

Insta-Lab

Wet Test
Which has more density, 50 drops of water or 10 mL of water? Add 50 drops to a graduate. Use a balance to find the mass of the water. Divide the mass of the water by the volume in mL. What did you find out?

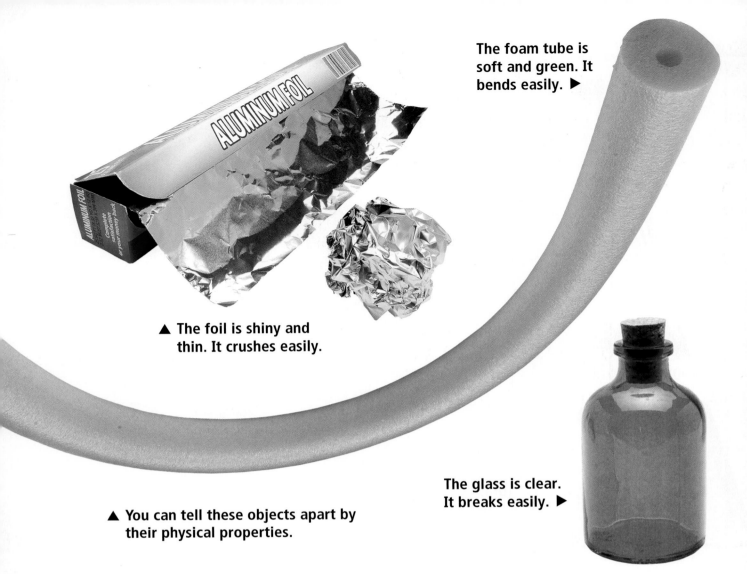

The foam tube is soft and green. It bends easily. ▶

▲ The foil is shiny and thin. It crushes easily.

The glass is clear. It breaks easily. ▶

▲ You can tell these objects apart by their physical properties.

Other Properties of Matter

Suppose two marbles have the same mass, volume, and density. How can you tell them apart? By their colors, of course! You can tell one object from another by their physical properties. You have learned that physical properties include mass, volume, and density.

Color is another physical property. Shape and texture are two more physical properties. You use your senses to detect physical properties.

In the next lesson, you will learn that another physical property of matter is state. Matter might be a liquid, a solid, or a gas.

The ability to transfer heat and electricity is another physical property. Some substances, such as copper, transfer heat and electricity easily. Others, such as plastic, do not.

You use physical properties to identify objects and substances every day.

 MAIN IDEA AND DETAILS What physical properties could you use to describe a rock?

1. MAIN IDEA AND DETAILS Draw and complete this graphic organizer.

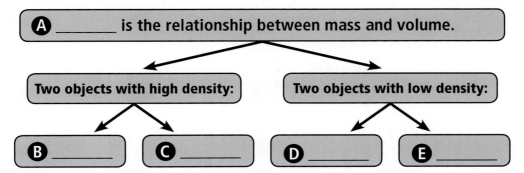

A _____ is the relationship between mass and volume.

Two objects with high density:

Two objects with low density:

B _____   **C** _____   **D** _____   **E** _____

2. SUMMARIZE Write a summary of the lesson by using the lesson vocabulary words in a paragraph.

3. DRAW CONCLUSIONS Two clear bags each contain a different unknown object. What physical properties can you use to tell the objects apart?

4. VOCABULARY In a sentence or two, explain why you must measure mass before you can determine density.

Test Prep

5. Critical Thinking Which senses help you determine an object's physical properties?

6. Which physical property can be the same for both a large marble and a small one?

A. color   **C.** volume

B. mass   **D.** weight

Links

Writing

Informative Writing
Suppose you are a scientist who has discovered a new substance. Write a **report** to describe its physical properties.

Math

Find the Density
A green ball has a mass of 100 grams and a volume of 200 cubic centimeters. A yellow ball has a mass of 50 grams and a volume of 10 cubic centimeters. Which ball has the greater density?

Physical Education

Catch This!
You can use an air pump to change the density of air inside a soccer ball or basketball. What happens when you pump more air into an inflated ball?

 For more links and activities, go to **www.hspscience.com**

How Does Matter Change States?

Fast Fact

Frozen Art Every March, ice artists like this one gather at the World Ice Art Championships in Fairbanks, Alaska. The artists depend on changing states of matter to shape and polish the giant sculptures. In the Investigate, you will have a chance to observe changes of state.

Melt, Boil, Evaporate

Materials
- 4 ice cubes
- hot plate
- safety goggles
- pot holders
- pan
- graduate

1. Draw the ice cubes and describe their physical properties. Be sure to tell how they look and feel.

2. **CAUTION: Put on safety goggles.** Put the ice in the pan. Your teacher will carefully heat the pan. If you must touch the handle, use a pot holder. Predict the changes you expect to see in the ice cubes.

3. When the ice cubes melt, your teacher will pour the hot water into the graduate. Record its volume.

4. Use a pot holder as you pour the water back into the pan. Your teacher will put it on the hot plate again. Let the water boil. Predict what will happen this time.

    CAUTION: Remember to turn off your hot plate. Remove the pan from the heat before it is dry. Place the pan on a burn-proof surface.

Step 2

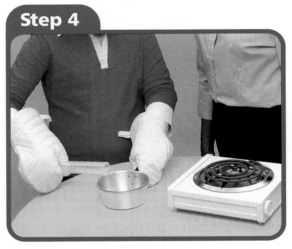
Step 4

Draw Conclusions

1. What caused the water to change?

2. **Inquiry Skill** Infer where the water is now. When it evaporated, what did the liquid water become?

Investigate Further

Using pot holders, pick up an ice cube in each hand. Push the cubes together without touching them with your hands. Explain what you observe.

VOCABULARY
state of matter p. 220
solid p. 220
liquid p. 220
gas p. 221

SCIENCE CONCEPTS
► what three states of matter are
► how temperature can change the state of a substance without matter being lost or gained

READING FOCUS SKILL
CAUSE AND EFFECT Look for things that cause changes in a state of matter.

| cause | → | effect |

States of Matter

Every day, you see and touch three **states of matter**: solid, liquid, and gas. But why is an apple solid, while milk is liquid? What makes the air you breathe a gas? The answer lies in the particles that you read about earlier.

All matter is made of particles. The way those particles are arranged determines whether the matter is a solid, a liquid, or a gas.

In a **solid**, the particles are packed together in a tight pattern. This pattern gives solids an exact shape, so the solid takes up a certain amount of space. When you roll a bowling ball, the particles stay tightly packed. As a result, the ball does not change its shape.

You learned that the particles in matter are always moving. Particles in solids are packed too tightly to move around. They vibrate in place instead.

Particles in **liquids** have more movement. They slide around, taking

Solids

Gems and bowling balls are solids. Their particles are packed together in tight patterns that give the objects their shape.

Liquids

Liquids take the shape of their containers and have definite volume.

Gases

Gases take the shape of their containers but have no definite volume.

the shape of their container. A liquid also takes up a certain amount of space. However, if you spill a liquid, its shape changes as its particles slide around.

A **gas** has no definite shape or volume. Particles move fastest in a gas. When you open a container and release a gas into the air, its particles move away quickly. That's why you smell perfume after it is sprayed. Then the scent gets weaker because its gas particles move away and spread out.

 CAUSE AND EFFECT What causes solids to keep their shape?

Insta-Lab

Spaces and Places

Fill a glass with water until the water bulges above the top. Next, slowly sprinkle 2 teaspoons of salt into the glass. The glass is full of water, so where does the salt go?

Changes in the State of Water

Water clearly shows how heating and cooling change the state of matter. Heat makes particles in matter move faster. If ice gains energy, its particles move faster. They begin to slide around each other. The solid loses its shape and becomes a liquid.

Particles in the liquid move around and take the shape of the container. If you pour the liquid into another container, the liquid particles take its shape. The volume of the water stays the same.

If you keep adding heat to the water, its particles move even faster. They evaporate into a gas—water vapor. The gas particles bounce into each other and spread out in all directions.

Cooling the gas particles slows their movement. The particles condense into a liquid. If the liquid gets cold enough, the particles freeze into solid ice again.

Although heat changes the state of matter, it does not change the amount of matter.

 CAUSE AND EFFECT How does heat change the state of water?

Heat Makes the Difference

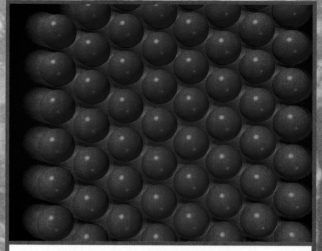

Ice is water in its solid state. The particles in a solid are arranged in a tight, evenly spaced pattern. The particles still vibrate.

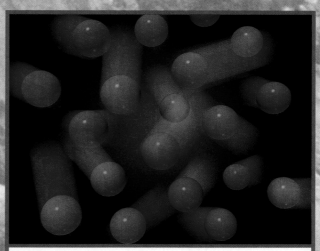

As ice warms, it melts into a liquid—water. As the particles warm up, they move and slide around one another. The even spaces between the particles become different-size spaces.

As the water is heated, the particles move faster and faster. The liquid boils and becomes a gas. The particles bounce off one another and fly out of the spout. If this water vapor cools, it will condense back into tiny drops of water.

 For more links and activities, go to www.hspscience.com

Other Materials Change States

Water is not the only material that changes state. Some materials change state in different ways. For example, dry ice is the solid form of carbon dioxide. Carbon dioxide changes directly from a solid into a gas.

Some gases change directly into solids. One example of a solid that forms this way is frost. Solid crystals of frost form from water vapor in the air.

 CAUSE AND EFFECT What causes dry ice to change state?

Freezing and Boiling Points

Almost anything will melt or boil if its temperature gets high enough or low enough. Which of these substances would be useful in an industry in which resistance to heat is important?

Substance	Melting Point	Boiling Point
Iron	1538°C (2800°F)	2862°C (5184°F)
Mercury	−39°C (−38°F)	357°C (675°F)
Nitrogen	−209°C (−344°F)	−196°C (−321°F)
Oxygen	−218°C (−360°F)	−183°C (−297°F)

Dry ice changes from a solid directly into a gas. ▼

Metals become liquid at very high temperatures. After a metal is cooled in a mold, it becomes a solid again. Then it has a new shape. ▶

224

1. CAUSE AND EFFECT Draw and complete each graphic organizer.

CAUSE → **EFFECT**

| Heat warms ice particles. | **A** _____ |

CAUSE → **EFFECT**

| **B** _____ | Water particles turn into gas. |

2. SUMMARIZE Write a summary of this lesson. Begin with this sentence: There are three common states of matter on Earth.

3. DRAW CONCLUSIONS What do you think happens when gas particles cool off?

4. VOCABULARY Make a crossword puzzle that has the vocabulary terms as answers. Write clear clues for the words.

Test Prep

5. Critical Thinking How can you change the state of water?

6. In which state of water are the particles the most organized?

  A. ice   **C.** liquid

  B. gas   **D.** water vapor

Links

Writing

Narrative Writing

Suppose you are a drop of water. Write a **story** about how you experience all three states of matter in one day.

Math 9÷3

Using Numbers

The metal mercury melts at about –40°C and boils at about 360°C. In which state is mercury at room temperature? How do you know?

Language Arts

Name Origins

We use two temperature scales: Celsius and Fahrenheit. Find out when and how these scales were created and named.

 For more links and activities, go to **www.hspscience.com**

What Are Mixtures and Solutions?

Fast Fact

Salty, Salty Seas Most lakes have fresh water, but some lakes are saltier than the ocean. Mono Lake, in California, has salts and minerals dissolved in it. In warm weather, its water evaporates, leaving behind some of the salts and minerals. When the lake's water level drops, a crust of minerals forms along its shore. In the Investigate, you will find out how salt and other solids dissolve in water.

Which Solids Will Dissolve?

Materials
- water
- teaspoon
- sand
- 4 clear containers
- stirrer
- salt
- sugar
- baking soda

Procedure

1. Half-fill each container with water.

2. Put 1 spoonful of sand into one container. Observe and record what happens.

3. Stir the mixture for 1 minute, and then record what you see.

4. Repeat Steps 2 and 3, using salt, sugar, and baking soda. Observe and record all the results.

Draw Conclusions

1. Which solid dissolved the most? Which did not dissolve at all?

2. **Inquiry Skill** Scientists often plan a simple investigation to test an idea quickly. What idea did this activity test? What is another simple investigation you could do with these materials?

Step 2

Step 3

Investigate Further

Dissolve table sugar and powdered sugar in separate containers of water. Compare how quickly the two kinds of sugar dissolve. Explain your results.

SI-2 Describe patterns/infer; **SI-3** Design and conduct simple investigations; **SK-2** Record results/data

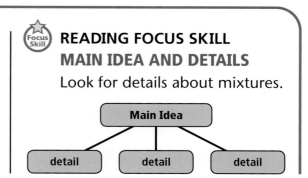

VOCABULARY
mixture p. 228
solution p. 230
solubility p. 231
suspension p. 232

SCIENCE CONCEPTS
▶ how a mixture, a solution, and a suspension differ
▶ differences in how substances dissolve

READING FOCUS SKILL
MAIN IDEA AND DETAILS
Look for details about mixtures.

Main Idea

detail   detail   detail

Mixtures

Do you like salad? Salad is a mixture. A **mixture** is two or more substances that are combined without changing any of them. These substances can be separated from each other again. For example, if you don't like onions, you can take them out of your salad.

Mixtures can contain different amounts of the substances. Your salad might have a lot of lettuce and just a little bit of onion.

oatmeal flakes

nuts

raisins

dried cranberries

This spoonful of granola is a mixture of good things to eat. ▶

Not all mixtures are made of solids. Salt water is a mixture of a solid and a liquid. Fog is a mixture of water drops and air. Air itself is a mixture of nitrogen, oxygen, carbon dioxide, and other gases.

The picture shows how one mixture can be separated. The mixture begins as a pile of rocks, dust, salt, and bits of iron. First, larger rocks and particles are strained from the mixture. Only the smaller particles can pass through the holes in the strainer.

Next, a magnet draws out the iron bits. Then, water is added to the remaining mixture. The wet dust and salt are poured through a filter. Water and dissolved salt pass through. The dust is left behind.

Finally, the salty water is heated. The water boils away, leaving the salt behind.

All the substances in the original mixture are separated. Being in the mixture did not change them.

MAIN IDEA AND DETAILS
Define the term *mixture*, and name three examples.

▲ The mixture begins as a pile of rocks, dust, dirt, salt, and bits of iron. The rocks are screened out first.

◄ A magnet takes away bits of iron.

◄ Water is added. Then the filter removes dust and dirt.

The salt water is heated. ▼

◄ The water is boiled away. Only salt is left behind.

Solutions

A solution is a kind of mixture. In a **solution**, different kinds of matter are mixed completely with each other. Salt water is a solution. The salt and the water are so evenly mixed that you can't see the salt. You can tell it is there by tasting the water. The air you breathe is also a solution.

On the other hand, a bowl of salad is not a solution. You can always tell the ingredients apart. The tomatoes might all be on top. Most of the lettuce might be on the bottom.

When a solid forms a solution with a liquid, the solid dissolves in the liquid. In the Investigate, you found that salt dissolves easily in water. The water particles pull the salt particles away from one another. All the particles are moving, so the salt particles spread evenly through the water.

However, sand doesn't dissolve in water. Water can't pull sand particles apart. Instead, they fall to the bottom. Sand in water is not a solution.

 MAIN IDEA AND DETAILS Why is pizza a mixture but not a solution?

Sugar crystals are added to water.

Water particles start pulling the sugar crystals apart.

The water has dissolved the sugar. The sugar bits are now too small to see, but you can taste them.

What would happen if sand dissolved in water as easily as salt does?

This salt was once dissolved in ocean water. After the water evaporated, particles of solid salt were left.

Solubility

You found in the Investigate that substances dissolve differently. **Solubility** (sahl•yoo•BIL•uh•tee) is a measure of how much of one material will dissolve in another. For example, 204 grams (7.2 oz) of sugar will dissolve in 100 milliliters (3.4 oz) of water at room temperature. So, sugar has a solubility of 204. However, no sand will dissolve in water. Sand has a solubility of zero.

 MAIN IDEA AND DETAILS Name two things besides sand that are not soluble in water.

Insta-Lab

Cool, Warm, or Hot?
Pour 10 mL of cold water into one cup. Into another, pour 10 mL of lukewarm water, and into a third, pour 10 mL of hot water. Add a small spoonful of sugar to each cup, and stir. In which cup of water does the most sugar dissolve?

Other Mixtures

In some mixtures, the ingredients are not spread out evenly. When these mixtures sit, some of the ingredients settle to the bottom. Other ingredients rise to the top. This kind of mixture is called a **suspension**. Particles of one ingredient are suspended, or floating, in another ingredient. Some suspensions you can eat are shown here.

If you have taken a walk on a foggy day, you have walked through a suspension. Drops of water are suspended in the air. If you dip water out of a muddy creek, you will see a suspension. Bits of soil are suspended in the water.

 MAIN IDEA AND DETAILS How can you tell whether a mixture is a suspension?

You must stir the orange juice in the glass because the pulp settles out of the juice. ▶

You must also shake most salad dressings. Otherwise, you might have just oil on your salad! ▶

Fog is a suspension of water droplets in air.

1. MAIN IDEA AND DETAILS Draw and complete this graphic organizer. List two details about each main idea.

```
  mixture              solution             suspension
  ↙    ↘              ↙    ↘              ↙    ↘
A____  B____        C____  D____        E____  F____
```

2. SUMMARIZE Use your completed graphic organizer to write a lesson summary.

3. DRAW CONCLUSIONS Why is lemonade made from a powdered mix a solution and not a suspension?

4. VOCABULARY Write two sentences. Use all four vocabulary words.

Test Prep

5. Critical Thinking Name two mixtures you have eaten in the past week. Explain whether each is a simple mixture, a solution, or a suspension.

6. Which of these is a mixture?
  A. apple   **C.** carrot stick
  B. broccoli   **D.** ham sandwich

Links

Writing

Narrative Writing
Suppose you are out walking on a rainy day. Write a **description** of what you see, and mention at least four mixtures. Include one solution and one suspension in your description.

Math

Make a Bar Graph
Use a graph to show the solubility of each of these substances in 100 mL of water at room temperature: sugar, 204 g; salt, 36 g; baking soda, 7 g; and sand, 0 g.

Social Studies

The Bronze Age
Bronze is a mixture of the metals tin and copper. Find out why people mix these two metals. Then research the Bronze Age. Find out what years it covered, and name an important event from that time.

 For more links and activities, go to **www.hspscience.com**

FIGHTING FIRES WITH DIAPERS

Firefighters usually use water and chemicals to fight wildfires. But firefighters battling a wildfire near Jackson, Wyoming, fought a fire with a new weapon: disposable diapers.

Well, actually, it is the chemical found in disposable diapers that is used. The chemical is now being used across the country as an effective weapon against fire.

Fire-Fighting Gel

Inside a disposable diaper is a chemical called *polyacrylate.* This chemical draws moisture away from babies' bottoms. Scientists have been able to use the chemical, in a gel form, as a fire retardant.

What happens is that when a fire breaks out near a house, firefighters can spray the gel, nicknamed "green slime," wherever they need it. The gel stays put for hours and can be rinsed off with a hose once danger has passed.

During the Jackson, Wyoming, fires, the gel was sprayed on nearly 200 houses. Because the green slime doesn't burn, it protects the houses from the fire. And as one fire department official said, "It is well worth being slimed to save your house."

THINK ABOUT IT

1. Why is it important that homeowners be able to wash the green slime away with water?
2. Why would putting the chemicals into a gel form help fight fires?

Find out more! Log on to
www.hspscience.com

ST-1 Explain how technology improves lives; **ST-2** Explain how technology meets needs

235

MARIE CURIE
Scientific Pioneer

Marie Curie (1867–1934) was a French scientist. She changed science forever and was the first woman to win the Nobel Prize.

Curie worked with her husband, Pierre. Together, they discovered the element radium. They also explored the idea of radiation. Now, doctors use radiation to find and treat diseases.

Marie Curie was born in Warsaw, Poland, on November 7, 1867. Her father inspired her to study science. He taught high school physics. Later, Curie moved to France. That's where she met and married Pierre Curie.

A Nobel Prize medal

Career   Nuclear Medicine Technologist

A nuclear medicine technologist uses radiation to take pictures inside a medical patient. First, the patient swallows a liquid that has a safe dose of radioactive material in it. The technologist then uses special cameras to take 3-D pictures. By looking at how the liquid moves through the patient, a doctor can learn if there are any problems.

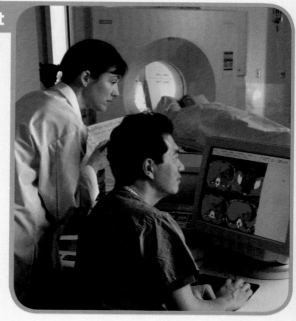

You Can Do It!

Quick and Easy Project

Don't Be Dense!

Materials
- deep container of water
- 2 identical marbles
- 2 balloons

Procedure

1. Find the mass of each marble to make sure they are identical.
2. Put a marble inside each balloon.
3. Knot one balloon close to the marble.
4. Blow some air into the other balloon, and knot the balloon close to its mouth.
5. Put both balloons in the water, and observe what happens.

Draw Conclusions

Which balloon has more mass? Which has more volume? Which has more density? Which balloon floats? Explain.

Design Your Own Investigation

Cooling Off

You have learned that particles move more slowly as their temperature drops. How could you use a round balloon, a tape measure, and a freezer to prove that air particles move closer together as they get colder? Write the steps for a procedure and the results you expect—your prediction. Then carry out the experiment to test your prediction.

SI-2 Describe patterns/infer;
SI-4 Control variables

Vocabulary Review

Use the terms below to complete the sentences. The page numbers tell you where to look in the chapter if you need help.

mass p. 213   solid p. 220
volume p. 214   liquid p. 220
density p. 214   solubility p. 231
state of matter p. 220   suspension p. 232

1. When some solids get warm enough, they become a _____.

2. When a liquid gets cool enough, it becomes a _____.

3. Mass divided by volume is _____.

4. The amount of a substance that can be dissolved in another substance is the measure of its_____.

5. Gas is one _____.

6. If particles settle out of a mixture, the mixture is a _____.

7. The amount of space an object takes up is its _____.

8. _____ is the measure of the amount of matter an object has.

Check Understanding

Write the letter of the best choice.

9. Which of these is made of matter?
   A. a dream   C. happiness
   B. a book   D. an idea

10. Which of these is a mixture?
    F. pail of sand and soil
    G. copper wire
    H. ring of pure gold
    J. pinch of salt

11. **MAIN IDEA AND DETAILS** Which of these is an example of a solution?
    A. granola   C. pizza
    B. iced tea   D. salad

12. Which of these has no definite volume?
    F. gas   H. matter
    G. liquid   J. solid

13. **CAUSE AND EFFECT** Which of these probably has the most mass?
    A. apple   C. brick
    B. balloon   D. golf ball

14. Which term best describes the contents of this glass?

    F. density   H. suspension
    G. mass   J. volume

15. Which is a measure of how closely particles are packed together?

    A. density   **C.** solubility

    B. matter   **D.** volume

16. Which has mass and takes up space?

    F. height   **H.** volume

    G. matter   **J.** weight

Inquiry Skills

17. Compare the arrangement of particles in a solid with the arrangement of particles in a gas.

18. Two boxes are the same size and density. What can you **infer** about their masses?

Critical Thinking

19. You have a red box and a black box that are exactly the same size. The red box is heavier than the black one. What does this tell you about the physical properties of the boxes?

Picture A

20. The air around us is a mixture of nitrogen, oxygen, carbon dioxide, and other gases. This morning, the air outside looked like Picture A below. Right now, the air outside looks like Picture B.

Part A Use the terms *solution* and *suspension* to describe the air this morning and the air right now.

Part B Explain how air can be a mixture, a solution, and a suspension.

Picture B

Lesson 1 What Is Matter Made Of?

Lesson 2 What Are Physical Changes in Matter?

Lesson 3 How Does Matter React Chemically?

Vocabulary

atom
element
change of state
physical change
physical property
chemical property
chemical change
chemical reaction
compound

What do **YOU** wonder?

The shrinking of a sea left this ship behind.
What happened to the sea floor? What is
happening to the outside of the ship?

What Is Matter Made Of?

Fast Fact

Tiny Circles Each of the little peaks on the oval marks an iron atom. Iron atoms are very tiny. It would take more than 40 million iron atoms to make a 1-cm-long line. In the Investigate, you'll observe larger, but still small, particles.

A Solution to the Problem

Materials
- iodized salt
- kosher salt
- sea salt
- granulated sugar
- powdered sugar
- brown sugar
- 6 spoons
- 6 plates
- 6 plastic cups
- water

Procedure

1. Place a small amount of each kind of salt and each kind of sugar on its own plate.

2. Compare the samples' colors and textures. Record your observations.

3. Compare the grain sizes of the samples. Record your observations.

4. Place the same amount of water in each of six cups. Use a clean spoon to place the same amount of each sample in its own cup. Stir. Record your observations.

Step 1

Draw Conclusions

1. Which samples—the light-colored ones or the dark-colored ones—mixed into the water more quickly?

2. Which samples—the ones with larger grains or the ones with smaller grains— mixed into the water more quickly?

3. **Inquiry Skill** Scientists interpret data to draw conclusions. What can you conclude about how color and grain size affect the speed at which a sample mixes into water?

Step 4

Investigate Further

Sequence the samples by how quickly they mixed into water. Predict where sugar cubes fit in your list. Test your prediction.

VOCABULARY
atom p. 246
element p. 248

SCIENCE CONCEPTS
▶ that matter is made up of atoms
▶ that an element is a substance made up of just one kind of atom

READING FOCUS SKILL
MAIN IDEA AND DETAILS
Look for details about atoms.

Main Idea

detail   detail   detail

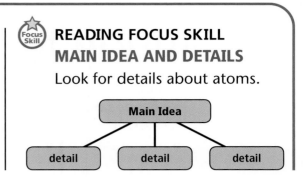

Basic Properties of Matter

What do your bed, the water in the ocean, and the air in your classroom all have in common? Not much, really. In fact, they have only one thing in common—they are all examples of matter. As you learned earlier, matter is anything that has mass and takes up space.

Sunlight is not matter. A light room does not have more mass than a dark room has. An idea also is not made of matter. Your brain doesn't take up more space when you think hard.

What is matter made of? What do matter's properties hint at about its particles? How do the particles combine to make the things you see and touch?

Like matter, these toy pieces can be put together to form objects of many shapes and sizes. Each object has mass and takes up space. ▶

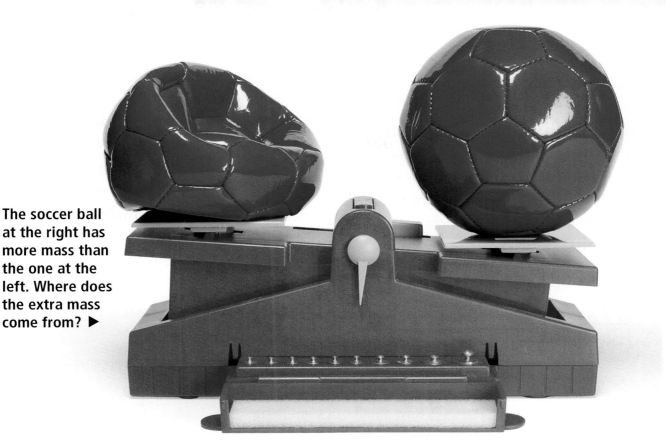

The soccer ball at the right has more mass than the one at the left. Where does the extra mass come from? ▶

Air is something around you every day. You need it to breathe. You know it is matter. The two balls on this page show that you can squeeze different amounts of it into a container.

The fact that you can squeeze more and more air into a container is evidence. It hints at the size of the particles of matter. You can't see the particles. But with an air pump, you can pack more and more of them into the same space. They must be very small.

Other properties of matter are also hints. Substances have properties such as solubility, mass, and hardness. As you learned in the Investigate, some materials act differently when mixed with water. You also know that metal objects are heavier and harder than

plastic ones. There are these differences because the tiny particles that make up matter are different. Some particles hold together more tightly or are heavier than others. In the rest of this lesson, you'll learn more about the particles.

 MAIN IDEA AND DETAILS How do scientists define *matter*?

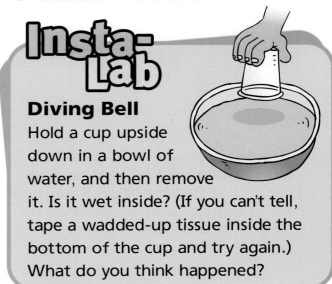

Insta-Lab

Diving Bell
Hold a cup upside down in a bowl of water, and then remove it. Is it wet inside? (If you can't tell, tape a wadded-up tissue inside the bottom of the cup and try again.) What do you think happened?

245

Particles of Matter

More than 2000 years ago, a Greek thinker named Democritus (dih•MAHK•ruh•tuhs) had an idea about matter. Democritus said that all matter is made up of tiny particles, or bits. He said that different kinds of matter are made up of different kinds of particles. And he thought that these particles could not be broken down into smaller parts.

Democritus didn't experiment or test his ideas in any way. Still, it turns out that he was right. We now know that any one substance can be broken down only so far. If you divide it into smaller and smaller parts, you end up with an atom. An **atom** is the smallest possible particle of a substance.

Science Up Close

1 How small can something get? Start with a bag of charcoal briquets. It is about a half meter long, and it has a fair amount of mass.

2 It's easy to break down the contents of the bag into smaller parts. This is one briquet. It is about 5 cm square, and it has a small mass.

3 Can you break the briquet into smaller pieces? Yes. Each of the large chunks is 1 or 2 cm across and has a smaller mass than a whole briquet.

As you might guess, an atom is very small. It's really, really small. In fact, it's so small that you can't see it. Even with a regular microscope, you couldn't see an atom. Why not? Because single atoms are too small to reflect light! So there's no way you can see a single atom at all unless you use a special microscope.

Democritus made up the word *atom.* It comes from a word that means "cannot be divided." Think about a tank of oxygen. You can divide all the oxygen inside into smaller and smaller parts. But when you get to an oxygen atom, you have to stop. If you break it up further, it isn't oxygen anymore.

 MAIN IDEA AND DETAILS What is an atom?

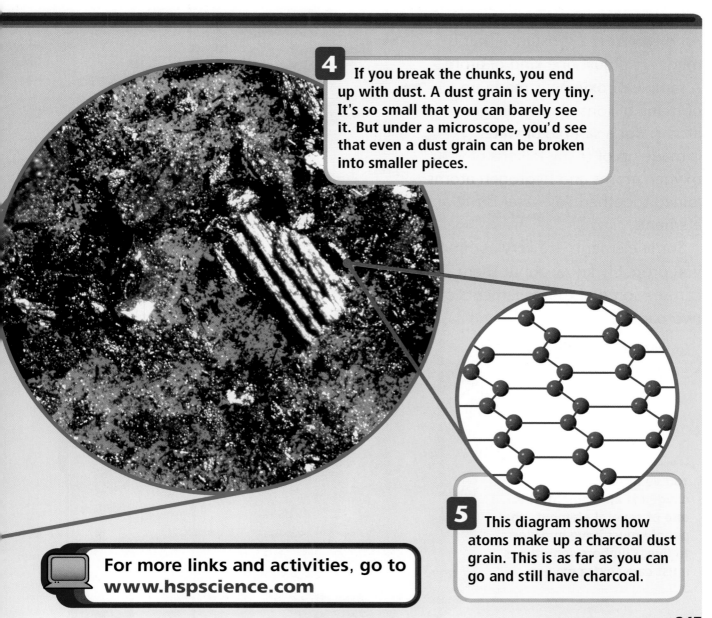

4 If you break the chunks, you end up with dust. A dust grain is very tiny. It's so small that you can barely see it. But under a microscope, you'd see that even a dust grain can be broken into smaller pieces.

5 This diagram shows how atoms make up a charcoal dust grain. This is as far as you can go and still have charcoal.

For more links and activities, go to www.hspscience.com

Elements

You just read that if you were to break down all the oxygen inside a tank into smaller and smaller parts, you would end up with an oxygen atom. What if you did the same thing with a drop of water? Would you end up with a single water atom? No, because there is no such thing as an atom of water. The smallest possible particle of water is made up of two different kinds of atoms—two hydrogen atoms and one oxygen atom.

Hydrogen and oxygen are elements. An **element** is a substance that is made up of just one kind of atom. A sample of oxygen is made up of many billions of only oxygen atoms. But a sample of water is made up of many billions of oxygen atoms and hydrogen atoms joined together. So, water is not an element.

Some elements are very common, and you probably know about them. You can see some of these elements on these two pages.

⭐ **MAIN IDEA AND DETAILS**
(Focus Skill) **What is an element?**

Remember the atoms in charcoal? They are carbon atoms. This pile of dark powder is pure carbon. Carbon is also the element that makes up most of the point of a pencil.

You've already read that oxygen is an element. It is one of several elements that people must have in order to live. Climbers sometimes must carry extra oxygen.

248

Have you ever seen a mercury switch inside a thermostat? As you can see here, mercury is a shiny, silver-colored element.

mercury in switch

Iron is another common element. You probably see things made of iron every day. You may also see things made of steel. Steel is made up of iron and a small amount of carbon.

Another shiny, silver-colored element is silver. Silver is somewhat rare. Many people call forks and spoons "silverware." However, only fancy, expensive silverware is really made of silver.

◀ Gold is an element. It is also a metal. It can be drawn out into thin wire that is used in jewelry and in electronics.

Sulfur is another element. It is a nonmetal. If you try to stretch it out, it breaks. ▶

Some Groups of Elements

You've probably noticed that scientists classify things into groups. Forming groups helps people see how things are like each other and different from each other. Scientists have classified elements into several groups. Two of these groups are metals and nonmetals.

Many metals, like iron, gold, and silver, are elements. However, not all metals are elements. Steel, for example, is made up of at least two elements, iron and carbon.

You already know about some metals. What are some ways metals are alike? For one thing, most metals are shiny. They can also be stretched out thin or drawn into long wires.

How are nonmetals different from metals? Nonmetals aren't shiny. They're dull. They can't be stretched out thin. Most nonmetals are brittle. They break instead of stretching. Some nonmetals, such as oxygen, aren't even solids.

 MAIN IDEA AND DETAILS Name two groups of elements.

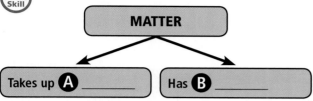

1. MAIN IDEA AND DETAILS Draw and complete this graphic organizer.

```
        MATTER                              ATOMS

  Takes up Ⓐ _____   Has Ⓑ _____   Building blocks of   Smallest piece of an
                                         Ⓒ _____           Ⓓ _____
```

2. SUMMARIZE Write a summary of this lesson by using each of the lesson vocabulary words in a sentence.

3. DRAW CONCLUSIONS The scientific name for table salt is sodium chloride. Why do you think this is so?

4. VOCABULARY Make a word puzzle by using the lesson vocabulary words. Be sure to write a clue for each word.

Test Prep

5. Critical Thinking Why is "anything you can touch and pick up" not a good definition of *matter*?

6. Which is the smallest particle of an element?

A. atom   **C.** chunk

B. bit   **D.** grain

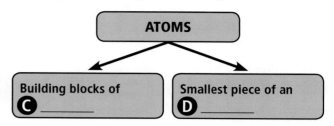

Links

Writing

Narrative Writing

Imagine that you have been shrunk down to the size of an atom. Write a short **story** about what you see and do.

Math

Identify Place Value

You have read that you would have to line up more than 40 million iron atoms to get a line of them 1 cm long. How do you write the numeral for 40 million?

Social Studies

Explore the History of Science

Did everyone accept Democritus' ideas about atoms 2000 years ago? Do some research. Then write a paragraph about people's reactions to Democritus' ideas.

 For more links and activities, go to www.hspscience.com

What Are Physical Changes in Matter?

Fast Fact

Bubble Life Span A scientist once kept a bubble in a jar for three months! It never popped, but it eventually shrank until the air in the bubble was gone. The shape of the bubble changed, but the substance didn't. In the Investigate, you'll observe changes like that in three liquids.

Drop by Drop

Materials
- 3 droppers
- water
- vegetable oil
- rubbing alcohol
- 3 plates
- safety goggles

Procedure

1. Wear safety goggles. Place 3 drops of water on one plate, 3 drops of vegetable oil on the second plate, and 3 drops of rubbing alcohol on the third plate. Be sure to use a different dropper for each liquid.

2. Record your observations of each liquid.

3. Repeat Step 2 every half hour for the rest of the school day.

Draw Conclusions

1. What did you observe at the end of the day?

2. **Inquiry Skill** When scientists give a possible explanation for what they observe, they are stating a hypothesis. Then the scientists test the hypothesis. What hypothesis can you make from your observations?

Step 1

Step 2

Investigate Further

What could you do to test your hypothesis? Plan and carry out an investigation to find out.

VOCABULARY
change of state p. 254
physical change p. 256

SCIENCE CONCEPTS
▶ that solid, liquid, and gas are three states of matter
▶ that physical changes do not make new substances

READING FOCUS SKILL
COMPARE AND CONTRAST
Look for similarities and differences in states of matter.

alike ——— different

States of Matter

Have you ever seen ice cubes melt in a glass? The ice becomes water. Or maybe you've seen water boil away on a stove. It seems to disappear. Whatever you've experienced, you probably figured out long ago that water, ice, and steam are all the same substance.

This fact isn't as easily known as you might think. After all, ice is cold and hard, and water is wet and soft. Steam is the same substance, too, but you can't see it. You wouldn't want to feel steam—it's very hot.

So, how is it that one substance can have three forms that are so different? Actually, every substance on Earth can exist as a solid, as a liquid, or as a gas. These are called the *three states of matter*.

A **change of state** occurs when a substance changes from one state to another. Each change of state has its

Liquid
The particles of water in this glass are close to each other. They move quickly and slide past each other easily.

These monkeys get warm by sitting in a hot spring. Around them are liquid water and the other two states. ▶

own name. If a solid is heated enough, it will eventually turn into a liquid. This is called *melting.* If a liquid is cooled enough, it will turn into a solid. This is called *freezing.*

If a liquid is heated enough, it will turn into a gas. This is called *boiling.* If a gas cools, it will turn into a liquid. This is called *condensing.*

You know that all matter is made up of tiny particles. These particles are always moving. Since ice, water, and steam are all the same substance, they are made up of the same kind of particles.

The difference between them is in the way the particles move. Ice particles don't move around at all; they just vibrate in place. Water particles move easily. Steam particles very quickly fly all over the place.

 COMPARE AND CONTRAST How are the particles in ice, water, and steam different? How are they the same?

Solid
The particles of ice are locked in place, although they're still vibrating.

Gas
The particles of air in this balloon are far apart and are moving very quickly.

Physical Changes

Look at the pictures of the icicles melting and the water boiling. What do they have in common? They both show changes of state.

Now look at the pictures on the next page. One sheet of paper is being shredded, another sheet of paper is being cut, and wood is being carved with a chain saw. The paper and wood are being changed, though none of the changes are changes of state. Still, the pictures on the next page have something in common with the pictures on this page. Do you know what it is?

All the pictures on these two pages show physical changes. A **physical change** is a change that does not result in a new substance. Changes of state are examples of physical changes. So are shredding, cutting, and carving.

Both of these pictures show physical changes taking place.

The water is boiling into steam, a gas you cannot see. Water and steam are two forms of the same thing. ▼

▲ The icicles are melting into water. Ice and water are two forms of the same thing.

The shredder is changing paper into many, many thin strips of paper. ▼

The scissors are changing a large piece of paper into smaller pieces of paper. ▶

This artist is using a chain saw to change a log into a deer statue and wood chips. ▼

How do you know that a change of state is a physical change? Well, you know that ice, water, and steam are all different forms of the same thing. If ice changes to water or water changes to steam, no new substance is made. So, that change is a physical change.

When you shred a sheet of paper, what do you get? You get shreds of paper. And when you cut a sheet of paper in two, you get two smaller pieces of paper. The size and shape are different, but you still have paper.

The chain saw makes lots and lots of wood chips. They're small, but they're still wood. Since wood is not being changed into another substance, the change is a physical change.

 COMPARE AND CONTRAST What do all physical changes have in common?

Insta-Lab

Change It
Take an everyday object, such as a piece of chalk or a sheet of paper. Describe its physical properties—is it smooth or rough, hard or soft, shiny or dull? Now break it or tear it. What are the physical properties of the pieces?

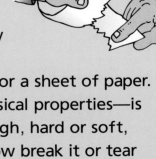

Dissolving

You know that a change of state is a kind of physical change. This picture shows another kind of physical change—*dissolving.* The sugar dissolves in, or becomes evenly mixed into, the hot water in the beaker.

How can you tell that dissolving is a physical change? You can let the water in the beaker *evaporate,* which is another physical change. After the water evaporates, the sugar is left behind in the beaker. The sugar doesn't change into another substance. It's still there.

Focus Skill **COMPARE AND CONTRAST** How is dissolving like evaporating?

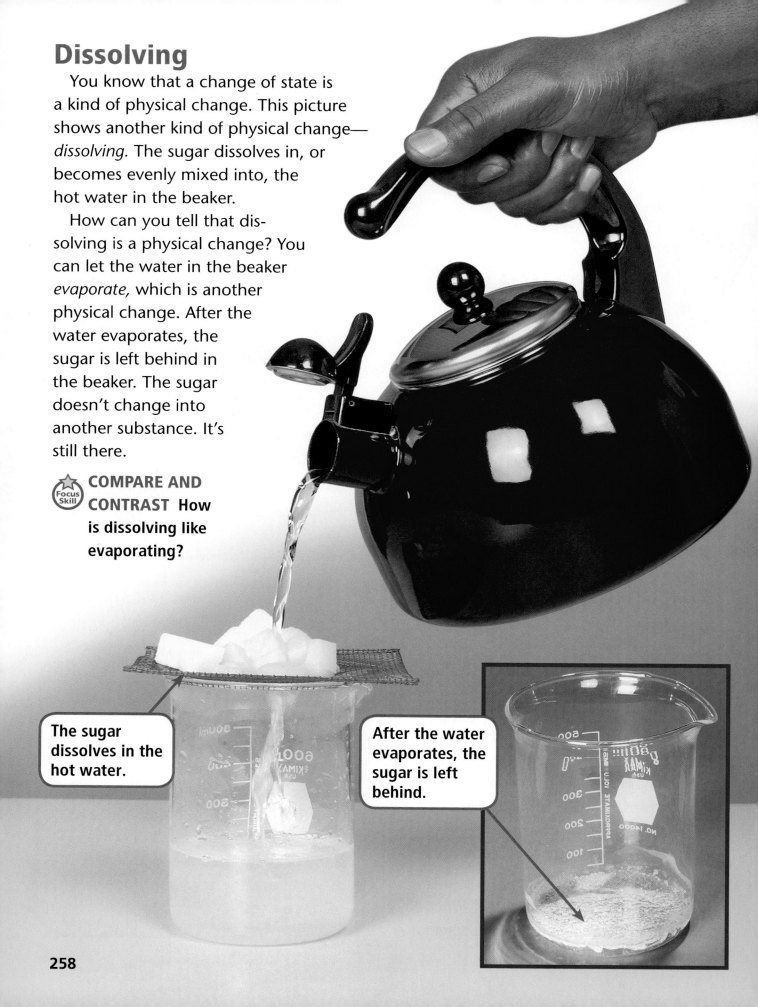

The sugar dissolves in the hot water.

After the water evaporates, the sugar is left behind.

1. COMPARE AND CONTRAST Complete the graphic organizer.

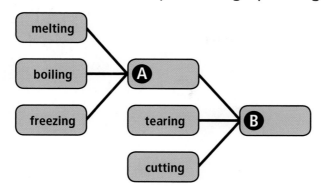

melting
boiling
freezing
A
tearing
B
cutting

2. SUMMARIZE Write a summary of this lesson. Begin with this sentence: *Matter can be in one of three states.*

3. DRAW CONCLUSIONS A glass falls on the floor and smashes into hundreds of tiny pieces. Is this a physical change? Why or why not?

4. VOCABULARY Write a fill-in-the-blank sentence for each vocabulary term. Show the right answers.

Test Prep

5. Critical Thinking A cook adds oil to vinegar and then mixes them to make salad dressing. Is this a physical change? Why or why not?

6. Which might occur if you heat a substance?

A. boiling   **C.** shredding

B. freezing   **D.** none of these

Links

Writing

Expository Writing
Imagine that you are helping a younger student learn about science. Write a short **explanation** of what changes occur when a substance goes through a change of state.

Math

Estimate Measurements
Nancy combines 950 mL of vinegar with 800 mL of oil. About how many liters is that in all?

Health

Food Changes
When you eat, your body changes food so that you can digest it. Make a diagram that shows two places in the body in which food undergoes a physical change. (Hint: Read about digestion.)

 For more links and activities, go to **www.hspscience.com**

How Does Matter React Chemically?

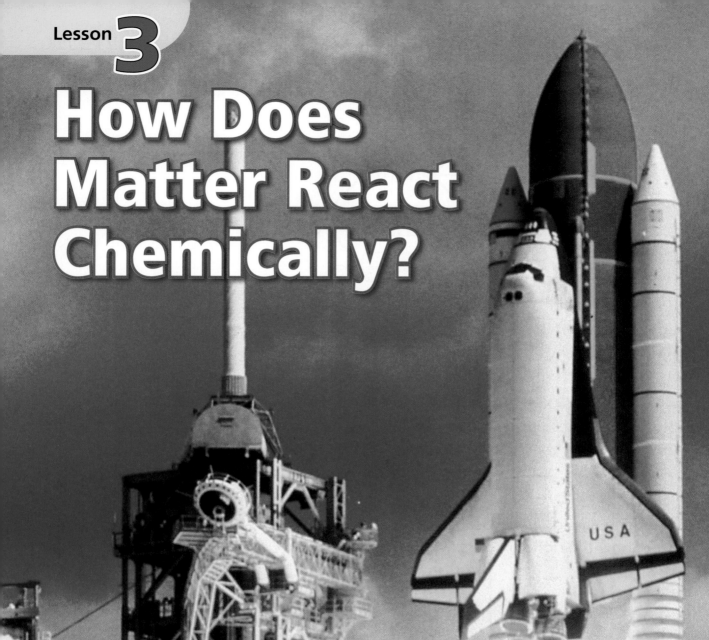

Fast Fact

Bang! Zoom! The energy made by two chemical reactions is enough to lift the space shuttle into orbit. Believe it or not, the substance that is made by one reaction is water. In the Investigate, you will find out about another reaction that involves water.

Wet Wool

Materials • 3 small pieces of steel wool • water
• 2 plates • bowl

Procedure

① Put one piece of steel wool on a plate.

② Soak another piece of steel wool in water. Then put it on the other plate.

③ Fill the bowl with water, and put the third piece of steel wool in the water. Make sure none of it sticks out above the water.

④ Place all three samples in the same area, away from direct sunlight. Examine them every day for a week. Record your observations.

Draw Conclusions

1. How do the three samples compare?

2. **Inquiry Skill** Scientists can draw conclusions from the results of their experiments. What two things can you conclude caused the changes?

Step 2

Step 3

Investigate Further

What do you predict will happen if you place the three samples in direct sunlight? Carry out a test to find out.

Reading in Science

VOCABULARY
physical property p. 263
chemical property p. 263
chemical change p. 264
chemical reaction p. 264
compound p. 264

SCIENCE CONCEPT
▶ that one or more new substances are produced during a chemical change

 READING FOCUS SKILL
COMPARE AND CONTRAST
Compare chemical changes to physical changes.

Physical and Chemical Properties

How would you describe a pencil? You might say that it's yellow, that it's long and thin, and that it has six sides. You might say that you use it to write and that the tip breaks easily.

All of these descriptions have something in common—they all describe the pencil by itself.

Can you also describe something in relation to another substance? Yes, you can. You can describe something by the way it interacts with other substances.

Think about the wood in the pencil. If there is oxygen near the wood and the temperature is hot enough, the wood will burn. So, another description of the pencil might be "It burns if there is oxygen near it and the temperature is very high."

	Physical Properties	
Water	• colorless • odorless • liquid at room temperature	• boils at 100°C • melts at 0°C
Silver	• shiny • soft • silver in color	• boils at 2163°C • melts at 962°C
Iron	• shiny • hard • grayish silver in color	• boils at 2861°C • melts at 1538°C
Sulfur	• dull • brittle • yellow	• boils at 445°C • melts at 115°C

So, now you know two different ways to describe a substance. One way is to tell about its physical properties. **Physical properties** are traits that involve a substance by itself.

Another way to describe a substance is to tell about its chemical properties. **Chemical properties** are properties that involve how a substance interacts with other substances.

Look at the table. You're probably familiar with most of these substances. You're probably also familiar with some of these changes. Have you ever seen rusted iron or tarnished silver?

 COMPARE AND CONTRAST How are physical properties different from chemical properties?

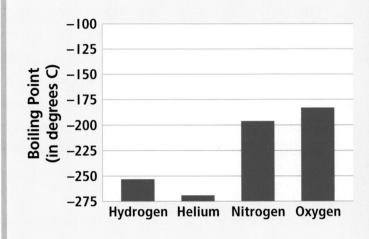

Math in Science
Interpret Data

Boiling Mad

Which substance in the graph has the highest boiling point? Which has the lowest boiling point?

Chemical Properties
• made up of hydrogen and oxygen • many substances dissolve easily in it
• does not react with many other substances • does not react with air • reacts with ozone or sulfur to form tarnish
• reacts easily with many other substances • reacts with oxygen to form the minerals hematite and magnetite • reacts with oxygen in presence of water to form rust
• reacts with any liquid element • reacts with any solid element except gold and platinum • reacts with oxygen to form sulfur dioxide, a form of air pollution

◀ Notice that in the table, one particular word is used in nearly every line. That word is *react* or *reacts*. What does that word mean in science? Well, it's a big topic, and you'll start reading about it on the next page.

263

Chemical Changes

You know that hydrogen and oxygen are usually gases. Do you know what happens when hydrogen burns? It combines with oxygen to form water.

This change results in a new substance—water. The formation of water is not a physical change. A physical change does not result in a new substance. This change that produces water is a chemical change. A **chemical change** is a change that results in one or more new substances. Another name for a chemical change is **chemical reaction**. Now you know what the word *react* or *reacts* means in the table on the previous page. It means "goes through a chemical change."

You know that an element is something made up of only one kind of atom. Since water is made up of hydrogen and oxygen atoms, it is not an element. It's a compound. A **compound** is made up of two or more different elements that have chemically combined.

 COMPARE AND CONTRAST How is a chemical change different from a physical change?

Bubble, Bubble, Bubble!

Use a funnel to pour some water into a balloon. Then put half of a foaming antacid tablet inside, and tie the balloon closed. What happens inside the balloon? How can you tell?

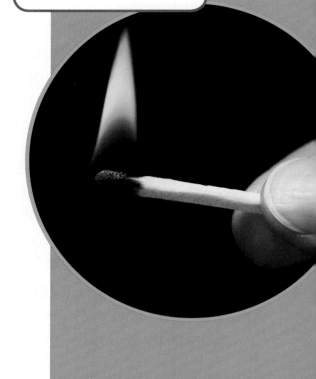

Sulfur in the match head is what helps the match light quickly.

Iron reacts with oxygen in the presence of water to form rust.

Silver reacts with sulfur to form tarnish. This helps you know that either sulfur or compounds that contain sulfur were in the air.

Sulfur reacts with oxygen to form sulfur dioxide. Often *a substance reacts with oxygen* means that the substance burns.

Recognizing Chemical Changes

Water is made up of two gases—oxygen and hydrogen. They react to form a liquid. It's easy to understand that a chemical reaction took place. Water is a liquid, not a gas!

There are clues that help you know that chemical changes are probably taking place. Some of them are listed in the table below. But remember that none of these clues is perfect. For example, when water freezes, it becomes solid—a new physical property. But freezing is a physical change, not a chemical change.

 COMPARE AND CONTRAST
Suppose you bake bread. Suppose you draw with a marker on paper. How are the changes in color that occur different from one another?

Before bread dough is baked, it's white or very pale tan.

After the bread is baked, its crust is dark brown. That's because baking causes a chemical change.

The smell of eggs frying tells you that a chemical change is taking place. So does seeing the egg yolk change from a runny liquid to a solid. ▶

Clues to Chemical Changes		
Clue	**Example**	**Description**
Color Change	Bread dough baking	Changes from white to brown
Smell	Eggs rotting	Gives off a terrible smell
New Physical Property	Iron rusting	Changes from hard and silvery to brittle and reddish brown
Substance Given Off	Wood burning	Smoke is released into the air
Heat Given Off	Sulfur burning	Fire is hot

1. COMPARE AND CONTRAST Copy and complete the graphic organizer.

	PHYSICAL	BOTH	CHEMICAL
Properties	deal with a substance by itself	**A** _____	**B** _____
Changes	**C** _____	involve a change in appearance	**D** _____

2. SUMMARIZE Write a summary of this lesson by using the lesson vocabulary terms in a paragraph.

3. DRAW CONCLUSIONS A car engine uses gasoline and oxygen. It gives off water and the gas carbon dioxide. Is there a chemical reaction in the engine? Explain.

4. VOCABULARY Use each of the lesson vocabulary terms in a sentence.

Test Prep

5. Critical Thinking Explain why the burning of wood is a chemical change. List as many clues as you can.

6. Which is a chemical property of a substance?

  A. its color

  B. whether it floats

  C. whether it burns when oxygen is present

  D. its melting temperature

Links

Writing

Expository Writing

It is often easier to remember something you've learned if you describe it to someone else. Write a **friendly letter** telling a relative what you learned in this lesson.

Math

Estimate Sums

A lab has 22 grams of iron, 14 g of sulfur, 31 g of sodium, and 29 g of potassium. Estimate the total mass of these four chemicals.

Art

Illustrate a Reaction

Choose one of the chemical reactions described in this lesson. Draw or paint a picture illustrating this reaction.

Dear Aunt Suzie, Today we did a fun science lab.

 For more links and activities, go to www.hspscience.com

WHAT A Taste Test

What do you get when you cross blueberries with meat? Sometimes you get a blueberry hamburger! Some scientists hope that blueberry burgers will soon be on your school cafeteria's menu.

Food scientist Al Bushway told *Weekly Reader* (*WR*) that his lab has experimented with adding blueberry powder and blueberry puree (pyoo•RAY) to beef, chicken, and turkey. Puree is a thick paste. It's made when fruit is mashed in a blender.

Why the odd food combination? Bushway says it's a way to increase the nutrition in meat and to make school lunches

more healthful. Blueberries are rich in special chemicals that help fight diseases such as cancer. A serving of blueberries can give kids plenty of calcium, magnesium, vitamin C, and vitamin A. The combination of the vitamins and minerals in the meat and the fruit makes for a healthier meal than just meat alone.

A Colorful Combo?

Do blueberries turn the meat blue? "In beef, you can't see the difference," Bushway told *WR*. "However, ground turkey turns a grayish blue color."

So far, many adult taste tasters have been giving the food the thumbs up. But will it be a hit with kids? One 8-year-old from Illinois said she would love to try a blueberry burger. Her 11-year-old sister didn't feel the same. "I like my hamburger with ketchup," she said.

At-Home Taste Test

With an adult's help, kids can try this fruit-and-meat combo at home. Allow about one-half to one ounce of frozen blueberries to come to room temperature. Then, again with an adult's help, use a blender to puree them. Finally, add the puree to ground hamburger meat. Be sure the mix is cooked. Then taste it.

THINK ABOUT IT

1. What other foods can help you stay healthy?
2. What are some food combinations that you like to eat?

Spin-In

Find out more! Log on to
www.hspscience.com

ST-1 explain how technology improves lives; **ST-2** Explain how technology meets needs

HIGH-FLYING SCIENTIST

In 1991, the United States government sent chemist Peter Daum to the Middle East. Daum was not there to fight in the first Persian Gulf War, however. He was sent there to study the environmental effects of the oil fires set by the retreating Iraqi army during the war.

Daum works for the U.S. Department of Energy's Brookhaven Laboratory. He studies pollution that is in Earth's atmosphere.

When Daum is at home in the United States, he and other scientists spend a lot of time flying in a plane that is an airborne laboratory. The plane's equipment can measure the levels of pollutants in the air.

Career Food Manufacturer

This is a job to sink your teeth into. People who make food, or manufacture it, work with raw fruits, vegetables, grains, meats, and dairy products. They change the raw materials into finished, packaged goods to sell to grocery stores or restaurants.

You Can Do It!

Quick and Easy Project

Practicing Changes

Materials
- 3 ordinary disposable objects

Procedure

1. Gather three ordinary objects—for example, a sheet of paper, an old button, and a tissue.
2. List at least four physical properties of each object.
3. For each object, try to change each of the properties you listed without changing the substance itself. In other words, put the object through physical changes but not chemical changes.

Draw Conclusions

Which physical properties could be altered by physical changes? Which physical properties could not be altered by physical changes?

Design Your Own Investigation

Demonstrate Basic Properties

Imagine that you are teaching a science class. Some students are having trouble understanding that air has mass and takes up space. Design an investigation that will demonstrate this in a way that is different from the two procedures from Lesson 1. Gather the materials, and carry out the investigation.

Review and Test Preparation

Vocabulary Review

Write the term that fits each definition or description. The page numbers tell you where to look in the chapter if you need help.

> **atom** p. 246
> **element** p. 248
> **change of state** p. 254
> **physical change** p. 256
> **physical property** p. 263
> **chemical property** p. 263
> **chemical change** p. 264
> **chemical reaction** p. 264
> **compound** p. 264

1. A substance having atoms of more than one element that are combined chemically

2. Describes a substance by itself

3. Results in a new substance

4. Describes how a substance reacts with other substances

5. Process of melting or freezing

6. Another name for *chemical change*

7. Process of boiling

8. Substance having just one kind of atom

9. The smallest possible particle of an element

10. Does not result in a new substance

Check Understanding

Write the letter of best choice.

11. What is all matter made of?
  A. atoms
  B. oxygen
  C. water
  D. wood

12. Which statement about atoms is true?
  F. They are all the same.
  G. All substances are made of just one kind.
  H. You can see them with your eyes.
  J. They are too small to be seen with an ordinary microscope.

13. The diagrams show iron, oxygen, carbon dioxide, and hydrogen.

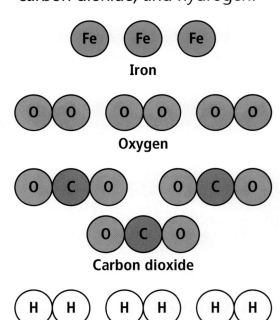

Iron

Oxygen

Carbon dioxide

Hydrogen

Which of these is a compound?
  A. iron
  B. oxygen
  C. carbon dioxide
  D. hydrogen

14. An element is made up of how many kinds of atoms?

   F. none

   G. one

   H. two

   J. two or more

15. **MAIN IDEA AND DETAILS** Which always happens during a chemical change?

   A. Matter disappears.

   B. A smell is produced.

   C. A gas is formed.

   D. A new substance is produced.

16. **COMPARE AND CONTRAST** How are physical properties and chemical properties similar?

   F. They both describe how one substance reacts with another.

   G. They both describe a substance.

   H. They both describe the size of a substance.

   J. They both describe a substance by itself.

Inquiry Skills

17. You're watching a chemist work. She mixes a green powder with a blue liquid and then heats the mixture. A yellow gas rises out of the beaker. When she is done, all that remains in the beaker is a crumbly orange solid. Do you think a chemical reaction took place? Explain your **conclusion**.

18. Next, the chemist places a whitish solid in a beaker and heats it. Before long, the solid has turned into a clear liquid. **Hypothesize** what might happen if she continues to heat the beaker.

Critical Thinking

19. Do you think butter can have a change of state? Why or why not?

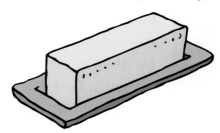

20. Suppose you leave a metal hand tool in a garden for a few weeks. Your area gets rain several times. When you finally pick up the tool, you see orange-brown spots on it.

Part A What are the spots?

Part B Explain what caused the orange-brown spots on the tool.

Building Fort Ancient

In southwest Ohio, you can find one of the oldest places built by people in North America. Fort Ancient was built 2000 years ago by the Hopewell Indians. The Hopewell did not have shovels or wheelbarrows. They built the huge walls by digging and piling the dirt using simple tools such as bones and shells.

Fort Ancient, in Warren County, Ohio, is one of the oldest structures in North America.

The Hopewell did not call the site Fort Ancient. No one knows what ancient people called the site. And ancient people did not use the site as a fort. The walls were not built for protection. The Hopewell used the site for special ceremonies. It was also a place to trade for food and goods.

You can still see Fort Ancient today. The structure has 5500 meters (18,000 ft) of walls. There are more than 67 openings in the fort. On certain days, the sun or moon shines straight through an opening. When the Hopewell saw the sun or moon shine through, they knew it was a special day. It might be time to plant crops or to have a special ceremony. In this way, the Hopewell used Fort Ancient as a kind of calendar.

How Did the Hopewell Indians Build Fort Ancient?

The Hopewell did not have modern tools to build Fort Ancient. Instead, they made tools from stones, trees, antlers, and shells. To dig through dirt, the Indians used long pointed sticks. The Hopewell also used the antlers from elk and the shoulder blades of deer to dig. They used hoes made from clamshells and animal bones to break up clumps of soil. They piled the soil into hand-woven baskets. Each basket weighed about 18 kg (40 lbs) when it was full. The Hopewell Indians carried these baskets up a high hill to add the dirt to the walls. Then they went back down and filled the baskets with more dirt. They kept working until the walls were complete.

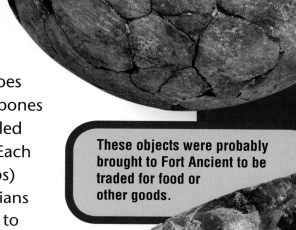

These objects were probably brought to Fort Ancient to be traded for food or other goods.

Think and Do

 1. SCIENCE AND TECHNOLOGY Imagine you had a wooden stick, a clamshell, a woven basket, and a big dirt pile. What could you build? Draw a picture showing what you would build. Write labels that tell how you would use each of your tools.

 2. SCIENTIFIC THINKING Fort Ancient was built with simple tools. It was also used as a calendar. Does this make Fort Ancient itself a tool? Write a paragraph explaining your answer.

Roscoe Village

Columbus

The Canal at Roscoe Village

Roscoe Village shows what travel was like in the early 1800s.

When you go to Roscoe Village it's like going back in time. In the early 1800s, Roscoe Village was a busy port. It served travelers on the Ohio and Erie Canal. Today, the village is a part of a larger town. Coshocton is a modern town in central Ohio. But Roscoe Village has been restored. A trip to the village shows what it was like to live in Ohio two hundred years ago.

Moving goods from place to place could be hard in the early 1800s. Settlers needed food and supplies from the east. The supplies were shipped to ports on Lake Erie. Settlers had to get the goods to their homes in south Ohio. It was too far to drive a wagon. The answer was to use boats, but there was no river between the lake and the Ohio River. So a canal was dug instead. When the canal was finished, boats could pass through to move supplies and people to ports like Roscoe Village.

Mule Power vs. Train Power

The canal boats were fueled by "mule" power. Mules were tied to long ropes, called tow lines, which pulled the canal boats. The boats moved only at about 6 km (4 mi) an hour, but they were the cheapest way to move goods.

The canal boat captain and his family lived on the boat. Everyone in the family helped with the work. To imagine what life was like in those days, visit Roscoe Village. You can climb aboard a canal boat. During the summer you can even ride down a portion of the restored canal.

Roscoe Village was important until the railroads came. Then the canal boats could not compete with fast-moving trains. The boats disappeared from the village. Many people left, too. It was more than 140 years before people realized the importance of Roscoe Village to Ohio's history.

Boats like this moved food and supplies through the Ohio and Erie Canal.

Think and Do

1. SCIENCE AND TECHNOLOGY The Ohio and Erie Canal stretched from Cleveland in the north to Portsmouth in the south. The entire canal was dug by hand. But trains soon put the canal boats out of work. Why do you think trains were a better technology? Make a list of your reasons.

2. SCIENTIFIC THINKING Suppose you were asked to restore a part of your town. What would you want to show people about the past? What do you think people would learn? Write a paragraph explaining what you would like to restore.

Zanesville

Columbus

The Y Bridge of Zanesville

Most people pay little attention to the bridges they cross. But in Zanesville, Ohio, some people come just to look at the bridge. Since 1814, the Y bridges in Zanesville have been famous because of how they were built. Today's bridge is so well known that airline pilots use it as a landmark.

Zanesville sits where two big rivers flow together. The rivers split the land into three sections. In order to reach each section, the bridge is built in a "Y"shape, with three arms.

The first bridge was built in 1814. It was made of wood and stone. Logs and planks formed the road. This bridge stood for six years until it fell in the river.

In 1819, another Y bridge was built in the same area. The designer used a truss system to make the bridge stronger. Trusses are joined beams that help support a bridge. The second bridge stood for 13 years. Then a flood weakened the structure. The people of Zanesville tried to repair the bridge, but it had to be replaced.

Aerial view of the Zanesville Y bridge

More Construction

The third Y bridge was built in 1832. It was similar to the second bridge. This bridge stood until 1900. During this time, most of the traffic was wagons and carriages.

The fourth Y bridge was built to be used by a lot of traffic. It was crossed by people on foot and in wagons, cars, and trucks. By 1979, bigger cars and trucks meant that the bridge was no longer safe. It had to be replaced.

The fifth Y bridge opened in 1984. It was made using strong steel girders so it could bear heavy loads. The bridge is expected to last for a long time. But someday there may be a new advance in bridge technology. If that happens, a new bridge in Zanesville probably won't be far behind.

Street level view of the present day Zanesville Y bridge

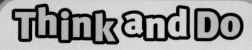

Think and Do

1. SCIENCE AND TECHNOLOGY The Y bridge has been built and rebuilt five times. Does this make the bridge a failure? Write a paragraph explaining why or why not.

2. SCIENTIFIC THINKING It might be simpler to have a single bridge that crosses each river. Draw a diagram showing how it would look with separate bridges instead of the Y bridge. List the pros and cons of this approach. What would you choose to build?

ST-1 Explain how technology improves lives; **ST-2** Explain how technology meets needs; **ST-3** Describe design process

279

How Can You Make Things Warmer?

Materials

Paper clip

Rubber band

Cup of water

Thermometer

Safety goggles

Procedure

1. Put on your safety goggles.

2. Touch a paper clip and feel its temperature. Now unbend it. Now bend the paper clip along one of the straight areas. Do this several times. Feel the paper clip again.

3. Feel a rubber band. Stretch the rubber band back and forth rapidly about 20 times. Feel it again.

4. Measure the temperature of the water in the cup. Record it. Set the cup in the sun. Measure the temperature again.

5. Rub your hands together rapidly. What do you notice?

Draw Conclusions

1. What happened to each of the objects? Why?

2. What did you do to cause the change in each object?

3. What other ways can you think of to make objects warmer? Design an experiment. After it is approved by your teacher, do the experiment. Share the results with the class.

How Can You Lift Heavy Loads Without Heavy Machines?

Materials
A heavy book like a dictionary
30-cm ruler
Small box

Procedure

1. Lift your book with one hand.

2. Make a lever using the ruler and the small box. Place the ruler on top of the box. Make sure the box is near one end of the ruler. This box will serve as the fulcrum.

3. Put the book on the end of the ruler closest to the fulcrum, or box.

4. Press down on the other end of the ruler and lift the book.

Draw Conclusions

1. Was it easier to lift the book with your hand or with the lever? Why?

2. How would using a lever help in building canal boats and in building the Y bridge? Give examples.

References

Contents

Health Handbook

Your Skin R1

Your Digestive System. R2

Your Circulatory System R4

Your Skeletal System R6

Your Muscular System. R8

Your Senses. R10

Your Immune System R12

Staying Healthy R14

Reading in Science Handbook

Identify the Main Idea and Details. R16

Compare and Contrast R18

Cause and Effect R20

Sequence R22

Summarize R24

Draw Conclusions. R26

Math in Science Handbook   R28

Science Safety. R36

Glossary R37

Index. R46

Your Skin

Your skin is your body's largest organ. It provides your body with a tough protective covering. It produces sweat to help control your body temperature. It protects you from disease. Your skin also provides your sense of touch that allows you to feel pressure, textures, temperature, and pain. When you play hard or exercise, your body produces sweat, which cools you as it evaporates. The sweat from your skin also helps your body eliminate excess salts and other wastes.

▼ The skin is the body's largest organ.

Epidermis
Many layers of dead skin cells form the top of the epidermis. Cells in the lower part of the epidermis are always making new cells.

Oil Gland
Oil glands produce oil that keeps your skin soft and smooth.

Hair Follicle
Each hair follicle has a muscle that can contract and make the hair "stand on end."

Pore
These tiny holes on the surface of your skin lead to your dermis.

Sweat Gland
Sweat glands produce sweat, which contains water, salt, and various wastes.

Dermis
The dermis is much thicker than the epidermis. It is made up of tough, flexible fibers.

Fatty Tissue
This tissue layer beneath the dermis stores food, provides warmth, and attaches your skin to underlying bone and muscle.

Caring for Your Skin

- To protect your skin and to keep it healthy, you should wash your body, including your hair and your nails, every day. This helps remove germs, excess oils and sweat, and dead cells from the epidermis, the outer layer of your skin. Because you touch many things during the day, you should wash your hands with soap and water frequently.

- If you get a cut or scratch, you should wash it right away and cover it with a sterile bandage to prevent infection and promote healing.

- Protect your skin from cuts and scrapes by wearing proper safety equipment when you play sports or skate, or when you're riding your bike or scooter.

Your Digestive System

Your digestive system is a series of interconnected organs that breaks down the food you eat and disposes of the leftover wastes your body does not need.

Mouth to Stomach

Digestion begins when you chew your food. Chewing your food breaks it up and mixes it with saliva. When you swallow, the softened food travels down your esophagus to your stomach where it is mixed with digestive juices. These are strong acids that continue the process of breaking your food down into the nutrients your body needs to stay healthy. Your stomach churns your food and turns it into a thick liquid.

Small Intestine and Liver

Your food leaves your stomach and goes into your small intestine. This organ is a long tube just below your stomach. Your liver is an organ that sends bile into your small intestine to continue the process of digesting fats in the food. The walls of the small intestine are lined with millions of small, finger-shaped bumps called villi. Tiny blood vessels in these bumps absorb nutrients from the food as it moves through the small intestine.

Large Intestine

When the food has traveled all the way through your small intestine, it passes into your large intestine. This last organ of your digestive system absorbs water from the food. The remaining wastes are held there until you go to the bathroom.

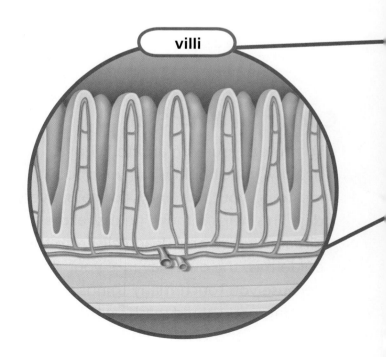

villi

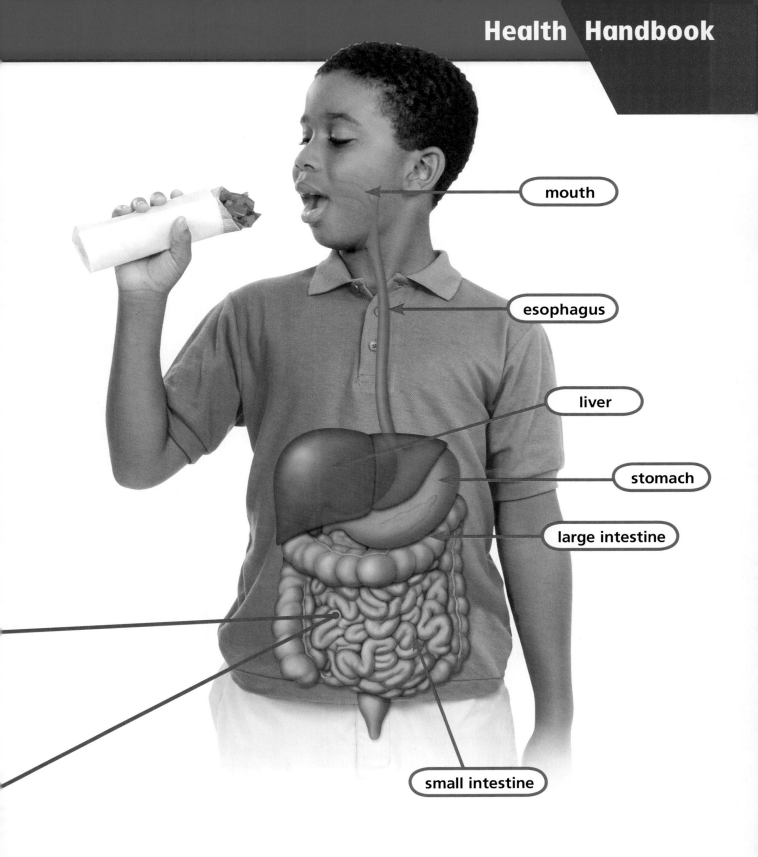

mouth

esophagus

liver

stomach

large intestine

small intestine

Your Circulatory System

You circulatory system carries to every cell in your body the nutrients your digestive system takes from food and the oxygen your lungs take from the air you breathe. As your blood moves throughout your body, it also helps your body fight infections, control your temperature, and remove wastes from your cells.

vein

heart

artery

Your Heart and Blood Vessels

Your heart is the organ that pumps your blood through your circulatory system. Your heart is a strong muscle that beats continuously. As you exercise, your heart adjusts itself to beat faster to deliver the energy and oxygen your muscles need to work harder.

Blood from your heart is pumped through veins into your lungs, where it releases carbon dioxide and picks up oxygen. Your blood then travels back to your heart to be pumped through your arteries to every part of your body.

Your Blood

The blood in your circulatory system is a mixture of fluids and specialized cells. The watery liquid part of your blood is called plasma. Plasma allows the cells in your blood to move through your blood vessels to every part of your body. It also plays an important role in helping your body control your temperature.

Blood Cells

There are three main types of cells in your blood. Each type of cell in your circulatory system plays a special part in keeping your body healthy and fit.

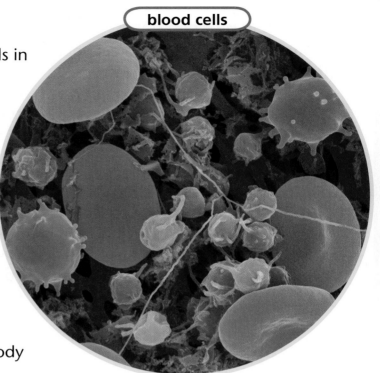

blood cells

Red Blood Cells are the most numerous cells in your blood. They carry oxygen from your lungs throughout your body. They also carry carbon dioxide back to your lungs from your cells, so you can breathe it out.

White Blood Cells help your body fight infections when you become ill.

Platelets help your body stop bleeding when you get a cut or other wound. Platelets clump together as soon as you start to bleed. The sticky clump of platelets traps red blood cells and forms a blood clot. The blood clot hardens to make a scab that seals the cut and lets your body begin healing the wound.

Caring for Your Circulatory System

- Eat foods that are low in fat and high in fiber. Fiber helps take away substances that can lead to fatty buildup in your blood vessels.

- Eat foods high in iron to help your red blood cells carry oxygen.

- Drink plenty of water to help your body replenish your blood.

- Avoid contact with another person's blood.

- Exercise regularly to keep your heart strong.

- Never smoke or use tobacco.

Your Skeletal System

Your skeletal system includes all of the bones in your body. These strong, hard parts of your body protect your internal organs, help you move, and allow you to sit and to stand up straight.

Your skeletal system works with your muscular system to hold your body up and to give it shape.

Your skeletal system includes more than two hundred bones. These bones come in many different shapes and sizes.

Your Skull

The wide flat bones of your skull fit tightly together to protect your brain. The bones in the front of your skull give your face its shape and allow the muscles in your face to express your thoughts and feelings.

Your Spine

Your spine, or backbone, is made up of nearly two dozen small, round bones. These bones fit together and connect your head to your pelvis. Each of these bones, or vertebrae, has a small round hole in the center like a doughnut. Your spinal cord is a bundle of nerves that carries information to and from your brain and the rest of your body. Your spinal cord runs from your brain down your back to your hips through the holes in your vertebrae. There is a soft, flexible disk of cartilage between each of your vertebrae. This allows you to bend and twist your spine. Your spine, pelvis, and leg bones work together to allow you to stand, sit, or move.

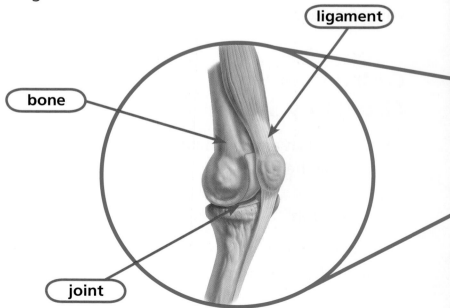

ligament

bone

joint

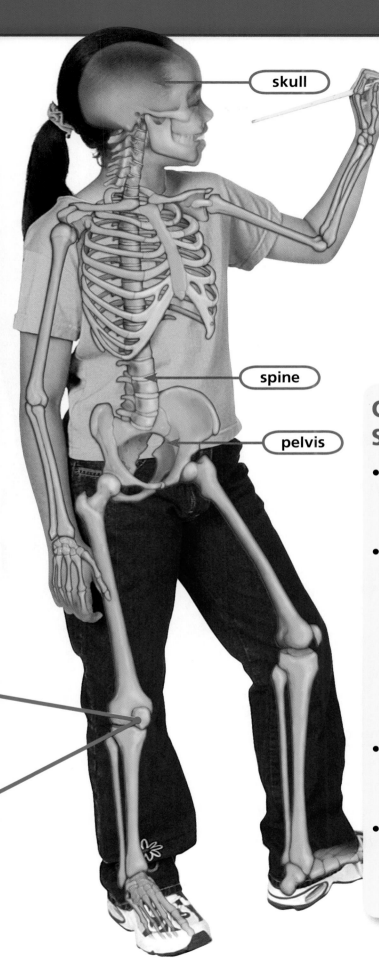

skull

spine

pelvis

Caring for Your Skeletal System

• Always wear a helmet and proper safety gear when you play sports, skate, or ride a bike or a scooter.

• Your bones are mostly made of calcium and other minerals. To keep your skeletal system strong and to help it grow, you should eat foods that are high in calcium like milk, cheese, and yogurt. Dark green, leafy vegetables like broccoli, spinach, and collard greens are also good sources of calcium.

• Exercise to help your bones stay strong and healthy. Get plenty of rest to help your bones grow.

• Stand and sit with good posture. Sitting slumped over puts strain on your muscles and on your bones.

Your Muscular System

A muscle is a body part that produces movement by contracting and relaxing. All of the muscles in your body make up the muscular system.

Voluntary and Involuntary Muscles

Voluntary Muscles are the muscles you use to move your arms and legs, your face, head, and fingers. You can make these muscles contract or stop to control the way your body moves.

Involuntary Muscles are responsible for movements you usually don't see or control. These muscles make up your heart, your stomach and digestive system, your diaphragm, and the muscles that control your eyelids. Your heart beats and your diaphragm powers your breathing without your thinking about them. You cannot stop the action of these muscles.

How Muscles Help You Move

All muscles pull when they contract. Moving your body in more than one direction takes more than one muscle. To reach out with your arm or to pull it back, you use a pair of muscles. As one muscle contracts to extend your arm, the other relaxes and stretches. As you pull your arm back, the muscles reverse their functions.

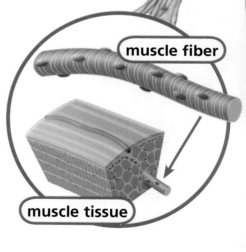

muscle fiber

muscle tissue

Your muscles let you do many kinds of things. The large muscles in your legs allow you to walk and run. Tiny muscles in your face allow you to smile.

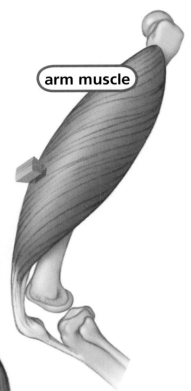

arm muscle

Your Muscles and Your Bones

The muscles that allow you to move your body work with your skeletal system. Muscles in your legs that allow you to kick a ball or ride a bicycle pull on the bones and joints of your legs and lower body. Your muscles are connected to your skeletal system by strong, cordlike tissues called tendons.

Your Achilles tendon, just above your heel, connects your calf muscles to your heel bone. When you contract those muscles, the tendon pulls on the heel bone and allows you to stand on your toes, jump, or push hard on your bicycle's pedals.

Caring for Your Muscular System

- Always stretch and warm your muscles up before exercising or playing sports. Do this by jogging or walking for at least ten minutes. This brings fresh blood and oxygen into your muscles and helps prevent injury or pain.

- Eat a balanced diet of foods to be sure your muscles have the nutrients they need to grow and remain strong.

- Drink plenty of water when you exercise or play sports. This helps your blood remove wastes from your muscles and helps you build endurance.

- Always cool down after you exercise. Walk or jog slowly for five or ten minutes to let your heartbeat slow and your breathing return to normal. This helps you avoid pain and stiffness after your muscles work hard.

- Stop exercising if your feel pain in your muscles.

- Get plenty of rest before and after you work your muscles hard. They need time to repair themselves and recover from working hard.

Your Eyes and Vision

Your eyes allow you to see light reflected by the things around you. This diagram shows how an eye works. Light enters through the clear outer surface called the cornea. It passes through the pupil. The lens bends the incoming light to focus it on the retina. The retina sends nerve signals along the optic nerve. Your brain uses the signals to form an image. This is what you "see."

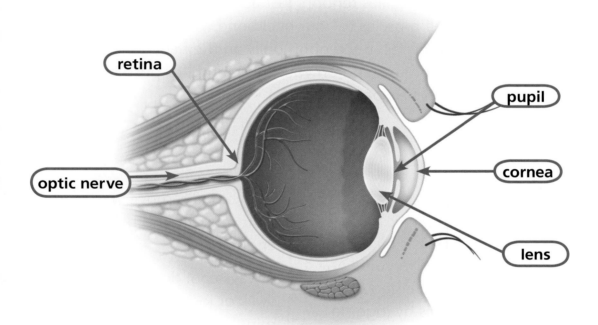

Caring for Your Eyes

- You should have a doctor check your eyesight every year. Tell your parents or your doctor if your vision becomes blurry or if you are having headaches or pain in your eyes.

- Never touch or rub your eyes.

- Protect your eyes from foreign objects by wearing safety glasses when you use tools or play sports.

- Wear goggles when you swim to protect your eyes from chlorine or contaminants in the water.

- Wear sunglasses to protect your eyes from very bright light. Looking directly at bright light or at the sun can damage your eyes permanently.

Your Ears and Hearing

Sounds travel through the air in waves. When some of those waves enter your ear you hear a sound. This diagram shows the inside of your ear.

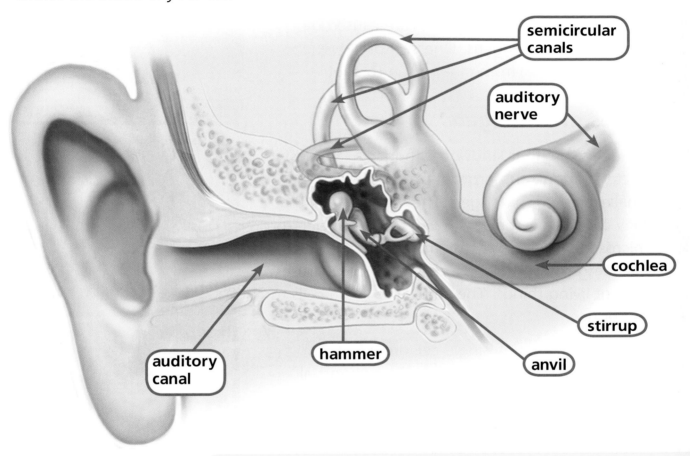

semicircular canals

auditory nerve

cochlea

stirrup

anvil

hammer

auditory canal

Caring for Your Ears

- Never put anything in your ears.

- Wear a helmet that covers your ears when you play sports.

- Keep your ears warm in winter.

- Avoid loud sounds and listening to loud music.

- Have your ears checked by a doctor if they hurt, leak fluid, or if you have any loss of hearing.

- Wear earplugs when you swim. Water in your ears can lead to infection.

Your Immune System

Pathogens and Illness

You may know someone who had a cold or the flu this year. These illnesses are caused by germs called pathogens. Illnesses spread when pathogens move from one person to another.

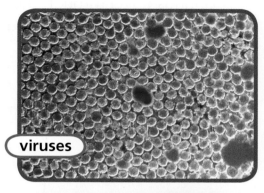
viruses

Types of Pathogens

There are four kinds of pathogens—viruses, bacteria, fungi, and protozoans. Viruses are the smallest kind of pathogen. They are so small that they can be seen only with very powerful electron microscopes. Viruses cause many types of illness, including colds, the flu, and chicken pox. Viruses are not living things. They must use living cells to reproduce.

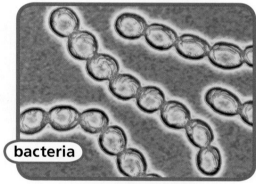
bacteria

Bacteria are tiny single-cell organisms that live in water, in the soil, and on almost all surfaces. Most bacteria can be seen only with a microscope. Not all bacteria cause illness. Your body needs some types of bacteria to work well.

fungi

The most common type of fungus infection is athlete's foot. This is a burning, itchy infection of the skin between your toes. Ringworm is another skin infection caused by a fungus. It causes itchy round patches to develop on the skin.

Protozoa are the fourth type of pathogen. They are single-cell organisms that are slightly larger than bacteria. They can cause disease when they grow in food or drinking water.

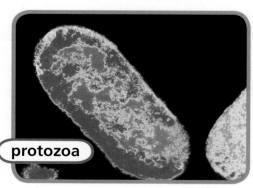
protozoa

Fighting Illness

Pathogens that can make you ill are everywhere. When you become ill, a doctor may be able to treat you. You also can practice healthful habits to protect yourself and others from the spread of pathogens and the illnesses they can cause.

The best way to avoid spreading pathogens is to wash your hands with warm water and soap. This floats germs off of your skin. You should wash your hands often. Always wash them before and after eating, after handling animals, and after using the bathroom. Avoid touching your mouth, eyes, and nose. Never share hats, combs, cups, or drinking straws. If you get a cut or scrape, pathogens can enter your body. It is important to wash cuts and scrapes carefully with soap and water. Then cover the injury with a sterile bandage.

When you are ill, you should avoid spreading pathogens to others. Cover your nose and mouth when you sneeze or cough.

Don't share anything that has touched your mouth or nose. Stay home from school until an adult or your doctor tells you that you are well enough to go back.

Even though pathogens are all around, most people become ill only once in a while because the body has systems that protect it from pathogens. These defenses keep pathogens from entering your body.

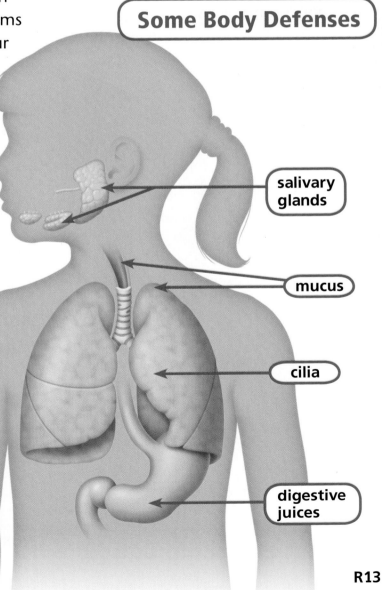

Some Body Defenses

salivary glands

mucus

cilia

digestive juices

Staying Healthy

Eat a Balanced Diet

Eating the foods that your body needs to grow and fight illness is the most important thing you can do to stay healthy. A balanced diet of healthful foods gives your body energy. Your body's systems need nutrients to function properly and work together.

Choosing unhealthful foods can cause you to gain excess weight and to lack energy. Inactivity and poor food choices can lead you to become ill more frequently. Unhealthful foods can also cause you to develop noncommunicable diseases. Unlike communicable diseases caused by germs, these illnesses occur because your body systems are not working right.

Exercise Regularly

Exercise keeps your body healthy. Regular exercise helps your heart, lungs, and muscles stay strong. It helps your body digest food. It also helps your body fight disease. Exercising to keep your body strong also helps prevent injury when you play sports.

Exercise allows your body to rest more effectively. Getting enough sleep prepares your body for the next day. It allows your muscles and bones to grow and recover from exercise. Resting also helps keep your mind alert so you can learn and play well.

Identify the Main Idea and Details

Focus Skill

Many of the lessons in this science book are written so that you can understand main ideas and the details that support them. You can use a graphic organizer like this one to show a main idea and details.

Main Idea: The most important idea of a selection

Detail: Information that tells more about the main idea	**Detail:** Information that tells more about the main idea	**Detail:** Information that tells more about the main idea

Tips for Identifying the Main Idea and Details

- To find the main idea, ask—*What is this mostly about?*

- Remember that the main idea is not always stated in the first sentence.

- Look for details that answer questions such as *who, what, where, when, why,* and *how*. Use pictures as clues.

Here is an example.

Main Idea

An environment that meets the needs of a living thing is called its habitat. The habitats of some are as big as a whole forest. This is often true for birds that fly from place to place. Some habitats can be very small. For example, fungi might grow in certain places on a forest floor.

Detail

Here is what you could record in the graphic organizer.

Main Idea: An environment that meets the needs of a living thing is called its habitat.

Detail: Some habitats can be as big as a whole forest.	**Detail:** A bird's habitat might be a whole forest.	**Detail:** Fungi might grow in certain places on a forest floor.

R16

More About Main Idea and Details

Sometimes the main idea is not at the beginning of a passage. If the main idea is not given, it can be understood from the details. Look at the graphic organizer. What do you think the main idea is?

Main Idea:

Detail:
Green plants are the producers in a food chain. They make their food.

Detail:
Consumers make up the next level of a food chain. They eat other things for energy.

Detail:
Decomposers are the next level. They feed on the wastes of consumers or on their remains.

Sometimes a paragraph's main idea might contain details of different types. In this paragraph, identify whether the details give reasons, examples, facts, steps, or descriptions.

A group of the same species living in the same place at the same time is called a population. A forest may have several populations of different kinds of trees. Trout may be one of several populations of fish in a stream. Deer may form a population among other animals in a meadow.

Skill Practice

Read the following paragraph. Use the Tips for Identifying the Main Idea and Details to answer the questions.

Animals do not get their energy directly from the sun. Many eat plants. The plants use sunlight to make food. Animals that don't eat plants still depend on the energy of sunlight. They eat animals that eat plants. The sun is the main source of energy for all living things.

1. What is the main idea of the paragraph?

2. What supporting details give more information about the main idea?

3. What details answer any of the questions *who, what, where, when, why,* and *how*?

Compare and Contrast

Some lessons are written to help you see how things are alike or different. You can use a graphic organizer like this one to compare and contrast.

> **Topic:** List the two things you are investigating.
>
> | **Alike** | **Different** |
> |---|---|
> | List ways the things are alike. | List ways the things are different. |

Tips for Comparing and Contrasting

- To compare, ask—*How are people, places, objects, ideas, or events alike?*

- To contrast, ask—*How are people, places, objects, ideas, or events different?*

- When you compare, look for signal words and phrases such as *similar, alike, both, the same as, too,* and *also.*

- When you contrast, look for signal words and phrases such as *unlike, different, however, yet,* and *but.*

Here is an example.

Compare

Mars and Venus are the two planets closest to Earth. They are known as inner planets. Venus and Earth are about the same size. But Mars is a little smaller. Venus does not have any moons. However, Mars has two moons.

Contrast

Here is what you could record in the graphic organizer.

> **Topic:** Mars and Venus
>
> | **Alike** | **Different** |
> |---|---|
> | Both are inner planets. | Mars is smaller than Venus. |
> | They are the planets closest to Earth. | Mars has two moons. |

More About Compare and Contrast

You can better understand new information about things when you know how they are alike and how they are different. Use the graphic organizer from page R18 to sort the following new information about Mars and Venus.

Mars	Venus
Mars is the fourth planet from the sun.	Venus is the second planet from the sun.
A year on Mars is 687 Earth days.	A year on Venus is 225 Earth days.
Mars has a diameter of 6794 kilometers.	Venus has a diameter of 12,104 kilometers.
The soil on Mars is a dark reddish brown.	Venus is dry and has a thick atmosphere.

Sometimes a paragraph compares and contrasts more than one topic. In the following paragraph, one topic being compared and contrasted is underlined. Find the second topic being compared and contrasted.

Radio telescopes and optical telescopes are two types of telescopes that are used to observe objects in space. A radio telescope collects radio waves with a large, bowl-shaped antenna. Optical telescopes use light. There are two types of optical telescopes. A refracting telescope uses lenses to magnify an object and a reflecting telescope uses a curved mirror to magnify an object.

Skill Practice

Read the following paragraph. Use the Tips for Comparing and Contrasting to answer the questions.

Both radio telescopes and optical telescopes work the same way. However, optical telescopes collect and focus light, while radio telescopes collect and focus invisible radio waves. Radio waves are not affected by clouds and poor weather. Computers can make pictures from data collected by radio telescopes.

1. How are radio and optical telescopes alike? Different?

2. What are two compare and contrast signal words in the paragraph?

Cause and Effect

Some of the lessons in this science book are written to help you understand why things happen. You can use a graphic organizer like this one to show cause and effect.

Cause	Effect
A cause is an action or event that makes something happen.	An effect is what happens as a result of an action or event.

Tips for Identifying Cause and Effect

- To find an effect, ask—*What happened?*

- To find a cause, ask—*Why did this happen?*

- Remember that events can have more than one cause or effect.

- Look for signal words and phrases, such as *because* and *as a result* to help you identify causes and effects.

Here is an example.

Cause

Effect

A pulley is a simple machine. It helps us do work. It is made up of a rope or chain and a wheel around which the rope fits. When you pull down on one rope end, the wheel turns and the other rope end moves up.

Here is what you could record in the graphic organizer.

Cause	Effect
One rope end is pulled down on a pulley.	The wheel of the pulley turns and the other rope end moves up.

More About Cause and Effect

Events can have more than one cause or effect. For example, suppose the paragraph on page R20 included a sentence that said *The pulley can be used to raise or lower something that is lightweight.* You could then identify two effects of operating a pulley.

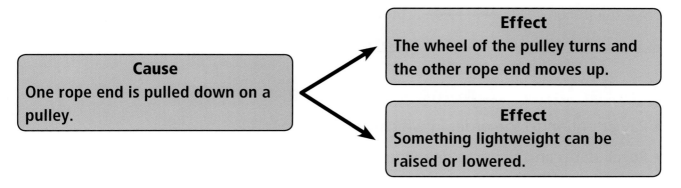

Cause
One rope end is pulled down on a pulley.

Effect
The wheel of the pulley turns and the other rope end moves up.

Effect
Something lightweight can be raised or lowered.

Some paragraphs contain more than one cause and effect. In the following paragraph, one cause and its effect are underlined. Find the second cause and its effect.

A fixed pulley and a movable pulley can be put together to make a compound machine. The movable pulley increases your force. As more movable pulleys are added to a system, the force is increased. The fixed pulley changes the direction of your force.

Skill Practice

Read the following paragraph. Use the Tips for Identifying Cause and Effect to help you answer the questions.

A lever can be used to open a paint can. The outer rim of the can is used as the fulcrum. Your hand supplies the effort force. The force put out by the end under the lid, or the resulting force, is greater than the effort force. As a result, the can is opened.

1. What causes the paint can to open?

2. What is the effect when an effort force is applied?

3. What signal phrase helped you identify the cause and effect in this paragraph?

Sequence

Some lessons in this science book are written to help you understand the order in which things happen. You can use a graphic organizer like this one to show a sequence.

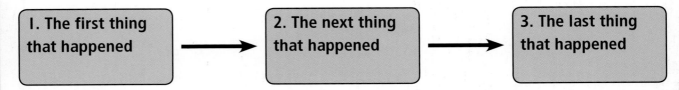

| 1. The first thing that happened | → | 2. The next thing that happened | → | 3. The last thing that happened |

Tips for Understanding a Sequence

- Pay attention to the order in which events happen.

- Recall dates and times to help you understand the sequence.

- Look for signal words such as *first, next, then, last,* and *finally.*

- Sometimes it is helpful to add your own time-order words to help you understand a sequence.

Here is an example.

Time-order word

Conduction is how thermal energy can be transferred from an electric stove burner to water in a metal pot. First, the burner gets hot and the particles in it move faster. Next, the particles in the burner bump into particles in the bottom of the pot. The bumping causes the particles in the pot to move faster and the pot becomes hotter. Then, the particles in the pot bump into the nearby particles of water. The bumping makes the water particles move faster, and the water gets hotter.

Here is what you could record in the graphic organizer.

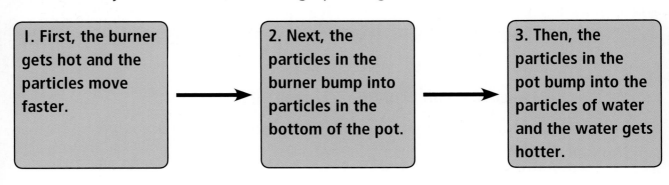

| 1. First, the burner gets hot and the particles move faster. | → | 2. Next, the particles in the burner bump into particles in the bottom of the pot. | → | 3. Then, the particles in the pot bump into the particles of water and the water gets hotter. |

More About Sequence

Sometimes information is sequenced by time. For example, an experiment can be done to measure temperature change over time. Use the graphic organizer to sequence the experiment.

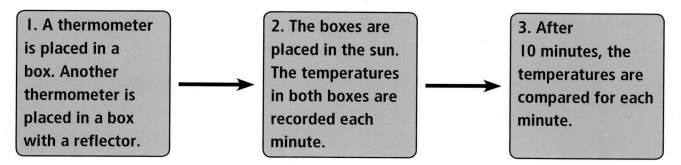

1. A thermometer is placed in a box. Another thermometer is placed in a box with a reflector.

2. The boxes are placed in the sun. The temperatures in both boxes are recorded each minute.

3. After 10 minutes, the temperatures are compared for each minute.

When time-order words are not given, add your own words to help you understand the sequence. In the paragraph below, one time-order word has been included and underlined. How many more time-order words can you add to understand the paragraph's sequence?

Convection is the transfer of thermal energy in a liquid or gas. As the air near a hot object gets hot, it expands. The hot air is forced up by the cooler, denser air around it. As the hot air is forced up, it warms the air around it. Then, the warm air slowly cools and sinks.

Skill Practice

Read the following paragraph. Use the Tips for Understanding a Sequence to answer the questions.

Solar energy can be used to heat water in a home. First, solar panels are placed on the roof of a house. Next, the panels absorb infrared radiation from the sun. Then, the radiation heats the water as it flows through the panels.

1. What is the first thing that happens in the sequence?

2. How many steps are involved in the process?

3. What three signal words helped you identify the sequence in this paragraph?

Summarize

At the end of every lesson in this science book, you will be asked to summarize. When you summarize, you use your own words to tell what something is about. In the lesson, you will be given ideas for writing your summary. You can also use a graphic organizer like this one to summarize.

Main Idea: Tell about the most important information you have read.	**Details:** Add details that answer important questions like who, what, where, when, why, and how.	**Summary:** Retell what you have just read and include only the most important details.

+ (between first two boxes) = (between last two boxes)

Tips for Summarizing

- To write a summary, ask—*What is the most important idea of the paragraph?*

- To add details, ask—*who, what, when, where, why,* and *how.*

- Remember to use fewer words than the original.

- Tell the information in your own words.

Here is an example.

Main Idea

Details

The water cycle is the constant recycling of water. As the sun warms the ocean, water particles leave the water and enter the air as water vapor. This is called evaporation, the process of a liquid changing to a gas. Clouds form when water vapor condenses high in the atmosphere. Condensation occurs when the water vapor rises, cools, and changes from a gas to liquid. When the drops of water are too large to stay up in the air, precipitation occurs.

Here is what you could record in the graphic organizer.

Main Idea: The water cycle is the constant recycling of water.	+	**Details:** Evaporation is water changing from a liquid to a gas. Condensation is changing from a gas to a liquid. Precipitation is water that falls to Earth.	=	**Summary:** The constant recycling of water is the water cycle. It consists of evaporation, condensation, and precipitation.

More About Summarizing

Sometimes a paragraph has details that are not important enough to be included in a summary. The graphic organizer remains the same because those details are not important to understanding the paragraph's main idea.

Skill Practice

Read the following paragraph. Use the Tips for Summarizing to answer the questions.

Tides are the changes in the ocean's water level each day. High tide is when much of the beach is covered with water. Low tide is when waves break farther away from the shore and less of the beach is under water. Every day most shorelines have two high tides and two low tides. High tides and low tides occur at regular times and are usually a little more than 6 hours apart.

1. If a friend asked you what this paragraph was about, what information would you include? What would you leave out?

2. What is the main idea of the paragraph?

3. Which two details would you include in a summary of the paragraph?

Draw Conclusions

At the end of each lesson in this science book, you will be asked to draw conclusions. To draw conclusions, use information from the text you are reading and what you already know. Drawing conclusions can help you understand what you read. You can use a graphic organizer like this.

What I Read Use facts from the text to help you understand.	+	**What I Know** Use your own experience to help you understand.	=	**Conclusion:** Combine facts and details in the text with prior knowledge or personal experience.

Tips for Drawing Conclusions

- To draw conclusions, ask—*What information do I need to think about?*

- To draw conclusions, ask—*What do I know from my own experience that could help me draw a conclusion?*

- Pay close attention to the information the author gives, as well as to your experience, to be sure the conclusions are valid, or make sense.

Here is an example.

Plants need air, nutrients, water, and light to live. A plant makes its own food by a process called photosynthesis. Photosynthesis takes place in the plant's leaves. In an experiment, a plant is placed in a dark room without any light. It is watered every day.

Story information

Here is what you could record in the graphic organizer.

What I Read A plant needs air, nutrients, water, and light to live.	+	**What I Know** Plants use light to make the food they need to live and grow.	=	**Conclusion:** The plant will die since it is not getting any light.

More About Drawing Conclusions

Sensible conclusions based on your experience and the facts you read are valid. For example, suppose the paragraph on page R26 included a sentence that said *After a day, the plant is removed from the dark room and placed in the sunlight.* You could then draw a different conclusion about the life of the plant.

What I Read		**What I Know**		**Conclusion:**
A plant needs air, nutrients, water, and light to live.	+	Plants use light to make the food they need to live and grow.	=	The plant will live.

Sometimes a paragraph might not contain enough information to draw a valid conclusion. Read the following paragraph. Think of one valid conclusion you could draw. Then, think of one conclusion that would be invalid.

Cacti are plants that are found in the desert. Sometimes it does not rain in the desert for months or even years. Cacti have thick stems. The roots of cacti plants grow just below the surface of the ground.

Skill Practice

Read the following paragraph. Use the Tips for Drawing Conclusions to answer the questions.

Animals behave in ways that help them meet their needs. Some animal behaviors are instincts and some are learned. Tiger cubs learn to hunt by watching their mothers hunt and by playing with other tiger cubs. They are not born knowing how to hunt.

1. What conclusion can you draw about a tiger cub if it is separated from its mother?

2. What information from your own experience helped you draw the conclusion?

3. What story information did you use to draw the conclusion?

Using Tables, Charts, and Graphs

As you do investigations in science, you collect, organize, display, and interpret data. Tables, charts, and graphs are good ways to organize and display data so that others can understand and interpret your data.

The tables, charts, and graphs in this Handbook will help you read and understand data. The Handbook will also help you choose the best ways to display data so that you can draw conclusions and make predictions.

Reading a Table

A scientist is studying the rainfall in Bangladesh. She wants to know when the monsoon season is, or the months in which the area receives the greatest amounts of rainfall. The table shows the data she has collected.

Monthly Rainfall in Chittagong, Bangladesh	
Month	Rainfall (inches)
January	1
February	2
March	3
April	6
May	10
June	21
July	23
August	10
September	13
October	7
November	2
December	1

Title

Headings

Data

How to Read a Table

1. **Read the title** to find out what the table is about.

2. **Read the headings** to find out what information is given.

3. **Study** the data. Look for patterns.

4. **Draw conclusions.** If you display the data in a graph, you might be able to see patterns easily.

By studying the table, you can see how much rain fell during each month. If the scientist wanted to look for patterns, she might display the data in a graph.

Reading a Bar Graph

The data in this bar graph is the same as in the table. A bar graph can be used to compare the data about different events or groups.

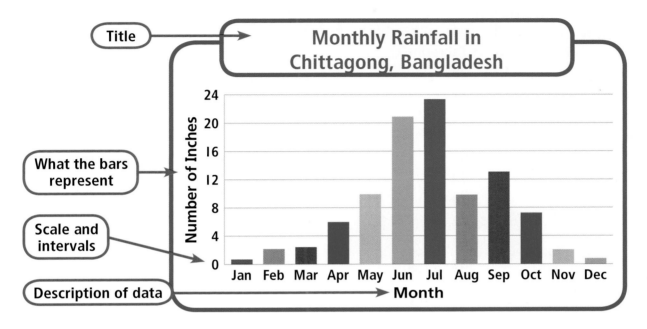

Title → **Monthly Rainfall in Chittagong, Bangladesh**

What the bars represent →

Scale and intervals →

Description of data →

How to Read a Bar Graph

1. **Look** at the graph to determine what kind of graph it is.

2. **Read** the graph. Use the numbers and labels to guide you.

3. **Analyze** the data. Study the bars to compare the measurements. Look for patterns.

4. **Draw conclusions.** Ask yourself questions like the ones under Skills Practice.

Skills Practice

1. In which two months does Chittagong receive the most rainfall?

2. Which months have the same amounts of rainfall?

3. **Predict** During which months are the roads likely to be flooded?

4. How does the bar graph help you identify the monsoon season and the rainfall amounts?

5. Was the bar graph a good choice for displaying this data?

Reading a Line Graph

A scientist collected this data about temperatures in Pittsburgh, Pennsylvania.

Average Temperatures in Pittsburgh	
Month	Temperature (degrees Fahrenheit)
January	28
February	29
March	39
April	50
May	60
June	68
July	74
August	72
September	63
October	52
November	43
December	32

How to Read a Line Graph

1. **Look** at the graph to determine what kind of graph it is.

2. **Read** the graph. Use the numbers and labels to guide you.

3. **Analyze** the data. Study the points along the lines. Look for patterns.

4. **Draw conclusions.** Ask yourself questions like the ones under Skills Practice.

Here is the same data displayed in a line graph. A line graph is used to show changes over time.

Title

What the points represent

Scale and intervals

Description of data

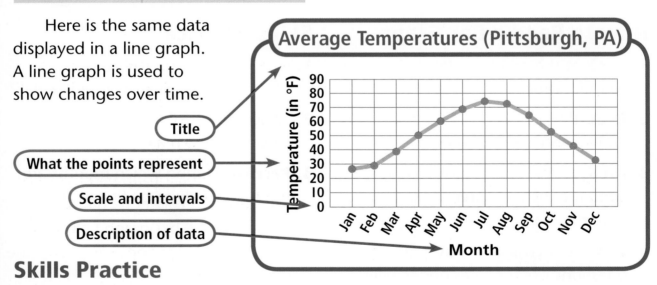

Average Temperatures (Pittsburgh, PA)

Skills Practice

1. In which three months are the temperatures the warmest in Pittsburgh?

2. **Predict** During which months are ponds in Pittsburgh likely to freeze?

3. Was the line graph a good choice for displaying this data? Explain why.

Reading a Circle Graph

Some scientists counted 100 animals at a park. The scientists wanted to know which animal group had the most animals. They classified the animals by making a table. Here is their data.

Animal Groups Observed at the Park

Animal Group	Number Observed
Mammals	7
Insects	63
Birds	22
Reptiles	5
Amphibians	3

The circle graph shows the same data as the table. A circle graph can be used to show data as a whole made up of parts.

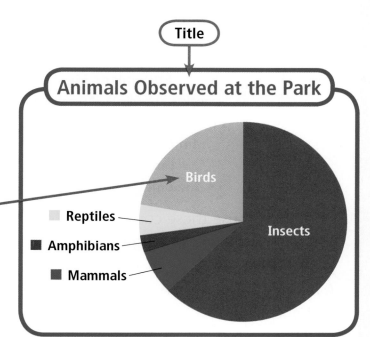

Title

Animals Observed at the Park

Label for a section

Birds

Reptiles

Amphibians

Mammals

Insects

How to Read a Circle Graph

1. **Look** at the title of the graph to learn what kind of information is shown.

2. **Read** the graph. Look at the label of each section to find out what information is shown.

3. **Analyze** the data. Compare the sizes of the sections to determine how they are related.

4. **Draw conclusions.** Ask yourself questions like the ones under Skills Practice.

Skills Practice

1. Which animal group had the most members? Which one had the fewest?

2. **Predict** If you visited a nearby park, would you expect to see more reptiles or more insects?

3. Was the circle graph a good choice for displaying this data? Explain why.

Measurements

When you measure, you compare an object to a standard unit of measure. Scientists almost always use the units of the metric system.

Measuring Length and Capacity in Metric Units

When you measure length, you find the distance between two points. The table shows the metric units of **length** and how they are related.

Equivalent Measures
1 centimeter (cm) = 10 millimeters (mm)
1 decimeter (dm) = 10 centimeters (cm)
1 meter (m) = 1000 millimeters
1 meter = 10 decimeters
1 kilometer (km) = 1000 meters

You can use these comparisons to help you learn the size of each metric unit of length:

A **millimeter (mm)** is about the thickness of a dime.	A **centimeter (cm)** is about the width of an index finger.	A **decimeter (dm)** is about the width of an adult's hand.	A **meter (m)** is about the width of a door.

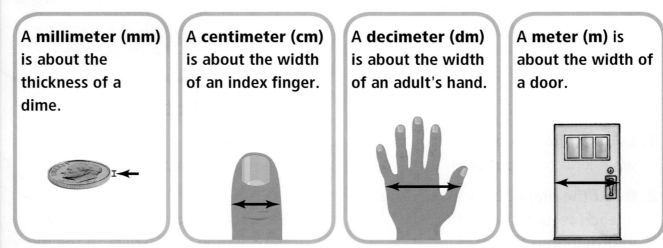

The following diagram shows how to multiply and divide to change to larger and smaller units.

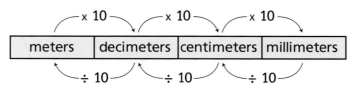

When you measure capacity, you find the amount a container can hold when it is filled. The images show the metric units of **capacity** and how they are related.

A **milliliter (mL)** is the amount of liquid that can fill part of a medicine dropper.

1 mL

A **liter (L)** is the amount of liquid that can fill a plastic bottle.

1 L = 1000 mL

You can use multiplication to change liters to milliliters.

You can use division to change milliliters to liters.

2 L = _____ mL	4000 mL = _____ L
Think: There are 1000 mL in 1 L.	Think: There are 1000 mL in 1 L.
2 L = 2 x 1000 = 2000 mL	4000 ÷ 1000 = 4
So, 2 L = 2000 mL.	So, 4000 mL = 4 L.

Skills Practice

Complete. Tell whether you multiply or divide.

1. 3 L = _____ mL

2. 5000 mL = _____ L

3. 7000 mL = _____ L

4. 6 L = _____ mL

5. 500 dm = _____ cm

6. 4 m = _____ mm

7. 8 _____ = 80 cm

8. _____ m = 1400 cm

Measuring Mass

Matter is what all objects are made of. **Mass** is the amount of matter that is in an object. The metric units of mass are the gram (g) and the kilogram (kg). You can use these comparisons to help you understand the masses of some everyday objects:

A paper clip is about **1 gram** (g).	A slice of wheat bread is about **20 grams.**	A box of 12 crayons is about **100 grams.**	A large wedge of cheese is **1 kilogram** (kg).

You can use multiplication to change kilograms to grams.

You can use division to change grams to kilograms.

2 kg = _____ g	4000 g = _____ kg
Think: There are 1000 g in 1 kg.	Think: There are 1000 g in 1 kg.
2 kg = 2 x 1000 = 2000 g	4000 ÷ 1000 = 4
So, 2 kg = 2000 g.	So, 4000 g = 4 kg.

Skills Practice

Complete. Tell whether you multiply or divide by 1000.

1. 5000 g = _____ kg

2. 3000 g = _____ kg

3. 4 kg = _____ g

4. 7 kg = _____ g

Measurement Systems

SI Measures (Metric)

Temperature
Ice melts at 0 degrees Celsius (°C).
Water freezes at 0°C.
Water boils at 100°C.

Length and Distance
1000 meters (m) =
                   1 kilometer (km)
100 centimeters (cm) = 1 m
10 millimeters (mm) = 1 cm

Force
1 newton (N) = 1 kilogram x
  1 meter/second/second (kg-m/s^2)

Volume
1 cubic meter (m^3) =
                   1 m x 1 m x 1 m
1 cubic centimeter (cm^3) =
                1 cm x 1 cm x 1 cm
1 liter (L) = 1000 millimeters (mL)
1 cm^3 = 1 mL

Area
1 square kilometer (km^2) =
                   1 km x 1 km
1 hectare = 10,000 m^2

Mass
1000 grams (g) = 1 kilogram (kg)
1000 milligrams (mg) = 1 g
1000 kilograms = 1 metric ton

Rates
km/hr = kilometers per hour
m/sec = meters per second

Customary Measures

Temperature
Ice melts at 32 degrees
   Fahrenheit (°F).
Water freezes at 32°F.
Water boils at 212°F.

Length and Distance
12 inches (in.) = 1 foot (ft)
3 ft = 1 yard (yd)
5280 ft = 1 mile (mi)

Force
16 ounces (oz) = 1 pound (lb)
2000 pounds = 1 ton (T)

Volume of Fluids
2 cups (c) = 1 pint (pt)
2 pt = 1 quart (qt)
4 qt = 1 gallon (gal)

Area
1 square mile (mi^2) = 1 mi x 1 mi
1 acre = 4840 sq ft

Rates
mph = miles per hour
ft/sec = feet per second

Safety in Science

Doing investigations in science can be fun, but you need to be sure you do them safely. Here are some rules to follow.

1. **Think ahead.** Study the steps of the investigation so you know what to expect. If you have any questions, ask your teacher. Be sure you understand any caution statements or safety reminders.

2. **Be neat.** Keep your work area clean. If you have long hair, pull it back so it doesn't get in the way. Roll or push up long sleeves to keep them away from your activity.

3. **Oops!** If you should spill or break something, or get cut, tell your teacher right away.

4. **Watch your eyes.** Wear safety goggles anytime you are directed to do so. If you get anything in your eyes, tell your teacher right away.

5. **Yuck!** Never eat or drink anything during a science activity.

6. **Don't get shocked.** Be especially careful if an electric appliance is used. Be sure that electric cords are in a safe place where you can't trip over them. Don't ever pull a plug out of an outlet by pulling on the cord.

7. **Keep it clean.** Always clean up when you have finished. Put everything away and wipe your work area. Wash your hands.

Visit the Multimedia Science Glossary to see illustrations of these words and to hear them pronounced.
www.hspscience.com

Glossary

As you read your science book, you will notice that new or unfamiliar terms have been respelled to help you pronounce them while you are reading. Those respellings are called *phonetic respellings.* In this Glossary you will see the same kind of respellings.

In phonetic respellings, syllables are separated by a bullet (•). Small uppercase letters show stressed syllables.

The boldfaced letters in the examples in the Pronunciation Key below show which letters and combinations of letters are pronounced in the respellings.

The page number (in parentheses) at the end of a definition tells you where to find the term, defined in context, in your book. Depending on the context in which it is used, a term may have more than one definition.

Pronunciation Key

Sound	As in	Phonetic Respelling	Sound	As in	Phonetic Respelling
a	b**a**t	(BAT)	oh	**o**ver	(OH•ver)
ah	l**o**ck	(LAHK)	oo	p**oo**l	(POOL)
air	r**a**re	(RAIR)	ow	**ou**t	(OWT)
ar	**ar**gue	(AR•gyoo)	oy	f**oi**l	(FOYL)
aw	l**a**w	(LAW)	s	**c**ell	(SEL)
ay	f**a**ce	(FAYS)		**s**it	(SIT)
ch	**ch**apel	(CHAP•uhl)	sh	**sh**eep	(SHEEP)
e	t**e**st	(TEST)	th	**th**at	(THAT)
	m**e**tric	(MEH•trik)		**th**in	(THIN)
ee	**ea**t	(EET)	u	p**u**ll	(PUL)
	f**ee**t	(FEET)	uh	med**a**l	(MED•uhl)
	sk**i**	(SKEE)		tal**e**nt	(TAL•uhnt)
er	pap**er**	(PAY•per)		penc**i**l	(PEN•suhl)
	f**er**n	(FERN)		**o**ni**o**n	(UHN•yuhn)
eye	**i**dea	(eye•DEE•uh)		play**fu**l	(PLAY•fuhl)
i	b**i**t	(BIT)		d**u**ll	(DUHL)
ing	go**ing**	(GOH•ing)	y	**y**es	(YES)
k	**c**ard	(KARD)		r**i**pe	(RYP)
	kite	(KYT)	z	bag**s**	(BAGZ)
ngk	ba**nk**	(BANGK)	zh	trea**s**ure	(TREZH•er)

abiotic [ay•by•AHT•ik] Of the nonliving parts of an ecosystem. **(168)**

air mass [AIR MAS] A large body of air that has a similar temperature and moisture level. **(54)**

anemometer [an•uh•MAHM•uht•er] A weather instrument that measures wind speed. **(60)**

angiosperm [AN•jee•oh•sperm] A flowering plant that has seeds protected by fruits. **(135)**

atom [AT•uhm] The smallest unit of an element that has all the properties of that element. **(246)**

balance [BAL•uhns] A tool that measures mass. **(8)**

barometer [buh•RAHM•uh•ter] A weather instrument used to measure air pressure. **(60)**

biotic [by•AHT•ik] Of the living parts of an ecosystem. **(166)**

carnivore [KAHR•nuh•vawr] An animal that eats only other animals. **(176)**

change of state [CHAYNJ uhv STAYT] A physical change that occurs when matter changes from one state to another, such as from a liquid to a gas. **(255)**

chemical change [KEM•ih•kuhl CHAYNJ] A reaction or change in a substance, produced by chemical means, that results in a different substance. **(264)**

chemical property [KEM•ih•kuhl PRAHP•er•tee] A property that involves how a substance interacts with other substances. **(263)**

chemical reaction [KEM•ih•kuhl ree•AK•shuhn] A chemical change. **(264)**

classify [KLAS•uh•fy] To group things that are alike. **(116)**

cold front [KOHLD FRUHNT] The boundary where a cold air mass moves under a warm air mass. **(56)**

community [kuh•MYOO•nuh•tee] All the populations of organisms living together in an environment. **(162)**

compound [KAHM•pownd] A substance made of two or more different elements. **(264)**

condensation [kahn•duhn•SAY•shuhn] The process by which a gas changes into a liquid. **(35)**

consumer [kuhn•SOOM•er] A living thing that can't make its own food and must eat other living things. **(174)**

decomposer [dee•kuhm•POHZ•er] A living thing that feeds on the wastes of plants and animals. **(178)**

density [DEN•suh•tee] The measure of how closely packed matter is in an object. **(214)**

deposition [dep•uh•ZISH•uhn] The dropping of bits of rock and soil by a river as it flows. **(84)**

diversity [duh•VER•suh•tee] A great variety of living things. **(172)**

earthquake [ERTH•kwayk] The shaking of Earth's surface caused by movement of rock in the crust. **(83)**

ecosystem [EE•koh•sis•tuhm] A community and its physical environment together. **(158)**

element [EL•uh•muhnt] A substance made up of only one kind of atom. **(248)**

energy pyramid [EN•er•jee PIR•uh•mid] A diagram showing how much energy is passed from one organism to the next in a food chain. **(188)**

environment [en•VY•ruhn•muhnt] All of the living and nonliving things that affect an organism. **(158)**

evaporation [ee•vap•uh•RAY•shuhn] The process by which a liquid changes into a gas. **(34)**

experiment [ek•SPAIR•uh•muhnt] A test of a hypothesis. **(15)**

extinction [ek•STINGK•shuhn] The dying out of an entire species. **(146)**

food chain [FOOD CHAYN] A series of organisms that depend on one another for food. **(184)**

food web [FOOD WEB] A group of food chains that overlap. **(186)**

fossil [FAHS•uhl] The remains of once-living things that have been preserved by being petrified or by leaving different kinds of imprints. **(90, 142)**

fossil record [FAHS•uhl REK•erd] The information about Earth's history that is contained in fossils. **(92)**

gas [GAS] The state of matter that does not have a definite shape or volume. **(221)**

germinate [JER•muh•nayt] To sprout. **(138)**

glacier [GLAY•sher] A large, moving block of ice. **(85)**

gymnosperm [JIM•noh•sperm] A plant with seeds that are not protected by fruits. **(134)**

habitat [HAB•ih•tat] An environment that meets the needs of an organism. **(182)**

hail [HAYL] Round pieces of ice formed when frozen rain is coated with water and refreezes. **(41)**

herbivore [HER•buh•vawr] An animal that eats only plants, or producers. **(176)**

hurricane [HER•ih•kayn] A large tropical storm that has winds of at least 74 miles per hour. **(42)**

hypothesis [hy•PAHTH•uh•sis] A statement of what you think will happen and why. **(15)**

inference [IN•fer•uhns] An untested conclusion based on your observations. **(12)**

land breeze [LAND BREEZ] A breeze that moves from the land to the sea. **(48)**

landform [LAND•fawrm] A natural feature on Earth's surface. **(72)**

liquid [LIK•wid] The state of matter that has a definite volume but no definite shape. **(220)**

mass [MAS] The amount of matter in an object. **(213)**

matter [MAT•er] Anything that has mass and takes up space. **(212, 244)**

microscope [MY•kruh•skohp] A tool that makes an object look several times bigger than it is. **(6)**

mixture [MIKS•cher] A blending of two or more types of matter that are not chemically combined. **(228)**

mountain [MOWNT•uhn] An area that is higher than the land around it. **(72)**

niche [NICH] The role of an organism in its habitat. **(183)**

nonvascular [nahn•VAS•kyuh•ler] Without vessels. Nonvascular plants do not have tubes to transport materials. **(120)**

observation [ahb•zer•VAY•shuhn] Information from your senses. **(12)**

omnivore [AHM•nih•vawr] An animal that eats both plants and other animals. **(176)**

phloem [FLOH•em] Vascular tissue that carries food from leaves to all plant cells. **(125)**

photosynthesis [foht•oh•SIN•thuh•sis] The process by which a plant makes food. **(128)**

physical change [FIZ•ih•kuhl CHAYNJ] A change in matter from one form to another that doesn't result in a different substance. **(256)**

physical property [FIZ•ih•kuhl PRAHP•er•tee] A property that involves a substance by itself. **(263)**

population [pahp•yuh•LAY•shuhn] All the individuals of the same kind living in the same environment. **(160)**

precipitation [pree•sip•uh•TAY•shuhn] Water that falls to Earth. **(32)**

predator [PRED•uh•ter] A consumer that eats prey. **(184)**

prey [PRAY] Consumers that are eaten by predators. **(184)**

producer [pruh•DOOS•er] A living thing, such as a plant, that can make its own food. **(174)**

rain [RAYN] Precipitation that is liquid water. **(41)**

rain shadow [RAYN SHAD•oh] The area on the side of a mountain range with less rain and cloud cover. **(50)**

scientific method [sy•uhn•TIF•ik METH•uhd] A way scientists find out how things work and affect each other. **(20)**

sea breeze [SEE BREEZ] A breeze that moves from the sea to the land. **(48)**

sleet [SLEET] Precipitation caused when rain falls through freezing air and turns to ice. **(41)**

snow [SNOH] Precipitation caused when water vapor turns directly into ice and forms ice crystals. **(41)**

solid [SAHL•id] The state of matter that has a definite shape and a definite volume. **(220)**

solubility [sahl•yoo•BIL•uh•tee] The measure of how much of a material will dissolve in another material. **(231)**

solution [suh•LOO•shuhn] A uniform mixture of two or more substances in a single state of matter. **(230)**

spore [SPAWR] A single reproductive cell that can grow into a new plant. **(132)**

spring scale [SPRING SKAYL] A tool that measures forces, such as weight. **(8)**

standard measure [STAN•derd MEZH•er] An accepted measurement. **(4)**

state of matter [STAYT uhv MAT•er] One of the three forms [solid, liquid, and gas] that matter can exist in. **(220)**

suspension [suh•SPEN•shuhn] A kind of mixture in which particles of one ingredient are floating in another ingredient. **(232)**

topography [tuh•PAHG•ruh•fee] The shape of landforms in an area. **(74)**

tornado [tawr•NAY•doh] A fast-spinning spiral of wind that touches the ground. **(42)**

vascular [VAS•kyuh•ler] Having vessels. Vascular plants have tubes that transport food and water to different parts of the plant. **(120)**

vascular tissue [VAS•kyuh•ler TISH•oo] Tissue that supports plants and carries water and food. **(125)**

volcano [vahl•KAY•noh] A mountain that forms as lava flows through a crack onto Earth's surface. **(82)**

volume [VAHL•yoom] The amount of space an object takes up. **(214)**

warm front [WAWRM FRUHNT] The boundary where a warm air mass moves over a cold air mass. **(56)**

water cycle [WAW•ter SY•kuhl] The movement of water from the surface of Earth into the air and back again. **(32)**

xylem [ZY•luhm] Vascular tissue that carries water and nutrients from roots to every part of a plant. **(125)**

Index

A

Abiotic factors, 168
climate, 170–171
Absorption in plants, 120
Age of Mammals, 94
Air
in ecosystems, 168
moisture level in, 54
Air masses, 54–56, 245
Air pressure, 59
Aleutian Islands (Alaska), 76
Algae, 145, 176
Alligators, 187
Alpine glaciers, 85
Amber, 91
Ammonites, 88
Anemometers, 60
Anemones, 185
Angiosperms, 135
Animals
climate and, 170
in ecosystems, 166, 167
in Everglades, 162
fossil, 91
populations of, 160
prey and predators, 186–187
producers vs. consumers,
176–177
Antarctic Ocean food web, 189
Antelope Canyon (Arizona), 69
Anther (plants), 136, 137
Aquanauts, 192–193
**Aquarius underwater
laboratory,** 192–193
Archaefructus sinensis, 145
Archer fish, 174
Atacama Desert (Chile), 164
Atoms, 246–248
Azaleas, 113, 118

B

Balances, 8
Ballard, Michael, 98
Bamboo, 117
Bar graphs, R29
Barometers, 60
Barrier islands, 76, 86
Beaches
erosion of, 106–107
formation of, 86
**Bees, plant reproduction
and,** 137
Birds, 150
in Everglades, 162
Blackbirds, 161
Blizzards, 42
Blood, R5
Blueberries, 268–269
Blue lupines, 194
Boiling point, 224
Bracket fungi, 180
Branches, 119
Breezes, 48
Bridges, Y, 278–279
British Isles, 76
Bubbles, 252
Buckeye tree, 117
Bug box, 6
Bushway, Al, 268–269
Butterflies, 198–199
Buttes, 74

C

Calories, 190
Canal boats, 276, 277
Canals, 276–277
Canopy (rain forests), 172
Canyons, 69, 73
Capacity, measuring, R33
Carbon, 248

Carbon dioxide, 128
Careers
food manufacturer, 270
nuclear medicine technologist,
236
Carnivores, 178, 179
Casts, fossil, 90
Caterpillars, 198
Cause and effect, R20–21
Cenozoic Era, 94
Change of state (matter),
254–255
chemical, 264–266
dissolving, 258
physical, 256–257
Chemical changes, 264–265
recognizing, 266
Chemical properties of matter,
262–263
Chemical reactions, 260, 263,
264
Chipmunks, 187
Chlorophyll, 128
Chloroplasts, 128
Chrysalis, 198
Cinder cone volcanoes, 82
Circle graphs, R31
Circulatory system, R4–5
Cirrus clouds, 57
Clams, 90
Classification, 13
of beans, 115
of plants, 116–120
Cliffs, weathering of, 86
Climate, 159, 170-171
fossil record of changes in, 93
Clouds
formation of, 32, 35
types of, 57
in water cycle, 33
Coastal plains, 74
Coin-sorting machine, 116
Cold air masses, 54–55

Cold fronts, 56, 58

Color, 216
on weather maps, 58–59

Communication, 16
food chain, 183
in scientific method, 22

Communities, 162

Comparison, 13
effects of water, 165
plants, 115
in reading, R18–19
spores and seeds, 131

Composite volcanoes, 82

Compounds, 264, 265

Condensation, 35

Cones (plant), 134

Conifer trees, 143

Consumers, 176–179, 188, 190

Contrasting (reading), R18–19

Control variables, 15

**Cooling, states of matter
and,** 222

Coral islands, 76

Coral reef habitat, 156, 185

Cordaites, 146

Core (Earth), 80

Cotyledons, 138

Crabs, 185

Crust (Earth), 80. *See also*
Landforms

Cryptoexplosion sites, 105

Cumbre Vieja volcano, 96–97

Cumulus clouds, 57

Curie, Marie, 236

Cycads, 143

D

Daisies, Lakeside, 202–203

Data, 16

Daum, Peter, 270

Day, Simon, 96–97

Deciduous trees, 117

Decomposers, 180

Deltas, 75, 84

Democritus, 246, 247

Density, 214–215
of water, 210

Deposition, 84

Deserts
climate of, 170, 171
habitats of, 164, 184

Details, supporting, R16–17

Diet, 14, R2–3

Digestive system, R1

Dinosaurs, 90–94

Diseases, human, R12–13

Displaying data, 16
densities of liquids, 211

Dissolving, 258

Distance, measuring, 4

Diversity (ecosystems), 172

Dogwoods, 113

Dragonflies, 161

Drawing conclusions, 16
germinating seeds, 141
in reading, R24–25
in scientific method, 22
solutions, 243
wet wool, 261

Drinking water, 36

Droppers, 5

Dunes, 75, 86

E

Ears, human, R11

Earth
fossil record and history
of, 92–93
geologic time scale of, 94
layers of, 80–81
See also Landforms

Earth Day, 64

Earthquakes, 83

Ecosystems, 158–159
climate and, 170–171
climate of, 159
communities, 162
coral, 156

definition of, 158
diversity in, 172
individuals in, 160
living things affecting,
166–167
nonliving things in, 168–169
populations of, 160–161

Eggs
dinosaur, 91, 93
in plant reproduction, 133,
134

Eidothea, 144

Elements, 248–249
definition of, 248
metals vs. nonmetals, 250

Elephants, 92

Embryo (plant), 137, 138

Emergent layer (rain forests),
172

Energy
food chains, 186–187
food webs, 188–189
photosynthesis and, 128
for seed growth, 138

Energy pyramids, 190

Environment, 158
fossil record of changes in, 93

Epidermis (leaves), 128

Eras, 94

Erie and Ohio Canal, 276

Erosion
of Lake Erie, 106–107
by wind and waves, 86

Evaporation, 34, 258

**Everglades National Park
(Florida),** 162

Evergreens, 117

Exercise, R15

Experiments, 15
in scientific method, 21
straw models, 19

Extinction
of dinosaurs, 94
of plants, 146

Eyes, R10

Farming, hydroponic, 148–149
Faults, 83
Ferns, 132, 133
   life cycle of, 133
   living vs. fossil, 142
Fertilization (plant reproduction), 133, 134
Fibrous roots, 126–127
Fiords, 85
Firefighting, 234–235
First-level consumers, 188
Floodplains, 74, 84
Floods, 38, 44
Flower beetles, 144
Flowering plants, 135–137
Food chains, 186–187
Food manufacturers, 270
Food webs, 188–189
Forceps, 6
Forests
   as ecosystem, 159
   rain-forest floor, 172
Fort Ancient (Ohio), 274–275
Fossil record, 92–93
Fossils, 90–91
   ammonites, 88
   definition of, 90
   formation of, 90
   on Kelleys Island, 103
   plant, 142–146
Franklin Park Conservatory (Ohio), 198–199
Freezing, 255
Freezing point, 224
Frogs, 160
Fronds
   ferns, 133
   palm trees, 117
Fronts (weather), 56, 58
Fruit
   plants with, 144–145
   plants without, 142–143
   seed dispersal for, 137
Fungi, 145

Gametophyte generation, 132, 133
Gases, 221, 254, 255
   changes in state of, 224
   condensation and, 35
   mixtures of, 229
   water vapor, 32
Gathering data, 16
   flood modeling, 39
Geologic time scale, 94
Georgia Dome (Atlanta), 10
Germination (seeds), 138
Glacial grooves, 102, 103
Glaciers, 85
   valley formation by, 73
Gold, 250
Graphs, R29–31
Grasses, 117
Grasslands
   climate of, 170
   as ecosystem, 158
Groundwater, 36
Gum Bumelia tree, 119
Gymnosperms, 134, 135
Gypsum, 75
Gypsy moths, 166

H

Habitats, 184–185
Hail, 32, 40, 41
Hand lenses, 6
Handling, tools for, 6
Hawai'i, 76
Hawks, 187
Hearing, R11
Heartwood, 127
Heat, states of matter and, 222
Henry I, King of England, 4
Herbivores, 178, 179
Hills, 72
Himalayas, 81
Hine's emerald dragonfly, 161

Holden Arboretum (Ohio), 200–201
Hopewell Indians, 274–275
Human body
   blood, R5
   diet for, 14, R2–3
   See also Systems (human body)
Hurricane Hunters, 62–63
Hurricanes, 42–43, 62–63
Hydroponics, 148–149
Hymenaea protera, 146
Hypothesizing, 15
   drops of liquids, 253
   in scientific method, 21

Ice Age, 92
Ice sheets, 85
Ice storms, 52
Identifying variables, 15
Illness, R12–13
Individuals (in ecosystems), 160, 161
Inference, 12
   barometers, 53
   melting, boiling, evaporation, 219
   salt to fresh water, 31
   vascular plant parts, 123
Inner core (Earth), 80
Inquiries
   skills for, 10–16
   tools for, 2–8
International System (SI), 14, R35. *See also* Metric system
Interpreting data, 16
   flood modeling, 39
Investigation, 15
Iron, 249
   atoms of, 242
   melting/boiling points of, 224
Islands, 76
   volcanic, 76, 81

Jaguars, 179

Kansas, fossils in, 93
Kelleys Island (Ohio), 102–103

Labrador Tea plants, 200–201
Lake Erie, 106–107
Lakeside Daisy State Nature Preserve (Ohio), 202–203
Land breezes, 48
Landforms
  canyons, 73
  deltas, 75
  dunes, 75
  earthquakes and, 83
  glaciers and, 85
  hills, 72
  islands, 76
  mountains, 72
  plains, 74
  plateaus, 74
  rivers and, 84
  valleys, 73
  volcanoes and, 81–83
  water cycle and, 48–50
  waves and, 86
  wind and, 86
Larva, 198
Leaves, 127, 128
Length, measuring, 4, R32
Lepidodendron, 146
Lichens, 145
Lightning, 50
Lilies, 118, 144
Line graphs, R30
Lion-fish, 185
Liquids, 220–221, 254, 255
  changes in state of, 254

condensation, 35
density of, 214–215
evaporation, 34
measuring, 5
mixtures of, 229
Liverworts, 145
Living things
  classification of. *See* Classification
  consumers, 176–179
  decomposers, 180
  in ecosystems, 158–159, 166–167
  energy pyramids, 190
  as environment, 158
  food chains, 186–187
  food webs, 188–189
  geologic time scale of, 94
  habitats, 184–185
  producers, 176
  roles of, 174–180

Magma, 80, 81
Magnifying boxes, 6
Magnifying lenses, 6
Magnolia fruit, 144
Main ideas (reading), R16–17
Mammoths, 92
Mangroves, 122, 127
Mangrove swamps, 161, 186
Mantle (Earth), 80
Maps, weather, 58–59
Marblehead Peninsula (Ohio), 202
Mars Rovers, 2, 18
Mass, 213, 244–245
  measuring, 8, R34
Matter, 212, 216
  basic properties of, 244–245
  chemical changes in, 264–265
  chemical properties of, 262–263
  definition of, 212, 244

density of, 214–215
elements, 248–249
mass of, 213
particles of, 246–247
physical changes in, 256–257
physical properties of, 216, 262–263
states of. *See* States of matter
volume of, 214
Measurement, 14
  of capacity, R33
  customary system of, R35
  decomposing bananas, 175
  of distance, 4
  of length, R32
  of mass, R34
  metric, R32–35
  with straws, 3
  systems of, R35
  tools for, 8
  of volume, 5
  of weather, 60
Measuring tape, 4
Melting, 255
Mercury (element), 249
  melting/boiling points of, 224
Mesas, 74
Mesozoic Era, 94
Metals, 250
  changes in state of, 224
Meter, 4
Metric system, 14, R32–35
  capacity measurement, R33
  length measurement, R32
  mass measurement, R34
Microscopes, 6, 7
Millipedes, 180
Minerals, in fossils, 90–91
Mixtures, 228–229
  solutions, 230
  suspensions, 232
Modeling, 14
  ecosystem, 157
  landforms, 71
  with straw, 11
  volcanic eruptions, 79

Moisture level (air), 54
Molds, fossil, 90
Mono Lake (California), 226
Mosquitoes, 162, 182
Mosses, 124, 132
  life cycle of, 132
  reproduction in, 132, 133
Mounds (Ohio), 104–105
Mountains, 72
  Himalayas, 81
  rain shadows, 50
  volcanoes, 82
Mount Saint Helens, 82, 98
Mullets, 186
Muscular system, R8–9

National Weather Service
  (NWS), 59
Natural resources, in Lake Erie,
  106–107
Niche, 185
Nimbostratus clouds, 57
Nitrogen, melting/boiling
  points of, 224
Nonliving things (in
  ecosystems), 158, 168–169
Nonmetals, 250
Nonvascular plants, 120, 124
Nuclear medicine technologists,
  236
Number skills. *See* Using
  numbers
Nutrition, 14, R2–3
NWS (National Weather
  Service), 59

Oak trees, 119
Observation, 12
  animal tracks, 89
  fossil events, 141
  heating land and water, 47

landform models, 71
in scientific method, 20
tools for, 6–7
Oceans
  food web in, 188–189
  fossil record and changes in,
    93
  new crust in, 81
  water in, 30
Ohio
  Fort Ancient, 274–275
  Franklin Park Conservatory,
    198–199
  Holden Arboretum, 200–201
  Kelleys Island, 102–103
  Lake Erie, 106–107
  Lakeside Daisy State Nature
    Preserve, 202–203
  Roscoe Village, 276–277
  Serpent Mound Memorial,
    104–105
  Y bridges, 278–279
Omnivores, 178, 179
One-celled organisms, 94
Ordering. *See* Classification
Oregon coast, 78
Organisms. *See* Living things
Outer core (Earth), 80
Ovary (plants), 136
Ovules (plants), 134, 136, 137
Oxygen, 248
  melting/boiling points of, 224
  in photosynthesis, 128

Pacific Ocean, coral islands in,
  76
Paleozoic Era, 94
Palm trees, 117, 143
Palo Duro Canyon, 73
Pan balances, 8
Parsley, 118
Particles (matter), 220–222,
  246–247

Pathogens, R12–13
Peninsulas, 49
Petals (plants), 136
Petrified Forest (Arizona), 91
Petrified wood, 91, 140, 143
Phloem, 125, 128
Photosynthesis, 128
Physical changes, 256–257
  dissolving, 258
Physical properties, 262–263
Phytoplankton, 189
Piersanti, Michaela, 64
Pine trees, 117
Plains, 74
Planning investigations
  (dissolving solids), 227
Plants
  branches, 119
  classification of, 116–120
  climate and, 170
  in ecosystems, 166, 167
  extinct, 146
  fossilized, 142–146
  with fruit, 144–145
  grasses, 117
  Labrador Tea, 200–201
  leaves, 128
  nonvascular, 124
  number of species of, 135
  reproduction in, 132–138
  roots, 126–127
  seed-bearing, 134–135
  seed germination, 138
  seed production in, 136–137
  spore reproduction in,
    132–133
  stems, 118, 127
  transport in, 120
  trees, 117
  vascular, 125
  without fruit, 142–143
Plateaus, 74
Plates, 80–81
  movement of, 81
  volcano formation and, 82
Pollen, 134

Pollen tube, 136
Pollinators, 130
    butterflies, 199
Polyacrylate, 235
Populations (ecosystems), 160–161
    balance in, 167
    in communities, 162
Prairie ecosystem, 158
Precambrian Era, 94
Precipitation
    air mass temperature and, 54–55
    definition of, 32
    formation of, 35
    with fronts, 56
    kinds of, 40–41
    in water cycle, 32, 33
Predators, 186–187
Prediction, 12
Pressure, air, 59
Prey, 186–187
Producers, 176, 190
Prop roots, 122
Pupa, 198

R

Rain, 32, 40
    climate and, 170
Rain forests, 172
    climates of, 170, 171
    layers of, 172
Rain gauges, 60
Rain shadows, 50
Recording data, 16
    flood modeling, 39
Red-winged blackbirds, 161
Reef fossils, 92
Reproduction, plant, 130, 132–138
Rhododendron, 118
River hogs, 179
Rivers, 84
    deltas, 75
    valley formation by, 73

Rocks
    magma, 80
    sedimentary, 90
Roots, 126–127
Roscoe Village (Ohio), 276–277
Rovers (spacecraft), 2, 18
Rulers, 4
Runoff, 36

S

Safety
    in science investigations, R36
    during severe weather, 44
Sagebrush, 184
Sago palm, 143
Salt, solubility of, 231
Salt water, 229, 230
Sand, solubility of, 231
Sand bars, 86
Sand dunes, 75, 86
Savanna climate, 170, 171
Scales, 8
Science activities
    glacial grooves, 108
    lifting heavy loads, 281
    making things warmer, 280
    parts of a flower, 204
    plant growth toward light, 205
    shoreline changes, 109
Science projects
    changes in physical properties, 271
    checking for air pollution, 195
    density, 237
    getting out dirt, 195
    leaf cast, 151
    making rain gauges, 65
    mass of air, 271
    rivers and landform changes, 99
    seismic waves, 99
    sunlight and chlorophyll, 151
    temperature and particle movement, 237
    weather and seasons, 65

Scientific inquiries. *See* **Inquiries**
Scientific method, 20–22
Sea arches, 86
Sea breezes, 48
Second-level consumers, 188
Sedimentary rocks, fossils in, 90
Seed-bearing plants
    reproduction in, 134–137
    seed germination, 138
Seed coat, 134, 137
Seismograms, 83
Sequence, R22–23
Serpent Mound Memorial (Ohio), 104–105
Shadows, rain, 50
Shape, 216
Shield volcanoes, 82
SI. *See* **International System**
Sidewinders, 184, 185
Silver, 249
Sirens, weather, 44
Skeletal system, R6–7
Skunk vine, 167
Sleet, 32, 40–41
Slot canyons, 69
Smith, Celia, 192–193
Snow, 32, 40–42
Soft stems, 118
Soil
    climate and, 170
    in ecosystems, 168
    in floodplains, 74
Solar energy
    evaporation and, 34
    water cycle and, 32
Solids, 220, 254, 255
    changes in state of, 224
    density of, 215
    measuring, 5
    mixtures of, 228
    in solution with liquids, 230
Solubility, 231
Solutions, 230
Sori, 133
Sow bugs, 180

Space shuttle, 260
Species of plants, 135
Sperm (plant reproduction), 132
Spores, 132, 133
Sporophyte generation, 132, 133
Spring scales, 8
Squall lines, 46
Standard measure, 4
States of matter, 216, 220–221
    changes in, 222, 224, 254–255
Stationary fronts, 56
Steel, 250
Stems, 118, 127
Stigma, 136, 137
Stomata, 128
Storms
    ice, 52
    safety during, 44
    sea breeze, 49
    types of, 42–43
Storm surges, 42
Stratus clouds, 57
Strike-slip faults, 83
Sugar, solubility of, 231
Sulfur, 250
Summarization (in reading), R26–27
Sunlight
    climate and, 170
    in ecosystems, 168
    in photosynthesis, 128
Supporting details, R16–17
Suspensions, 232
Systems (human body)
    circulatory, R4–5
    digestive, R1
    muscular, R8–9
    skeletal, R6–7
Systems (nature). *See* Ecosystems

Tables, reading, R28
Taiga ecosystems, 159, 162, 170, 171
Tapirs, 179
Taproots, 126
Tarantulas, 184
Temperate forest climate, 170, 171
Temperate rain forest climate, 170
Temperature
    of air over land vs. water, 48
    in Earth's core, 80
    on mountains, 72
    states of matter and, 222
    on weather maps, 58, 59
Texture, 216
Thermometers, 8
Three states of matter, 220, 254–255
Thunderstorms, 42, 46, 56
Time, geologic, 94
Time/space relationships, 14
Tissues, vascular, 125
Tools, 2–7
    at Fort Ancient, 274–275
    for measuring, 2–5
    for observing and handling, 6–7
Top-level consumers, 188
Topography, 74
Tornadoes, 42, 44
Trace fossils, 91
Transport (in plants), 120
Trees, 117, 125
    fossil, 91
    petrified, 140, 143
Trilobites, 92, 94
Tropical rain forest climate, 170, 171

Tsunamis, 97
Tundra ecosystems
    climate of, 170, 171
    diversity in, 172
Turf, 117

Understory (rain forests), 172
Upper mantle, 80
Upper St. Croix River gorge (Wisconsin), 70
Using numbers, 13

Valleys, 73
    rivers and formation of, 84
Vascular plants, 120, 125
Vision, R10
Volcanoes, 82
    Cumbre Vieja, 96–97
    islands created by, 76, 81
    Mount Saint Helens, 98
    studying, 98
Volume, 214
    measuring, 5
    metric system measurements, R33

Ward, Steven, 97
Warm air masses, 54, 55
Warm fronts, 56, 58
Water
    changes in state of, 254–256, 266
    densities of, 210
    in ecosystems, 168
    formation of, 264
    forms of, 35

groundwater, 36

in oceans, 30

rivers, 84

runoff, 36

states of, 222, 223

Water cycle, 32–33

kinds of precipitation in, 40

landforms and, 48–50

parts of, 34–35

weather related to. *See* Weather

Water lilies, 144, 160

Water vapor, 32, 34

Waves, landform changes from, 86

Weather

air masses, 54–55

cloud types, 57

fronts, 56

land breezes, 48

measuring, 60

precipitation, 40–41

rain shadows, 50

safety considerations, 44

sea breezes, 48

sea breeze storms, 49

storms, 42–43

Weather maps, 58–59

Weather stations, 59, 60

White Sands, New Mexico, 75

Wichtowski, Blake, 194

Wind, 86

in hurricanes, 42

landform changes from, 86

on weather maps, 59

Wind tunnels, 18

Wind vanes, 60

Wood, petrified, 91, 140, 143

Woody stems, 118

Woolly mammoths, 91

World Ice Art Championships (Alaska), 218

Wyoming, fossils in, 93

Xylem, 125, 126, 128

Y bridges (Ohio), 278–279

Yellowstone National Park, 160

Yukon, 29

Zanesville, Y bridge at, 278–279

Zebras, 170

Ziff, Khloe, 150

Zygotes, 133

KEY: (t) top, (b) bottom, (l) left, (r) right, (c) center, (bg) background, (fg) foreground

Introduction
x (c) S Frink/Masterfile; 2 (c) AP Photo/NASA; 7 (inset) Sinclair Stammers / Science Photo Library; 10 (c) AP Photo/David J.Phillip; 18 (c) National Research Council Canada; 20 (inset) Mark Gibson / Index Stock Imagery, Inc.; 20 (bc) Robert Llewellyn/CORBIS;

Unit A
27 Department of Natural Resources, Ohio; 28 SuperStock; 30 Jeff Greenberg/The Image Works; 38 David Sailors/CORBIS; 40 (b) Royalty-Free/CORBIS; 41 (b) Rob Atkins/Getty Images; 41(cr) Layne Kennedy/Dembinksy Photo Assoc.; 41 (tr) Oote Boe/Alamy Images; 42 (bl) Alaska Stock Images; 42 (tr) Royalty-Free/CORBIS; 43 (bg) Royalty-Free/CORBIS; 44 (cl) Gene Rhoden; 44 (br) Richard Cummins/CORBIS; 44 (bl) Silver Image; 44 (cr) Micheal Heller/911 Pictures ; 46 Alan R. Moller/Getty Images; 49 (c) NOAA/AP Photo; 52 Gene Rhoden/Peter Arnold, Inc.; 57 (tr) Tom Dietrich/Getty Images; 57 (cr) George Post/Photo Researchers; 57 (tl) Eastcott/Momatiuk/The Image Works; 57 (cl) John Eastcott & Yva Momatiuk/Getty Images; 57 (b) Getty Images; 60 (c) David Young-Wolff/Photo Edit; 60 (tcr) Burke/Triolo Productions/Getty Images; 60 (tc) Paul Seheult; Eye Ubiquitous/CORBIS; 65 (bg) Robert Carr/Bruce Coleman, Inc.; 67 (tl) Layne Kennedy/Dembinsky Photo Associates; 68 Mediacolor's/Alamy Images; 70 G. Alan Nelson Outdoor Dembinsky Photography; 72 (br) Darrell Gulin/CORBIS; 72 (bl) Paul A. Souders/CORBIS; 73 (inset) Gary Yeowell/Getty Images; 73 (bg) Josef Beck/Getty Images; 74 (bg) James Strachan/Getty Images; 74 (inset) AirphotoNA.com; 75 (t) NASA/CORBIS; 75 (b) David Muench/CORBIS; 76 (cr) Photri/Topham/The Image Works; 76 (b) Douglas Peebles; 78 Jean-Paul Ferrero/Ardea; 81 (b) David Paterson/Getty Images; 82 (b) Bernhard Edmaier/Science Photo Library; 83 (tr) David Butow/CORBIS SABA; 83 (br) David Hume Kennerly/Getty Images; 84 (tr) Ernest Manewal/Index Stock Imagery; 84 (br) Pat O'Hara/CORBIS; 85 (tr) Arnulf Husmo/Getty Images; 85 (tl) Harvey Lloyd/Getty Images; 86 (bg) M. T. O'Keefe/Robertstock.com; 86 (inset) Mark Gibson/Index Stock Imagery; 88 James L. Amos/CORBIS; 90 (bg) Runk/Schoenberger/Grant Heilman Photography, Inc.; 91 (c) Imagenes de Nuestro Mundo; 91 (tl) Francois Gohier/Photo Researchers; 91 (tr) Eberhard Grames/Bilderberg/Peter Arnold, Inc.; 92 (inset) Indiana Dept. of Natural Resources/Falls of the Ohio State Park; 92 (b) Indiana Dept. of Natural Resources/Falls of the Ohio River; 93 (cr) Sinclair Stammers/Photo Researchers; 99 (bg) James King-Holmes/Science Photo Library; 101 (bl) Martin Siepmann/AGE footstock; 102 (b) Jeff Herbst; 103 (c) Mike Williams/Department of Natural Resources, Ohio; 105 (c) Richard A. Cooke/CORBIS; 106 (cr) Mahan Photo/Sweetwater Visions; 106 (b) Mike Wiliams/Department of Natural Resources, Ohio; 107 (tr) U.S. Geological Survey; 107 (r) Department of Natural Resources, Ohio;

Unit B
111 (b) ThisWeek Newspapers, Columbus, Ohio; 112-113 Freeman Patterson/Masterfile; 114 E.R. Degginger/Color Pic, Inc.; 117 (tcl) Donald R. Wright/Science Photo Library; 117 (tr) Steven Lam/Getty Images; 117 (tl) Trevor Smithers ARPS/Alamy Images; 117 (tc) Patti Murray/Animals Animals/Earth Scenes; 117 (tcr) Premium Stock/CORBIS; 118 (cl) Fritz Poelking/Age Fotostock; 118 (br) Jeff Grenberg/Photo Edit; 119 (l) TH Foto-Werbun/Photo Researchers; 119 (r) Thomas Dressler/Age Fotostock; 119 (c) A Riedmiller/Peter Arnold, Inc.; 122 Luiz C. Marigo/Peter Arnold, Inc.; 124 (br) Fritz Polking/ Peter Arnold, Inc.; 124 (b) Ron Fehling/Masterfile; 125 (r) Sherman Hines/Masterfile; 126 (t) Ed Reschke/ Peter Arnold, Inc.; 126 (tl) Keate/Masterfile; 126 (tr) Walter H. Hodge/Peter Arnold, Inc.; 127 (r) J.A. Kraulis/Masterfile; 127 (br) Ed Reschke/Peter Arnold, Inc.; 128 (bg) Adam Hart-Davis/Science Photo Library; 128 (bc) Ed Reschke/Peter Arnold, Inc.; 130 Randy Miller/Masterfile; 132 (b) Tony Wharton/CORBIS; 133 (bl) Ed Reschke/Peter Arnold, Inc.; 133 (br) Ed Reschke/Peter Arnold, Inc.; 134 (br) James Richardson/Visuals Unlimited; 134 (bl) Patti Murray/Animals Animals; 135 (l) Lloyd Sutton/Masterfile; 135 (fg) BIOS/Peter Arnold, Inc.; 137 (bl) Tim Fitzharris/Masterfile; 137 (br) Royalty-Free/CORBIS; 138 (all) Dwight Kuhn; 140 (c) E.R.Degginger/Color Pic, Inc.; 142 (l) Bob Gibbons/Photo Researchers; 142 (br) John Cancalosi/DRK Photo; 143 (cl) Tom Bean Photography; 143 (tl) Christie Carter/Grant Heilman Photography, Inc.; 143 (tr) Color-pic/Animals Animals/Earth Scenes; 143 (cr) Dr. Carleton Ray/Photo Researchers; 144 (t) Neil Fletcher/dk Images; 144 (cr) Jack Clark/Animals Animals/Earth Scenes; 144 (bl) Peter Rae/Fairfax Photos; 144 (bc) Peter Weston/Royal Botanic Gardens, Australia; 144 (br) Ted Clutter/Photo Researchers; 145 (tl) www.terratreasures.com; 145 (r) David Dilcher & Ge Sun/Museum of Natural History, University of Florida; 145 (cl) E.R. Degginger/Color Pic, Inc.; 146 (tr) Louise Broman/Photo Researchers; 146 (cr) Dirk Wiersma/Photo Researchers; 146 (b) Breck P. Kent/Animals Animals/Earth Scenes; 148 AP/Wide World Photos, 149 (t) AP/Wide World Photos; 150 (t) Francois Gohier/Photo Researchers; 150 (bg) William H Hullins/Photo Researchers; 151 (bg) Bill Ross/CORBIS; 154 Tom and Pat Leeson; 156 Bob Thomas/Getty Images; 158 (cr) Bob & Clara Calhoun/Bruce Coleman; 158 (br) Beth Davidow/Visuals Unlimited; 158 (b) Cathy Melloan/PhotoEdit; 159 (t) E. R. Degginger/Bruce Coleman, Inc.; 159 (cl) George Sanker/Bruce Coleman, Inc.; 160 (t) Dennis MacDonald/PhotoEdit; 160 (tl) Dennis MacDonald/PhotoEdit; 161 (bl) Steve Maslowski/Visuals Unlimited; 161 (b) Kenneth Fink/Bruce Coleman, Inc.; 162 (cl) Jeremy Woodhous/Getty Images; 164 Karl Kummels/SuperStock; 166 (c) Jerome Wexler/Visuals Unlimited; 166 (bl) Adam Jones/Visuals Unlimited; 166 (br) Rob Simpson/Visuals Unlimited; 167 Dennis MacDonald/PhotoEdit; 167 (br) David L. Shirk/Animals Animals; 171 (tr) Greg Neise/Visuals Unlimited; 171 (cl) Adam Jones/Visuals Unlimited; 171 (tl) Julie Eggers/Bruce Coleman, Inc.; 171 (br) Eastcott-Momatiuk/The Image Works; 171 (bl) Patrick Endres/Visuals Unlimited; 171 (cr) Richard Thom/Visuals Unlimited; 174 Kim Taylor/Bruce Coleman, Inc.; 177 (br) D. Robert & Lorri Franz/CORBIS; 177 (tr) Lynn Stone/Animals Animals; 177 (tl) Darrell Gulin/CORBIS; 179 (bl) Michael Fogden/Animals Animals; 179 (cr) Bob Barber/Barber Nature Photography; 179 (tc) Lynn Stone/Animals Animals; 179 (cl) Kevin Schafer/CORBIS; 180 (cr) Wolfgang Kaehler/CORBIS; 180 (b) Jim Brandenburg/Minden Picures; 180 (cl) Ken Lucas/Visuals Unlimited; 181 (br) D.Hurst/Alamy Images; 182 CDC/PHIL/CORBIS; 184 (b) Royalty-Free/CORBIS; 184 (cr) Gerry Ellis / Minden Pictures; 184 (br) Darrell Gulin/CORBIS; 184 (tr) ZSSD/MINDEN PICTURES; 185 (br) Dale Sanders/Masterfile; 185 (tl) CORBIS; 185 (c) Andrew J. Martinez/Photo Researchers; 185 (tr) Dale Sanders/Masterfile; 186 (bl) M. Timothy O'Keefe/Bruce Coleman, Inc.; 186 (bg) Wolfgang Kaehler/CORBIS; 186 (br) Doug Perrine/SeaPics.com; 187 (bl) Joe McDonald/CORBIS; 187 (tc) Bill Brooks/Masterfile; 187 (cr) Barry Runk/Stan/Grant Heilman Photography; 187 (tl) Jim Zipp/Photo Researchers; 192-193 NOAA; 194 Index Stock; 194 (inset) Courtesy Mutual of Omaha; 195 (bg) Dennis MacDonald/Alamy Images; 198 (all) Franklin Park Conservatory; 200 (b) Brian Parsons/the Holden Arboretum; (tr) Ian Adams/The Holden Arboretum; 201 (all) Ian Adams/The Holden Arboretum; 202-203 (all) Department of Natural Resources, Ohio.

Unit C
207 Diana Blackford/Wapakoneta Daily News; 208 Science Photo Library/Photo Researchers; 210 Steve Shott/DK Images; 214 (tl) PhotoDisc/Getty Images; 215 (tc) Getty Images; 215

(tr) Charles D. Winters/Photo Researchers; 216 (cr) Flat Earth/FotoSearch; 218 Patrick J. Endres/AlaskaPhotoGraphics; 220 (bl) Charles D. Winters/Photo Researchers; 220 (br) Mike Hipple/Index Stock Imagery; 221 (tc) Spencer Jones/FoodPix/Getty Images; 221 (tl) David Bishop/FoodPix/Getty Images; 222 (br) Keate/Masterfile; 223 (br) Japack Company/CORBIS; 223 (bl) Keate/Masterfile; 224 (bg) Charles O'Rear/CORBIS; 224 (cl) Charles D. Winters/Photo Researchers; 226 David Whitten/Index Stock Imagery/PictureQuest; 231 (bg) Peter French/Bruce Coleman; 232 (bg) Tim Fitzharris/Minden Pictures; 237 (bg) SuperStock/PictureQuest; 239 (bc) Daryl Benson/Masterfile; 239 (br) John Warden/Index Stock Imagery; 240 Gerd Ludwig/VISUM/The Image Works; 247 (cl) Richard Megna/Fundamental Photographs; 248 (br) Tony O'Brien/The Image Works; 248 (tr) Charles D. Winters/Photo Researchers; 248 (bl) Bill Aron/Photo Edit; 249 (bc) Jeff J. Daly/Fundamental Photographs; 249 (tr) Russ Lappa/Photo Researchers; 249 (cr) Tom Pantages/AGPix; 249 (c) Richard Cummins/CORBIS; 249 (br) Ryan McVay/Getty Images; 250 (tl) Elio Ciol/CORBIS; 250 (cr) Richard Treptow/Photo Researchers; 252 Rommel/Masterfile; 254 (tcr) Gary Buss/Getty Images; 254 (br) Joseph Van Os/Getty Images; 255 (cr) Royalty-Free/CORBIS; 256 Kjell Sandved/Bruce Coleman; 256 (br) Michael Dalton/Fundamental Photographs; 257 (tl) PhotoDisc/Getty Images; 257 (cr) Bonnie Kamin/PhotoEdit; 260 NASA/Science Photo Library; 262 Andrew Lambert Photography/Science Photo Library/Photo Researchers; 262 (bcl) Tom Pantages/AGPix; 262 (bcl) Scott Haag; 264 Fotomorgana/ CORBIS; 264 (tr) SuperStock; 264 (br) Fife/Photo Researchers; 265 (br) Richard Megna/Fundamental Photographs; 266 (cr) Grant Heilman/Grant Heilman Photography; 266 (bc) Burke/Triolo/Brand X Pictures/PictureQuest; 266 (tr) Grant Heilman/Grant Heilman Photography; 270 (t) Daum photos; 270 (b) Layne Kennedy/CORBIS; 271 (bg) Royalty-Free/CORBIS; 274 University of Cincinnati/CERHAS; 275 (t) Courtesy Ohio Historical Society; 275 (cr) Werner Forman/Art Resource; 276 Layne Kennedy/CORBIS; 277 Courtesy Roscoe Village, OH; 278 Courtesy the Ohio Historical Society/P259; 279 Zanesville Chamber of Commerce;

Health Handbook
R5 Dennis Kunkel/Phototake; R12 (t) CNRI/Science Photo Library/Photo Researchers; R12 (tc) A. Pasieka/Photo Researchers; R12 (bc) CNRI/Science Photo Library/Photo Researchers; R12 (b) Custom Medical Stock Photo; R15 (inset) David Young-Wolff/PhotoEdit; R15 (b) Bill O'Connor/Peter Arnold, Inc.;

All other photos © Harcourt School Publishers. Harcourt Photos provided by the Harcourt Index, Harcourt IPR, and Harcourt photographers; Weronica Ankarorn, Victoria Bowen, Eric Camden, Doug Dukane, Ken Kinzie, April Riehm, and Steve Williams.

BEHAVIOR Playing helps wolf cubs develop strength and hunting skills.

HOWLING Wolves howl to communicate with other wolves or sometimes just for fun.

BEHAVIOR Wolves bare their teeth when they are angry.

SPEED Wolves can run up to 56 kilometers per hour.

SENSES Wolves can hear prey up to 12 km away, can smell prey up to 3 km away, and have excellent eyesight.